About Island Press

Since 1984, the nonprofit organization Island Press has been stimulating, shaping, and communicating ideas that are essential for solving environmental problems worldwide. With more than 800 titles in print and some 40 new releases each year, we are the nation's leading publisher on environmental issues. We identify innovative thinkers and emerging trends in the environmental field. We work with world-renowned experts and authors to develop cross-disciplinary solutions to environmental challenges.

Island Press designs and executes educational campaigns in conjunction with our authors to communicate their critical messages in print, in person, and online using the latest technologies, innovative programs, and the media. Our goal is to reach targeted audiences—scientists, policymakers, environmental advocates, urban planners, the media, and concerned citizens—with information that can be used to create the framework for long-term ecological health and human well-being.

Island Press gratefully acknowledges major support of our work by The Agua Fund, The Andrew W. Mellon Foundation, Betsy & Jesse Fink Foundation, The Bobolink Foundation, The Curtis and Edith Munson Foundation, Forrest C. and Frances H. Lattner Foundation, G.O. Forward Fund of the Saint Paul Foundation, Gordon and Betty Moore Foundation, The Kresge Foundation, The Margaret A. Cargill Foundation, New Mexico Water Initiative, a project of Hanuman Foundation, The Overbrook Foundation, The S.D. Bechtel, Jr. Foundation, The Summit Charitable Foundation, Inc., V. Kann Rasmussen Foundation, The Wallace Alexander Gerbode Foundation, and other generous supporters.

The opinions expressed in this book are those of the author(s) and do not necessarily reflect the views of our supporters.

Next Generation Infrastructure

Next Generation Infrastructure

Principles for Post-Industrial Public Works

By Hillary Brown

⬤ **ISLAND**PRESS Washington | Covelo | London

Island Press is a trademark of The Center for Resource Economics.

Island Press would like to thank Furthermore, a program of the J. M. Kaplan Fund, for generous support of the design and printing of this book.

Library of Congress Cataloging-in-Publication Data

Brown, Hillary.
  Next generation infrastructure / Hillary Brown.
    pages cm
  Includes bibliographical references and index.
   ISBN 978-1-59726-805-9 (hardback)—ISBN 1-59726-805-4 (cloth)—ISBN 978-1-61091-181-8 (paper) 1. Infrastructure (Economics)—Environmental aspects—United States. 2. Infrastructure (Economics)—Government policy—United States. I. Title.
  HC110.C3B76 2014
  363.60973--dc23

                                        2013039889

 Printed on recycled, acid-free paper

Manufactured in the United States of America
10 9 8 7 6 5 4 3 2 1

Keywords: biomass, bioremediation, carbon reduction, climate change adaptation, climate change mitigation, coastal resilience, distributed energy systems, geothermal energy, green streets, hydrogen power, infrastructural ecology, renewable energy, siting public utilities, smart grid, solar power, storm-water management, urban resilience, waste combustion, water scarcity, waste-to-energy facilities, water treatment and storage

For *Jeanne* and *George*

Contents

Foreword

David W. Orr

An hour north of New York City, the Omega Institute operates a solar-powered wastewater system that looks and works like a tropical greenhouse. It was designed by John Todd and BNIM Architects to process 50,000 gallons of wastewater each day. The system combines indoor and outdoor wetlands to purify sewage without chlorine, aluminum salts, or other chemicals, and without fossil fuels. Plants, animals, and some of the most ancient organisms on Earth remove nitrogen and phosphorus from the waste stream and detoxify contaminants. It is a model of smart ecological design, good engineering, full-cost economics, and foresight. But the Omega Institute facility is only one small example of next-generation design applied to energy, water, transport, and waste-management systems. There are many others around the world that are revolutionizing infrastructure, reducing costs, and improving resilience, as reported here by Hillary Brown.

Our existing infrastructure of wastewater plants, bridges, the electrical grid, pipelines, roads, and dams is rapidly deteriorating. The American Society of Civil Engineers estimates that its repair or replacement will cost $3.6 trillion. For financial reasons alone it is a good time to rethink the way we design, build, and invest in public infrastructure. But the design assumptions underlying our existing infrastructure are crumbling along with the concrete, steel, wires, and pipes. The designers of the industrial infrastructure presumed an inexhaustible supply of cheap energy, the efficacy of simple and single-purpose solutions to complex problems, and the necessity of brute-force mastery of nature, all executed with a bulletproof confidence in endless economic growth on a finite planet. The fatal shortcomings of that paradigm are massively documented and are becoming a daily bad-news story in our increasingly precarious experience.

But a new ecological paradigm is reshaping the mindsets of the designers of the systems that provision us with food, energy, materials, transport, shelter, waste cycling, and security. Ecological designers and ecological engineers begin with the imperative to design with, not against, natural processes and flows. Following Kentucky writer Wendell Berry they are asking: What is here? What will nature let us do here? What will nature help us do here? The answers, particularly to the last question, are surprisingly positive and point the way to a far more cost-effective, resilient, and sustainable infrastructure. Properly engaged, nature will in fact do a great deal of the work in engineered systems for free. The detailed knowledge of how nature utilizes sunlight, purifies waste, and builds elegant structures without fossil fuels or toxic chemicals is changing the design of human systems. Without much fanfare, emerging fields such as biomimicry, ecological engineering, and ecological design are quietly transforming architecture, engineering, agriculture, forestry, urban planning, and infrastructure development.

The precepts of ecological design are straightforward: (1) use nature as the standard, not something to be overcome; (2) eliminate waste so that everything is food for other organisms; (3) use only renewable energy; (4) preserve and enhance biodiversity; (5) distribute costs and benefits fairly within and across generations. The operating instructions derived from those precepts are: (1) "solve for pattern" across traditional boundaries of disciplines and bureaucratic silos so that every solution solves more than one problem and causes no new ones; (2) design systems that are resilient and repairable with redundant components; (3) emphasize proximity so that supply chains are mostly local or regional, as urban historian Jane Jacobs once proposed.

Short-term economic thinking is often used as an excuse for poor design. But the fact is that sooner or later we pay for sustainable and resilient infrastructure (and lots of other things) whether we get it or not. We pay for ecologically incoherent design in human health, vulnerability to terrorism or acts of God, climate change, injustice, loss of biodiversity, and excessive operating and maintenance costs. Accounting for full life-cycle costs should cause us to reconsider the rules for investment in public infrastructure from a broader and longer-term perspective. Low first costs are not always cheaper. Avoided future costs, including those of disasters such as Hurricane Sandy, ought to be calculated into infrastructure budgets. Investments that improve resilience and reduce our vulnerability to climate destabilization are a smart use of public and private capital. The point is that we will need to be as creative about financing new infrastructure are we are about designing it.

It is possible to design and build infrastructure for transportation, water management, and energy that reduces ecological damage, climate risks, and construction and maintenance costs, while improving human health and creating the economic foundation for broad-based and sustainable prosperity. This is not a distant possibility. In *Next Generation Infrastructure*, Hillary Brown shows that the design know-how already exists and is being creatively deployed across the world in dozens of good examples. Next-generation infrastructure is not a luxury for the well-to-do. It is coming on line just as the climate forecast, for rich and poor alike virtually everywhere, is for much higher temperatures, longer droughts, bigger storms, and higher-velocity winds. We will need a new infrastructure that is resilient in the face of much greater stresses than humans have ever experienced before.

Hillary Brown is a brilliant guide to one of the most important, if mostly overlooked, aspects of a resilient society. In her work as the originator and co-author of two important publications for New York City, *High Performance Building Guidelines* and *High Performance Infrastructure Guidelines*, and in her subsequent work as a designer, author, and teacher she has developed an extraordinary depth of insight and experience. *Next Generation Infrastructure* is a vital chapter in the narrative we are writing about the human future and should be mandatory reading for planners, financiers, and public officials at all levels.

Acknowledgments

Since a valuable portion of my career was spent in city government, I offer this book to the many individuals involved in public works who inspired and mentored me. A special debt of gratitude also goes to Michael Singer and Jason Bregman at Michael Singer Studio. Grateful nods especially to Christina Lazarus and to Nancy Levinson for help with earlier writings. Thanks especially to the many friends and colleagues who have supported my emerging interests in this field in notable ways: Andrea Woodner, Claire Weisz, Don Watson, Byron Stigge, Jim Russell, Bill Reed, and Paul Mankiewicz.

Thanks go out to individuals interviewed: David Burke, Paul Chamberlin, Christine Holowacz, Mark Horn, Dave Hyams, Penny Lee, Erika Mantz, Charles McKinney, Thomas Paino, Linda Pollack, Stephanie Reichlin, James Roche, Margie Ruddick, Anthony Shorris, Ken Smith, George Stockton, Laura Truettner, Jurgen van der Heijden, Peter Op 't Veld, Ariane Volz, David Waggonner, and Kate Zidar.

I'm indebted to those who helped in myriad ways in the development of this manuscript: Rachel Spellman, Cara Turett, Miriam Ward. The work has received support through the generosity of the Bernard and Anne Spitzer School of Architecture Fund. I am grateful for Sandra Chizinski's sharp editorial eye and ear, and for the unfailing support of editor Heather Boyer at Island Press. Finally, this book is also dedicated to my brother Richard and nephews Eliot and Nicholas with love.

1. Introduction: Bold Endeavors Needed

There are sufficient resources to retrofit cities if we
practice integrative infrastructure management … if
we begin to manage the city as if it really were a living
ecosystem, which of course it is, or was, and should be.

— Kenny Ausubel,
Nature's Operating Instructions:
The True Biotechnologies

On August 1, 2007, four of the eight lanes of Minnesota's I-35W highway bridge were closed to accommodate roadbed repairs. Evening rush-hour traffic was diverted into the four open lanes, creating an asymmetrical stress that compounded an underlying weakness in the bridge's support system. When the center span collapsed, 17 of the 111 vehicles on the bridge were cast into the Mississippi River, 108 feet below, killing 13 people and injuring 145 (fig. 1-1).[1]

The I-35W tragedy quickly became symbolic of the debilitated state of the once-noble Interstate Highway System—and of what many critics see as America's disinvestment in its infrastructure. But it also called attention to a broader problem: that a narrow focus on optimizing the various parts of complex systems may undermine the sustainability of the whole.

According to an evaluation conducted by the National Transportation Safety Board (NTSB), the primary cause of the failure was the initial undersizing of the steel plates that joined critical members of the bridge's steel truss system, compromising the bridge's structural redundancy, or ability to withstand extra stress. The NTSB highlighted four additional factors: subsequent additions to the bridge deck had increased the dead weight of the structure;[2] safety inspectors, who tended to focus on corrosion and cracks, had failed to notice the slight

Figure 1-1. Cars remain on the collapsed portion of I-35W Mississippi River Bridge, in Minneapolis, Minnesota, four days after the August 2007 collapse. (Courtesy of Kevin Rofidal, US Coast Guard.)

bowing—evident from photos—of the steel plates caused by structural stress;[3] 270 tons of repair-related loads, including raw materials, equipment, and personnel, had been positioned above the bridge's weakest points just hours before the collapse; and traffic controllers had unwittingly added further stress to the structure.

What the NTSB's account does not address, however, is an increasingly common problem in the design and management of complex systems: the failure to see and to appreciate the workings of the whole. In the case of the bridge collapse, any knowledge of existing problems likely remained within each of the separate departments responsible for design, repair, inspection, maintenance, and operations. Thus, it might be argued that better information flow among "bureaucratic silos" might have had produced a different outcome, perhaps even preventing the tragedy. As Paul Hawken, Amory B. Lovins, and L. Hunter Lovins observe in *Natural Capitalism*,

> optimizing components in isolation tends to pessimize the whole system. . . . You can actually make a system less efficient while making each of its parts more efficient, simply by not properly linking up those components. If they're not designed to work with one another, they'll tend to work against one another.[4]

This book explores how we can optimize, rather than "pessimize," the facilities and assets of public services—primarily energy, water, and waste management. The book arises from the confluence of several streams of thought. First, if we're to chart a course for global sustainability, we must begin to decouple carbon-intensive and ecologically harmful technologies from critical infrastructure systems, namely the essential systems for contemporary society: water, wastewater, power, solid waste, transportation, and communication. Second, we have the opportunity, through the power of systems thinking, to imagine an alternative future and to take bold steps toward that potential. Lastly, although we possess the scientific and technological know-how to move forward, we are critically lacking a policy and implementation framework to support such efforts.

Churning its way across the New York / New Jersey metropolitan region, Hurricane Sandy vividly demonstrated the extreme vulnerability of urban systems to storm surges, which are becoming stronger and more frequent due to climate change. It especially highlighted the interdependencies among infrastructure sectors. Inundating New York City's vital arteries, floodwaters overwhelmed tunnels and sewers; closed bridges; shut down the electrical substations that control mass transit; curtailed gas supplies; and destroyed streets, buildings, and whole neighborhoods. For days and even weeks, failures triggered by floodwaters deprived millions of electrical, heat, and water services.

One premise of this book is that our current patterns of infrastructure development reflect an industrialized worldview—one that, in the interests of convenience, efficiency, and bureaucratic control, has largely isolated the various elements of our infrastructural systems. A post-industrial viewpoint, by contrast, focuses on understanding how the parts of such systems relate to each other and to the whole. From this perspective, the "hardware" of energy, water, and waste management is essentially viewed along ecological lines. Next-generation infrastructure means moving beyond compartmentalized thinking toward new, integrated approaches to planning, financing, constructing, operating, and maintaining infrastructure. In both their conception and design, the innovative projects highlighted in this book are less "object focused" and more "outcome driven." They encourage us to move forward with greater sensitivity to the larger infrastructural context; to consider a location in terms of its economic, environmental, and social resources; and to share resources across different systems, thereby reducing costs and extending benefits. Through a systems approach to lifeline services, we can begin to move more rapidly toward sustainability.

The Scope of the Problem

In *Bold Endeavors: How Our Government Built America, and Why It Must Rebuild Now*, Felix Rohatyn recounts the story of America's entrepreneurial investments in infrastructure—from the transcontinental railroads and the Panama Canal to rural electrification and the Interstate Highway System—chronicling the unusual foresight and intrepid leadership behind each initiative and highlighting the manifold rewards, particularly economic growth.[5] In the face of the imperative to repair and strengthen existing assets or to reinvent them altogether, what needs to be done, and where are we to begin?

In 2009, the American Society of Civil Engineers awarded US infrastructure an average grade of D for adequacy and safety—a grade that was raised to D+ in 2013, thanks to a pickup in incremental investments. The same 2013 report contended that repairing US infrastructure assets to achieve a "good" condition (essentially a grade of B) will require an estimated cumulative investment of $3.6 trillion by 2020—a figure that does not even begin to address growth or expansion.[6] The following are some highlights from a few recent assessments:

- The United States loses 1.7 trillion gallons of drinking water annually through system leakage and 240,000 water main breaks per year.[7] The cost to upgrade distribution, treatment, and storage would be $334.8 billion over 20 years.[8]
- Each year, more than 75,000 overflows from combined storm and sewage drains discharge 900 billion gallons of untreated sewage into US waterways.[9] The estimated cost of updating and expanding wastewater and stormwater systems is $298 billion over 20 years.[10]
- The number of significant power outages has risen from 76 in 2007 to 307 in 2011.[11] Between 2005 and 2009 the United States experienced 264 large-scale blackouts. Estimates for electrical-system upgrades call for $1.5 to 2.0 trillion in expenditures over 20 years.[12]
- Ensuring the safety and efficiency of existing mass-transit systems will require between $18.2 and $29.6 billion in annual improvements in 2012 dollars.[13]
- As of 2012, 11 percent of bridges were classified as structurally deficient. To repair or replace substandard structures by 2028 would cost an estimated $76 billion.[14]

Funded at about 3.5 percent of total non-defense spending, and at roughly the same level since 1976, US infrastructure funding lags behind that of both developed and developing nations.[15] Although the United States is roughly two and a half times the area of the European Union, the US will spend annually, on average, $150 billion—less than 1 percent of our GDP, compared to the European Union's $300 billion during the decade 2010 to 2020.[16] Infrastructure investment in the developing world also outpaces ours: relative to their GDPs,

India and China spend 8 and 9 percent, respectively, on public works.[17]

In April 2013, President Obama was pushing for investment in US infrastructure—one of his key priorities—for perhaps the fifth time. Among his proposed initiatives were a $50 billion economic stimulus based primarily on transportation investments, and $10 billion in public funding that would leverage private investment through a newly created, independent National Infrastructure Bank[18]—pleas that have repeatedly fallen on the deaf ears of a Congress preoccupied with austerity. Yet Obama's proposals parallel those of others around the world.

In the United States, those who fear that forestalling infrastructure investment will cost the US its competitive edge, both economically and politically, are sounding the clarion call for action. The degraded state of US lifeline systems has failed to capture public attention. Infrastructure repairs and upkeep are notoriously unsexy expenditures, and politicians are more invested in cutting ribbons at new projects than in funding basic maintenance, a trend that has further undercut the condition of our existing systems. Thus, despite the intermittent alarms sounded after catastrophic failures, there is little sense of urgency—or recognition that infrastructure systems are vital lifelines to economic growth, public health and safety, and other desirable social goals. Even more unusual is any understanding of how those lifelines are linked, directly or indirectly, to the integrity of natural systems.

Nature and Infrastructure

Human life depends on ecological services provided by nature—from water purification to waste digestion to the regulation of natural hazards.[19] These services originate in ecosystems: self-organized aggregations of living and nonliving elements that exist in a state of symbiosis, sharing energy, information, and matter for mutual benefit.

Human-engineered energy, water, and waste infrastructure systems are, like natural ecosystems, tightly coupled.[20] Electrical power generation, for instance, relies on water cooling, while water distribution and wastewater treatment require electricity; electrical energy still relies on coal transported by rail. Transportation services, water treatment, and electricity generation all rely on information technology.[21] Nonetheless, since the advent of the industrial era, the convention has been to disaggregate the elements of infrastructural systems into different sectors, both physically and jurisdictionally, and to dissociate them from the natural ecosystem services on which they ultimately depend.

The industrial paradigm was largely responsible for estranging public works from the ecosystem services upon which they depend. Few infrastructural transactions remain visible; most services are distributed below grade or are wired high—and almost unseen—above. Power, water, and waste facilities are typically removed from populous areas. The web that connects public services, daily life, and the environment is rarely brought to mind: we don't think "polluting coal combustion" as we flick on a light switch, and a refuse chute or garbage bin doesn't summon images of vast landfills.

There are direct but not readily visible correspondences between ecosystem services and human-made systems. Water filtration and treatment are analogous to the natural ground infiltration that supplies aquifers and reservoirs, and also to the purification accomplished by wetlands. Incinerating waste or relegating it to a landfill are imperfect counterparts to natural microbial decomposition. And when we "generate" energy, we are essentially releasing the solar power stored in biomass.

As the unparalleled costs associated with the hurricanes of the past decade demonstrate, we suppress or deny the interdependence of constructed systems, as well as their combined reliance on natural systems, at our peril. An evolving post-industrial viewpoint—one that reflects the holistic perspective associated with sustainability—emphasizes interconnectedness rather than separation. From this perspective, the constructed world is nested within the natural one and depends on its health and productivity. Natural ecosystems and human-made infrastructures are not simply a universe of discrete objects but rather are vital working parts embedded in networks that share energy, matter, and information.

When we move from an industrial to a post-industrial worldview, the question is no longer "How can we direct nature?" but "How can we capitalize on the connectedness of our critical systems to nature and to each other?"[22] What if, for example, the services provided by power plants, sewage treatment plants, and other elements of infrastructure were based on an ecological model of interdependency, instead of an industrial model of segregation?

Infrastructural Ecology

Nature's operating patterns depend on integration rather than segregation of functions. We know, for example, that planting legumes near other crops may eliminate the need for chemical fertilizers; that spacing tree rows so that certain companion crops can be grown under and between them maximizes yield; and that planting nut-producing trees among wheat, soy, or other crop rows helps to protect against wind and to stabilize topsoil. These examples, drawn from the discipline of permaculture, have an analogy in the realm of infrastructure: as we begin to recognize the beneficial links among infrastructural systems, we can capitalize on the efficiencies that emerge when shared components perform more than one function, or when energy, water, or waste is exchanged among them. Collectively, such synergies may lower carbon emissions, save resources, reduce or eliminate waste, and provide auxiliary civic benefits.

As David Holmgren, one of the founders of the practice of permaculture, has observed, "Integration of previously segregated systems appears to be a fundamental principle driving post-industrial design."[23] Such integration is at the root of infrastructural ecology. Like the discipline of permaculture, infrastructural ecology takes its cue from the way that nature, when left undisturbed, already works: by optimizing the flows of resources and information in ways that are specific to the environmental context. For example, biotic systems—relying solely on energy gathered from the sun—"cascade," or pass along energy, water, and nutrients in a closed-loop arrangement that leaves no residual waste.

The term *industrial symbiosis* was coined in the late 1980s to describe innovative ways to locate energy infrastructure, industry, and other commercial entities together for mutual benefit. The classic example of the "eco-industrial park," established in Kalundborg, Denmark, in the 1960s and 1970s, resulted from a collaboration among public and private entities driven by a common interest: to optimize energy and resource use (fig. 1-2). Kalundborg's hub is a coal-fired power plant whose waste heat warms greenhouses, a fish farm, and 3,500 homes. The power plant shares surplus steam with an oil refinery and a pharmaceutical company, eliminating heat pollution from the receiving waters. Fly ash scrubbed from the power plant's waste stack replaces two-thirds of the virgin gypsum that would otherwise

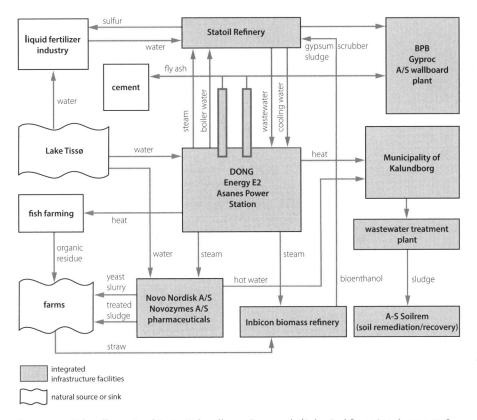

Figure 1-2. Kalundborg Symbiosis, Kalundborg, Denmark. (Adapted from Jacobsen 2006, Domenech and Davies 2011.)

be needed to manufacture sheetrock in the factory next door. Waste nutrients from the pharmaceutical plant feed a local pig farm, and waste from the fish farm is used locally as crop fertilizer. This web of waste reduction and reuse (22 separate exchanges as of 2011) generates new revenues for the partners, whose $60 million investment in the exchange infrastructure has produced $15 million in annual savings. Annually, moreover, CO_2 emissions are reduced by 64,460 tons, and 3.9 million cubic meters (137.7 million cubic feet) of water were saved.[24]

Kalundborg's mutually beneficial exchanges provide a model for what will be referred to here as *post-industrial* infrastructural systems. This term highlights new ways of thinking in which constructed systems are continuous with and dependent upon natural systems *and upon each other*, and hegemony over nature is not assumed. A post-industrial outlook also implies less emphasis on things and more emphasis on relationships; greater attention to reciprocity between systems; more contextual, or "situated" knowledge; and, ultimately, more-adaptable regulatory institutions.

The End of the Industrial Paradigm

The critical infrastructural services that form the backbone of the US economy are largely a product of the modern industrial epoch. But these "legacy systems" are associated with a broad array of challenges. First, because a significant majority of the urban infrastructural systems in the US have deteriorated in performance or are nearing the end of their useful life, they will require costly replacements or upgrades. Second, carbon- and chemical-intensive facilities and processes pollute our air, water, and soil. Third, urbanization pressures require the expansion of existing facilities or the addition of new ones—but public awareness of the potential for associated encumbrances and harms (as well as public disappointment with past practices) have made the selection of appropriate sites increasingly difficult. Finally, legacy structures and services have proven vulnerable to extreme weather, storm surges, flooding, and drought, and scientists predict that we will see an increase in the frequency and intensity of these natural events due to a changing climate. Posing an even greater risk to the systems, perhaps, are the entrenched ways that we think about them. By separating naturally interdependent infrastructural systems into discrete, self-contained regimes, we amplify vulnerabilities while foregoing efficiencies, cost savings, and other valuable dividends.

In 2000–2001, Californians endured multiple large-scale blackouts precipitated in part by drought and heat waves, and in part by energy traders' manipulations of electricity prices. The resulting disruptions in the production and distribution of oil and natural gas caused major losses in Silicon Valley and in metallurgy-dominated economies in the northwestern part of the state.[25] When the power outages triggered by Hurricane Katrina shut down petroleum pipelines on the Gulf Coast, nearly 10 percent of the US supply was affected, and the economic effects rippled throughout the US economy.[26] In 2007, a severe drought emptied the hydroelectric dam on Ecuador's Paute River, causing rolling blackouts in Quito, Guayaquil, and other major cities.[27] In 2010, during the hottest July on record in New Haven, Connecticut, increases in water demand, both for irrigation and for the cooling towers of power plants and other buildings, boosted the flow rates in water mains, which scoured the sediment from water piping and yielded disconcerting (though still usable) muddy brown tap water.[28]

How can our complex, increasingly interdependent utilities continue to support a rapidly urbanizing world, subject to both carbon constraints and the impacts of a destabilizing climate? How might these critical technical networks be reimagined, to be made more efficient, less environmentally damaging, and more resilient? Such questions are at the heart of the approaches and initiatives explored in this book. With a better understanding of the connections and potential synergies among different services, we can not only reduce inadvertent disruptions but also take advantage of constructive exchanges, thereby achieving crosscutting benefits and lower costs—in short, optimizing the whole. To continue to provide lifeline services, we must undertake such optimization much more effectively than we do now.

Organization of This Book

The alternative paradigm proposed in this volume calls for more diversified, distributed, and interconnected infrastructural assets that simulate the behavior of natural systems. At their best, such systems are based on five key principles:

1. Systems should be multipurpose, interconnected, and synergistic.
2. Infrastructure should contribute few or no carbon emissions.
3. Infrastructure should work with natural processes.
4. Infrastructure should improve social contexts and serve local constituencies.
5. Infrastructure should be resilient and adapt to predicted changes brought about by an unstable global climate.

The chapters that follow highlight each of these characteristics in turn (climate resilience is addressed in two chapters); the concluding chapter considers policy approaches to the development of next-generation infrastructure. Although the projects illustrating a given principle in each chapter also have other attributes associated with post-industrial development, they were selected because they are particularly compelling examples of that chapter's principal focus.

Chapter 2, "Toward Infrastructural Ecologies," illustrates the economies of scale, energy efficiencies, reductions in waste output, and other dividends that can be achieved when projects are colocated and designed to capture synergies and to fulfill more than one function. The projects examined in chapter 3, "Greening Heat and Power," have diversified the energy mix by leveraging nearby biomass, geothermal heat, landfill gas, or waste combustion, or by locating utilities adjacent to renewable-energy sources or "sinks." By distributing power generation—and thereby reducing transmission losses—such approaches can also help us move in the direction of a "smart grid," in which consumers who are also producers help control energy demands, maximize energy efficiencies, provide backup power, and improve the overall stability of the power supply.

Chapter 4, "Advancing Soft-Path Water Infrastructure," highlights projects that rely upon natural or bioengineered systems for localized water capture, cleaning, storage, treatment, and reuse. These features also clean and cool air, digest or detoxify waste, and bolster biodiversity. By rejuvenating natural systems, such initiatives may also help offset other losses globally. Chapter 5, "Destigmatizing Infrastructure," focuses on the social context of technical networks, suggesting how multiple services might be beneficially integrated into both the fabric of neighborhoods and the broader cultural landscape. Chapters 6 and 7, "Creating Resilient Coastlines and Waterways" and "Combating Water Stress and Scarcity," focus on multipurpose assets specifically designed to cope with events such as storm surges, inland flooding, water scarcity, prolonged drought, and extreme heat. "Ways Forward," the final chapter in the book, suggests that in the absence of a national infrastructure agenda, enlightened and proactive state and local officials, developers, and a concerned public can leverage existing policy tools and investment vehicles to create "future-proof" public works.

In the United States, energy, water, communications, and transportation command an estimated 69 percent of total energy consumption;[29] further, they contribute more than 50 percent of US greenhouse-gas emissions.[30] They also leave behind uncountable tons of chemical residue as well as organic and inorganic waste that must be assimilated. According to a 2010 study conducted by the World Wide Fund for Nature, "business as usual (BAU)"—that is, continuing to invest in carbon-intensive, environmentally-taxing development—is likely to double carbon emissions in just three decades.[31] Given the typically long life of infrastructure investments, BAU will commit us to environmental harm for decades to come. Investments in lower-carbon, more environmentally benign structures and services, in contrast, will reduce or offset environmental damage over the useful life of those investments. Thus, decisions made today will determine whether we remain on the path of environmental degradation or begin living within our planetary means.[32]

While nature relies on the self-organizing affinities of healthy ecosystems, our efforts will need to be driven by a self-conscious design process. David Holmgren suggests that our cultural predisposition "to see and believe in predatory and competitive relationships, and discount cooperative and symbiotic relationships" has led us to isolate and optimize the parts, and thereby discount the potential yield of cooperative relationships.[33] If we were to deliberately design our systems to mimic natural ecosystems, what key principles would such systems possess? This book proposes five bold organizing objectives that, in the hands of decision makers and designers, will help bring about a future of multipurpose, low-carbon, resilient infrastructure that is tightly coordinated with natural systems, well integrated into social contexts, and capable of adapting to a changing climate.

Although the examples discussed in subsequent chapters vary widely in their complexity (some benefit from simple adjacency, whereas others are enmeshed in tightly woven, synergistic webs), all of them move beyond compartmentalized practices and reflect heightened sensitivity to economic, environmental, and social contexts. By taking advantage of the potential for resource exchanges across different infrastructural systems, these progressive projects improve efficiency, reduce costs, and yield meaningful social dividends. Such holistic, systems-oriented initiatives offer promising approaches for moving planning, regulatory, investment, and operating policies toward higher ground.

Hope for the Future

Within three days after the collapse of the I-35W bridge, Congress had funded a new structure, and the Minnesota Department of Transportation quickly selected a project management team and initiated an accelerated approach to construction procurement. The St. Anthony Falls Bridge, the replacement for the collapsed structure, was designed and built in less than nine months—record time.

The new bridge (fig. 1-3), which opened to great fanfare on September 18, 2008, demonstrated that America has not yet lost its historic prowess in producing forward-looking public works. Designed to accommodate multiple transit modes, including future bus and rail lines, the bridge was also conceived with energy and greenhouse-gas-emission reductions in mind. The concrete structure incorporates waste material from the previous bridge and residual products from coal-fired power plants, offsetting the amount of energy-intensive cement used in construction. Ornamental elements feature a new product: a self-cleaning cement that decomposes air pollutants and abates noxious gases. New LED (light-emitting diode) lighting reduces annual energy consumption by 15 percent and requires re-lamping only every 15 years.

Other next-generation enhancements include "smart technology" that provides real-time monitoring of both the

Figure 1-3. View under the reconstructed St. Anthony Falls Bridge, under nighttime illumination, Minneapolis, Minnesota. (Courtesy of Collin Anderson.)

bridge's structural components and its operations. In an effort to address the increasing frequency of severe meteorological events, the bridge also features an anti-icing system and signs that automatically report adverse conditions.

Both bridge users and the community at large participated in the planning process, weighing in on design decisions and various approaches to integrating the structure into the river landscape. Participants in public meetings and workshops chose native local stone and vivid ornamental lighting. Handsome viewing platforms enhance the visitor's experience of the river, and the bridge design accommodates the future construction of a separate carriageway for walkers and bikers that will connect to trail systems on both sides of the Mississippi. Schoolchildren installed their own handmade commemorative mosaic tiles on one of the bridge abutments.

2. Toward Infrastructural Ecologies: Interconnected, Multipurpose, and Synergistic Systems

Completed in May 2007, the 9.7-km (6-mi.) Storm Water Management and Road Tunnel (SMART), in Kuala Lumpur, Malaysia—a densely developed city of 1.6 million—marries two seemingly incompatible uses. Most of the time, the tunnel diverts automobile traffic from the congested central business district, reducing travel time by as much as 75 percent (and reducing the associated air pollution from vehicles otherwise idling in traffic jams.)[1] During heavy rains the tunnel also serves to retain stormwater from the flood-prone areas downtown. The tunnel's 3-million-cubic-meter (105.9-million-cubic-foot) storage capacity diverts up to 90 percent of stormwater in a heavy storm.[2]

The structure has three modes: during a light rainfall, no water is diverted into the tunnel, and traffic continues to flow; during moderate storms, water is directed into the tunnel's lowest section; during the heavy storms that occur once or twice annually, vehicles are evacuated and all sections of the tunnel receive floodwater. Within 48 hours, driven by gravity, most of the water will recede; pumps evacuate the remainder. The tunnel is desilted, washed down, and returned to its vehicular use.[3] Thanks to sophisticated controls, SMART can rapidly transform its operating conditions to whatever mode is required, and thereby protect the city from inundation.

The value-added component of the motorway made the behemoth stormwater diversion project feasible. One project with two functions costs less, uses fewer resources, and is generally less disruptive than two separate projects. In this instance, the vehicular use pays its own way: much of the construction cost is being recovered through toll collection.[4] The SMART project was included in the 2011 UN Habitat "Scroll of Honor" for its innovative and resource-savvy solution to multiple urban problems.[5]

Whereas the legacy of industrial-era infrastructure is one of independent, single-purpose assets and "non-reimbursed," or one-way flows, post-industrial solutions are modeled on the multifunctional, closed-loop exchanges characteristic of natural ecosystems. This chapter offers insight into the why and how of such systems. The featured examples were selected because they exemplify the first principle of the post-industrial paradigm: systems should be multipurpose, interconnected, and, ideally, synergistic.

At the most basic level, connected projects may simply be in close physical proximity. In such forms of colocation, two dissimilar entities achieve economies by efficiently sharing space or structure, though they do not significantly interact. The key assets and distribution networks of public works and utilities typically occupy segregated, dedicated space or easements, above or below grade. Colocation affords efficient use of real estate by bringing together unrelated but compatible functions in one locale, typically at a combined construction cost that is lower than the sum of the individual outlays would have been.

"Coupled" projects are those whose spatial proximity allows one system to make use of the productive or distributive functions of another, minimizing the resources leaving the system. Coupled projects may not only cross sectors (e.g., power, communications, and transportation), but may also cover a range of jurisdictional scales: from a neighborhood to a city to a region. A waste-to-energy plant located in Hiroshima, Japan, for example, generates electricity for the urban grid, shares its waste heat to warm a nearby recreation center (including a swimming pool), and incorporates a regional visitors center that highlights the benefits of waste reduction.[6] (Coupled projects are discussed later in the chapter.)

Examples of Simple Colocation

Across the United States, urban transportation departments must continually grapple with the disruptions that occur when various utility companies jackhammer their way into the tangle of water pipes, sewage and gas mains, electric cables, steam tunnels, and phone and telecommunications cables lying beneath public rights-of-way.[7] At its simplest, joint trenching means using a single ditch, instead of separate trenches, to accommodate multiple utilities. Upfront coordination not only reduces installation and maintenance costs but decreases the space requirements in the right-of-way. The city of Tallahassee, Florida, which began using joint trenches in 2000—primarily to service large, newly planned communities—has also found that joint trenches minimize environmental impact (because they require fewer surface cuts) and improve worker safety.[8]

Common utility ducts (also called "utilidors") improve upon joint trenches. These are usually made of metal or concrete, are typically insulated in cold climates, and are placed either above or below ground. They have shared, easy-to-find access points. Examples abound in Japan, but common utility ducts can also be found in the new Poundbury Village settlement, in the United Kingdom,[9] and in Bremen, Germany, where the ducts are located under bikeways or footpaths. Singapore's subgrade "common services tunnel" combines telecom cables, power lines, water and wastewater infrastructure, and district cooling—and also includes pneumatic refuse-collection pipes. Wet utilities are segregated from dry.[10] This type of duct is designed for ease of maintenance and expansion, as well as for utility protection during natural disasters. In the United States, the ducts have been deployed in Florida's Disney World in the form of underground service tunnels.[11]

Utilidors were pioneered in Taipei, Taiwan, in the mid-1990s, where they were colocated with the city's rapid-transit line. One such project, which cut typical construction time by six months, also saved NT$44.64 million for the Taipei city government through its single, spatially efficient, one-time coordinated construction.[12] Because of their higher initial costs, utilidors have been underutilized, but those now in use illustrate the multiple benefits of simple infrastructural colocation, including maximizing the use of subsurface space, decreased construction and maintenance costs, minimal traffic disruption, and simplified access for repairs.

Another example of simple colocation is the photovoltaic noise barrier (PVNB). These are typically grid-connected solar-panel arrays, which are mounted to the sound barriers often erected to shield nearby communities from the noise of railways or highways. Like building-integrated solar-power applications, PVNBs save material and construction costs by piggybacking on existing structures. Since the late 1980s, these opportunistic colocations have been successfully producing electricity for the grid while deflecting noise away from homes and other occupied areas. The structures achieve economy of scale and save real estate, as both functions are sited within the transportation easement; the arrangement also supports servicing, as both systems can be cleaned and serviced by one set of maintenance vehicles.[13]

A large-scale, 220-kilowatt (kW) grid-connected system with 2,000 square feet of PVNB, located along the A9 highway near Ouderkerk aan de Amstel (Amsterdam, the Netherlands), produces some 176 megawatt-hours (MWh) of electrical power annually. Another example is the 5,035-square-meter (1.2-acre) PV/sound barrier along a 1-km (about 0.6-mi.) length of a motorway near Trento, Italy, which brings noise levels in the adjacent municipality of Isera into compliance with codes. Its peak power rate of 730 kW meets the annual energy demand of 600 people, which reduces CO_2 emissions by more than 420 tons, and decreases day- and nighttime noise levels by 10 decibels (dB).[14]

Another installation is a hybrid: the glass surfaces of the PV arrays deflect sound, eliminating the need for a separate acoustic barrier. East- and west-facing PVNBs installed along a motorway viaduct near Zurich, Switzerland, offer yet another advantage: a back-to-back configuration that redirects sound waves. Moreover, exposure to morning and evening sun effectively doubles electricity production, putting the yield on par with that of the more typical, south-facing installations.[15]

A 2005 study of existing and planned transportation infrastructure concluded that photo-voltaic noise barriers, extending the total length of appropriately oriented roads and rails, could produce as much as 5–6 percent of the electricity needed for the European Union.[16] In increasingly congested cities and along suburban routes where sound protection may become imperative, it would be advisable to begin planning for integrated PVNB systems as part of major roadwork upgrades or new construction currently under way.

Utilities have been known to take the high road, conjoined with transportation bridges across water bodies. Bangladesh's Bangabandhu Bridge, for example, forged a vital conduit between the eastern and western halves of that nation, which had long been separated by the Jamuna River. Completed in 1998, it supports an uninterrupted international road and rail link between Southeast Asia and northwestern Europe.[17] Before the bridge was constructed, two studies—one for a combined rail and road bridge, and another for a separate gas pipeline link—revealed that neither project was economically feasible on its own. Today, these functions are combined in a multipurpose structure that also conveys high-voltage and telecommunication cables.[18]

The Enneüs Heerma Bridge (fig. 2-1), which connects Amsterdam with a new urban development on the neighboring island of IJburg, consists of five spans suspended between two graceful arches. The bridge accommodates two lanes of

Figure 2-1. Enneüs Heerma Bridge (with tram) between Amsterdam and Island of IJburg, the Netherlands. (Courtesy of S. Sepp.)

vehicular traffic, two tramlines, two bicycle lanes, and pedestrian footpaths, while also carrying pipelines for water, sewage, and other public utility services between island and mainland.

The energy sector and the information and communications technology (ICT) sector offer a number of intriguing examples of cross-sector couplings. Wind streams are inherently variable in velocity and direction—and, as US use of wind energy scales up, greater precision is needed for measuring and predicting wind patterns. Strategically placed wind sensors can yield forecast data, allowing electricity-system operators to optimize wind energy's contribution to the electric grid.

In Texas, sensors developed by Onesemble, a wind data provider, have been placed on cell phone towers at heights of 80–100 meters (262–328 feet)—where most turbine blades rotate. The network of 100 sensor hubs tracks wind speed, direction, and temperature for nearly 95 percent of the wind farms in Texas, providing the Electric Reliability Council of Texas, an independent operator that manages 85 percent of the state's electric load, with six predictions per hour.[19]

The ubiquitous electrical substation—housing transformers, switchgear, metering, and other equipment—typically converts high-transmission voltage to levels appropriate for local distribution. Substations are frequently housed at grade in security-fenced enclosures, or underground, or within special-purpose buildings (particularly in cities, where these mostly unmanned substations are treated as infrastructural pariahs, given the not-unreasonable public concerns about noise, electromagnetic emissions, and unsightliness).

In an approach that is more common outside the United States than within, high-voltage electrical substations have been integrated into buildings or other complexes.[20] Containment generally eliminates the objectionable noise from transformers; controls effluents that may result from any equipment spills; increases resilience to flooding, climate stress, and seismic activity; and eliminates redundant excavation and foundations. Moreover, innovations in gas-insulated substation technology and highly integrated switchgears may be able to reduce space requirements for substations by as much as 30 percent.[21]

In Japan, substations are commonly concealed beneath other structures. Tokyo Electric Power Company's Higashi-Uchisaiwai-cho Substation, for example, sits five levels (100 feet) beneath three tiers of subsurface parking, an at-grade commercial facility, and 22 residential floors. In another example, an unusual one, Chubu Electric constructed a substation beneath a parking lot near Meijo Castle, a seventeenth-century Nagoya landmark. In a useful synergy, an above-grade ornamental fountain, added to help cool the electrical equipment, also cancels mechanical noise.

The Haymarket bulk-power substation in Sydney, Australia, is a multi-tiered example located in the dense central business district. Its components are integrated into a shopping complex: some parts are above the publicly occupied areas, but most of the primary equipment is situated below an underground parking structure.[22] In St. Gallen, Switzerland, a two-story substation is sited completely invisibly beneath Breitfield Soccer Stadium.[23] London substations are sometimes located beneath public parks or sidewalks.

In many US cities, substations are categorized as nuisances and are therefore confined by zoning laws to industrial or manufacturing districts (or, in the case of very small substations, to commercial districts). With the decline of their manufacturing base, however, many cities are rezoning—and foregoing manufacturing ("M") designations on much of their real estate. At the same time, neighborhood demands for electrical power are increasing, and real estate prices are rising—making the locations of new substations problematic. Were it not for zoning interdictions, the logical answer would lie in colocation—that is, stacking substations with other compatible facilities.[24]

A rare US example—one grandfathered in (inside a 1967 building that was destroyed on September 11, 2001)—is the rebuilt substation that powers much of Lower Manhattan. Today it occupies four stories within the eleven-story concrete bunker that makes up the base of the new Seven World Trade Center office tower.[25] Housing three 20-foot-tall transformers (with room for up to ten more), the substation is inside a plinth, artfully concealed by stainless steel panels with integrated louvers that allow for ventilation. It provides 40 megawatts (MW) of electricity and has the capacity to meet the growing power demand anticipated for a reconstructed and expanded Lower Manhattan.

In another rare example of substation colocation in the United States, a public utility—after extensive community input and involvement—sited two 50-MVA (megavolt-ampere), sixty-nine 12-kV (kilovolt) transformers deep within a hillside of a high-income residential area in East Anaheim, California. This subterranean, gas-insulated facility, the first of its kind in the United States, serves 25,000 residents and operates virtually noiselessly beneath a two-acre neighborhood park. The $19.5-million project may serve as a prototype for other utilities, not only in California but across the nation.[26]

Colocating infrastructure with other land uses can bring collateral benefits, including reduced costs for equipment, access roads, and utilities, and sometimes for direct power provision. Agriculture and wind generation coexist quite compatibly, for example; wind farms have become increasingly prevalent on lands long dedicated to agriculture or the grazing of livestock. Wind energy, of course, has been used historically, as in the Netherlands, for milling grain, or for draining and maintaining farmland.[27]

Conflicts arising from shared use are usually manageable or can be mitigated. These include the sacrifice of some productive land to accommodate the towers supporting the turbines and interconnecting roads and transmission lines for industrial-scale wind operations. Other reparable concerns include erosion or other damage resulting from wind turbine construction.[28]

Community-scale wind farms are excellent examples of colocation across different sectors. In these installations, planned with local input and/or farmer-ownership or lease agreements, power feeds back into agricultural operations while most is sold to the grid. The Minwind projects near Luverne, Minnesota, are among the first farmer-owned turbines (2004) to take advantage of US Department of Agriculture renewable-energy grants. Involving more than 200 local investors, the farming cooperative secured long-term power-purchase and interconnection agreements with Xcel Energy. In addition to its dual yields, the project's multiple benefits include diverse local employment opportunities and an increase in the local tax base.[29]

On the west coast of Australia, north of Perth, the Alinta Walkaway wind farm is one of that country's largest wind-energy complexes. Its 54 turbines supply 90 MW of power to approximately 60,000 homes, reducing carbon dioxide emissions by 400,000 tons annually (equivalent to removing 80,000 cars from the roads). A major tourist attraction, the development also includes a nearby 35-hectare conservation park, a visitors center, and a viewing platform.[30] Optimally spaced turbines across open farming country may be compatible with both broadacre crops (e.g., cereals, oilseeds, sugarcane, legumes, hops, cotton, hay, and silage) and stock grazing. With the roadbeds for turbine access integrated into the farm's existing track network, and internal power cables placed at a depth to allow cropping over the top, typically less than 1 percent of farmland has been appropriated.[31]

Brazil stands to become the fifth largest wind-energy producer globally. Intensive investments in wind energy have been made in the country's northeast area specifically to rebalance its energy mix. A decade ago, Brazil's dependency on hydropower (91 percent of installed capacity) precipitated an energy shortage and a related economic crisis when this section of the country was struck by drought. Here, development of wind farms has been strategically synergistic in two ways: first, in Brazil wind power is accepted as highly compatible with both agriculture and ranching, and private wind developers contribute land-lease payments to this rural agricultural sector. Second, wind power's potential is greatest during the annual dry season, when wind speeds are at their peak, whereas hydropower is then at its lowest ebb.[32]

Like land-based installations, offshore wind farms offer opportunities for colocation with other activities, including fisheries (aquaculture in particular) and maritime traffic. As of September 2013, 520 MW of offshore wind capacity was being connected to Germany's grid, but by 2030 the Federal Government hopes to reach a North Sea capacity of 25,000 MW.[33] With aquaculture one of the world's fastest-growing food-production sectors, experts have been reviewing the possibilities for combining and coordinating these emerging industries in multipurpose marine areas. Initial studies have proven the biological and technical feasibility of using the groundings of these turbines as armatures for cultures of mussels and sugar kelp.[34] A partnership could benefit both groups through the co-management of operations and maintenance: for example, the sharing of maritime offshore infrastructure (logistics platforms, vessels), as well as general maritime skills and knowledge. With the right regulatory policies in place, along with proactive administration of the industry interfaces, both sectors could reap the economic efficiencies of combined use.[35]

Underground Wastewater Treatment in Barcelona

Barcelona's Besos Wastewater Treatment Plant is a uniquely creative example of colocation. This seaside city has a unitary sewer system (combined sewage and stormwater). By the late 1980s, Barcelona's regional rivers were among the most polluted and degraded in Western Europe. After the 1991 European Union directive on urban wastewater, the municipality undertook comprehensive upgrades of its water treatment infrastructure, including the Besos Plant. Improvements to the plant were implemented as part of a 40-hectare urban renewal project. The urban renewal site encompassed Barcelona's old industrial waterfront, Porta Vell. What is now known as the Barcelona Forum is a 74-acre, world-class harbor development featuring restaurants, a commercial center (the Maremagnum), Sea World, an IMAX theatre, luxury hotels, a concert arena, a convention center, and a public square—all connected via a pedestrian bridge across an upgraded marina to Las Ramblas, the city's major tree-lined pedestrian corridor. Barcelona used EU and local public-sector funding to leverage private investment, a familiar technique today but less common 15 years ago, when the project was undertaken.

Before the upgrade and expansion of the plant, residents and tourists had suffered from the noxious odors of hydrogen sulfide and ammonia that were being discharged into the water. Barcelona's Ministry of the Environment dealt with the harbor's space limitations by constructing the plant completely underground. The new, 920,000-square-foot facility sits directly beneath the premium space of the Forum, and treats more than 70 percent of the wastewater from Barcelona and the surrounding towns—more than two million people. It was the plant's positioning beneath a prestigious public venue that intensified the demand for absolute odor control, which is accomplished, by a combination of physical and chemical means, through the use of absorptive media in the ventilation system.[36]

When it comes to integrating freight transportation modes (e.g., sea to rail to truck), multinational corporations have largely led the way—developing seamlessly integrated logistics systems, using consolidated, single-contract service providers, and promoting packaging infrastructure such as containerization.[37] Internationalized markets have also helped foster the integration of transportation modes. Maritime ports—including Vancouver, Canada; the Port Authority of New York and New Jersey; Rotterdam, the Netherlands; and Hamburg, Germany—are working to integrate shipping facilities and container, train, and trucking yards to enable cargo to move more smoothly from one conveyance to another; some ports are even linked to airports.

An intermodal (also called multimodal) approach to transportation is as transformative an idea for moving people as it is for moving goods. In addition to improving connectivity between various forms of transportation, such an approach has the added advantage of reducing the environmental impacts associated with the unimodal infrastructure of heavily used highways, rights-of-way, and parking lots. Ultimately, intermodal complexes can help shift investment away from the construction and repair of roadways, and toward features that support public transit and nonmechanical modes of transportation: sidewalks, pedestrian amenities, bike routes, and bike-storage facilities.[38]

The US federal government's recognition of the efficiencies associated with multimodal public transportation can be seen in the 1991 passage of the Intermodal Surface Transportation Efficiency Act (ISTEA). A 1994 report by the National Commission on Intermodal Transportation cited the following benefits:

> *(1) lowering overall transportation costs by allowing each mode to be used for the portion of the trip to which it is best suited; (2) increasing economic productivity and efficiency, thereby enhancing the Nation's global competitiveness; (3) reducing congestion and the burden on overstressed infrastructure components; (4) generating higher returns from public and private infrastructure investments; (5) improving mobility for the elderly, disabled, isolated, and economically disadvantaged; (6) reducing energy consumption and contributing to improved air quality and environmental conditions.[39]*

Today's transportation hubs are perhaps the best examples of the shift away from the capitalization of single-mode infrastructure in favor of integrated, multimodal assets. The key attributes of such facilities are (1) convenient connectivity between rail, bus, and air, and (2) safe links to auto parking, cycling, and other pedestrian amenities. Travel schedules, ticketing, and information are integrated through logical connections between trip origins and destinations—allowing broader service choices as well as greater comfort and convenience, and potentially luring travelers away from private vehicles and toward public transit.

Through its Multimodal Discretionary Grants (TIGER) Program, the 2009 American Resource and Recovery Act is helping to fund numerous mixed-use, intermodal ventures. Cities including St. Paul, Minnesota; Normal, Illinois; and Kent, Ohio, are constructing urban hubs that support more-seamless transfer between different modes of travel, save travel time, and reduce greenhouse-gas emissions, while in many cases eliminating redundancies in facilities.

The City of Raleigh, North Carolina, will use a $36.5-million TIGER grant matched by $6 million from its own coffers and $9 million from North Carolina's Department of Transportation to repurpose a former warehouse in the west end of its downtown into a regional multimodal transit station. The facility will incorporate waiting areas, mixed use, and civic space for current and future demand for intercity passenger rail, commuter rail, light rail, city bus, regional bus, taxis, bicycles, and other transportation modes. Designs feature a grand pedestrian plaza and a large stormwater park adjacent to the complex. It is expected to boost economic development in the area once it is completed in 2017.[40]

San Francisco's Transbay Transit Center

At the 2013 ground breaking for the Transbay Transit Center (TTC), San Francisco's $4.1-billion multimodal facility, shovel-wielding officials signified the active involvement of federal, state, county, and local governments in the creation of this infrastructural showpiece. Celebrated as a "project of national significance" by Congresswoman Nancy Pelosi,[41] the TTC is an intermodal facility situated within a mixed-use, multi-tiered 13-tower complex that will reshape the city skyline. Part of the San Francisco Redevelopment Agency's plan for a refurbished South of Market financial district, the project is the centerpiece of San Francisco's broader strategies to reduce sprawl, green-house-gas emissions, and heat islands; bolster environmental quality; and stimulate local economic growth.

Currently the best embodiment of US efforts to shift away from single-mode solutions at a dense urban scale, the TTC represents a new kind of compound asset, one that originates in collaboration between multiple planning and operating agencies, and also reflects a team approach to land-use decision making and complex spatial problem solving. When completed in 2017, it will exemplify the strategic use of intensified real estate development to generate a funding stream capable not only of supporting transportation infrastructure development but also achieving additional societal benefits both locally and regionwide. Proceeds from development of the adjoining parcels will help finance the hub, which is designed to stitch together 11 existing transportation systems, and funding requirements ensure that the terminal and extensions are constructed as a single, integrated project.[42] As a holistic engine of redevelopment, the full, three-phase build-out of this plan is predicted to increase the gross regional product of the Bay Area by $80 million.[43]

The project, which was in its early construction phases at the time of writing, is the offspring of a generations-old policy. In 1973, the San Francisco Board of Supervisors passed the Transit First resolution, which discouraged freeway development and assigned priority to public transit. The TTC is an outstanding example of one of the goals of ISTEA: "to reduce energy consumption and air pollution while promoting economic development."[44]

Thanks to the Muni and BART municipal light-rail systems, the San Francisco Bay Area enjoys a strong public transportation network, but many outlying suburbs are still largely auto dependent. The project replaces a more than 70-year-old terminal that was already a toll-financed, multimodal destination. In the early 1940s, commuter train services that entered the city via the San Francisco/Oakland Bay Bridge were eliminated and replaced by buses. The new center will revive these lost connections. It will efficiently link and expand local, commuter, and long-distance bus lines; rail travel; and AC (Alameda–Contra Costa) Transit. It will connect to the more remotely situated Caltrain commuter-rail service. By offering more suburban residents convenient and direct rail access to downtown, it will take drivers off the road and eliminate an estimated 36,000 tons of carbon dioxide annually. The new center will dignify the experience of arrival, departure, and transfer among multiple modes on different levels, and include retail along its full-length pedestrian concourse one level below grade (fig. 2-2). Lastly, planned high-speed rail service from Los Angeles/Anaheim will add national intercity service to this seamless passenger exchange among regional operators.

A generous roof, accessible from the street level via escalator or elevator, shades the sidewalk plaza. A 5.4-acre rooftop park that runs the full quarter-mile length of the site features walking paths, lawns, gardens and play gardens, ponds, an outdoor theater, restaurants, and retail. Captured stormwater will irrigate the greenery, which will in turn filter and cool the air, thus reducing the heat-island effect. Large, domed light wells will help illuminate the floors; provide natural ventilation to passively cool the complex at night; and visually unify the complex, helping to orient visitors. An animated public "plaza-in-the-sky," the living roof is the visual focal point for the surrounding new towers.

The build-out of the adopted 2005 Redevelopment Plan is carefully coordinated through development controls and design guidelines. Three million square feet of office and hotel are coupled with 100,000 square feet of commercial retail con-

Figure 2-2. Cross-section rendering, Transbay Transit Center, San Francisco, California. (Project Architect: Pelli Clarke Pelli. Renderings courtesy of the Transbay Joint Power Authority.)

centrated on immediately adjacent parcels. Careful placement of low, mid-rise, and high-rise buildings maintain sunlight in the public spaces below. Appropriately, this transit-oriented mixed-use development, equipped with bike facilities, pedestrian alleys, and other amenities, serves as a gateway to downtown and revitalizes the space vacated by the bridge ramps, made unnecessary by the new design, that were demolished.

The San Francisco Redevelopment Agency will finance the TCC's $1.59-million budget through multiple funding sources, including the implementation of its full plan with assistance from the city, state, and federal governments, using tax-increment financing, interest income, and the sale of agency bonds, assessments, and loans.[45] The agency received a federal loan of $171 million from USDOT's Transportation Infrastructure Finance and Innovation Act (TIFIA) and an award of $400 million in ARRA stimulus funds. Land sales valued at $429 million are joined with regional toll funding valued at almost $250 million, along with contributions from AC Transit, San Mateo County sales tax, and San Francisco Proposition K 0.5 percent sales tax for public transit improvements. Further, property taxes allocated from the redevelopment area are expected to generate as much as $430,000 million in net tax-increment financing for the Center's construction and operating costs at its anticipated opening in 2017.[46]

Local comprehensive plans, development regulations, and planned capital improvements are to be implemented under the aegis of the Redevelopment Agency and the Transbay Joint Powers Authority (TJPA).[47] An unprecedented collaboration across Bay Area government and transportation bodies, the TJPA was formed to undertake the development of the Transbay Transit Center.

While retaining its "primary jurisdiction," the TJPA also made provisions for redevelopment input from local landowners, extending preferences to businesses at the site wishing to remain in the project area. Years of stakeholder participation, overseen by the TJPA's Citizen's Advisory Committee, helped develop new urban and design objectives. The TJPA was able to provide technical solutions to regional transit problems by convening the full range of government, NGO (nongovernmental organization), and private entities in order to produce a cooperative regional transport system. It successfully overcame physical, financial, and community opposition, as well as environmental constraints, by turning impediments into catalysts to bridge traditional modal boundaries. If all goes according to plan, the completed Transbay Transit Center will demonstrate how a complex, yet holistically conceived project can function better than the sum of its parts.

Coupling: Beyond Colocation

The remaining examples in this chapter highlight an ideal attribute of post-industrial infrastructure: symbiotic exchanges across different infrastructural systems, whereby output from one system supports the functions of another. For example, waste heat from data processing can be recovered for urban district heating, or useable biomethane can be retrieved from sewage to power a large data system. Combined heat and power, or cogeneration, similarly recovers the otherwise-wasted process heat from electrical generation in the form of steam, which is then used for industrial or domestic (district or home heating) applications.

Data centers house large-scale server systems and associated components, such as backup power supplies and telecommunications equipment. They are prodigious consumers of electrical energy (the power draw for large data centers can be as high as tens of megawatts) and producers of waste heat, the elimination of which accounts for more than half of their energy use.[48] For large organizations, data centers may represent as much as 30 percent of corporate energy consumption. With more than 1.5 billion people online around the world, scientists estimate that the energy footprint of the Internet is growing by more than 10 percent annually.[49] Measured by the US Environmental Protection Agency (EPA) in 2006, this sector consumed about 61 billion kilowatt-hours (kWh), or 1.5 percent of total US electricity consumption, double the rate measured in 2000.[50]

For the burgeoning information technology (IT) sector, finding use-compatible sites for data centers is important, given their significant energy and cooling needs. A growing number of IT companies are examining the prospects of utilizing the natural conditions found in underground data bunkers—the surrounding thermal mass, and, in the case of some limestone caves, naturally flowing cold air. Cavern Technologies of Kansas City, Kansas (whose motto is "We set IT in stone"), houses a data center 125 feet underground. In addition to the subterranean protection from natural disasters or deliberate attack (the limestone structure is three times stronger than concrete), the ambient 68°F temperature significantly reduces cooling costs (by as much as 50 percent), enabling Cavern Technologies to offer services to consumers at price points significantly below those of competitors.[51]

At the world's first 100 percent wind-cooled data center, operated in Billingham, United Kingdom, by Hewlett-Packard, fans suck cold North Sea air into the air-filtration and under-floor air-delivery system to keep the center at about 75°F. Here, efficiency is compounded by the use of white walls and light-colored server racks, which, by better reflecting light, reduce the need for additional lighting by 40 percent, saving about $7 million a year. In total, the facility reduced its annual energy use from 27,500 to 20,000 MWh, and its annual CO_2 production from 17,500 to 8,770 metric tons, thus cutting its carbon footprint in half.[52]

A partnership between the IT company Academica of Helsinki, Finland, and Helsinki Energia (a for-profit energy company owned by the city) resulted in the colocation of a new 2-MW data-server center. The IT infrastructure is sited underneath the nineteenth-century Uspenski Cathedral, an Eastern Orthodox landmark and a popular tourist destination. This new center, situated within a subterranean chamber of the cathedral that also served as a bomb shelter during World War II, holds hundreds of computer servers. The waste heat from the computers is transferred by heat pumps into the city's district heating network, first developed in the 1950s, providing domestic heat for approximately 500 detached homes. At the same time, district cooling, produced by heat pumps from thermal energy, seawater, or the city's energy generation, provides cooling to the data center. The center's energy needs for cooling have been reduced by nearly 80 percent, saving $200,000 annually and shrinking Academica's carbon footprint by 1,600 tons.[53] Another synergy offered by this unusual siting is, of course, the added security of the data center's entombment.

In an unusual feasibility study, five scientists at Hewlett-Packard's Sustainable IT Ecosystem Laboratory examined the potential for symbiotic exchanges between dairy farms and data center. The data center's waste heat would be used to accelerate the anaerobic processing of cow manure, and the resulting methane would fuel electric generation for the data center. This coupling would not only dispose of noxious and polluting solid waste (as a greenhouse gas, methane is 21 times more damaging than carbon dioxide), but would also provide additional income to dairy farmers. In this case, a 10,000-cow dairy operation could support the energy requirements of a 1-MW (that is, a medium-sized) data center with surplus power left for use in farm heating or refrigeration. After two years, the study estimates, farmers could break even and then go on to earn as much as $2 million annually from processing bovine by-product for power sales to the data center.[54] While HP is not currently exploring where this approach might be put to work, the technology, according to the authors of the study, is readily available for implementation. The idea does not seem too far off. Microsoft announced in November 2012 that its new

$5.5-million 200-kW data center in Cheyenne, Wyoming, would operate off the grid, using processed methane (biogas) from the city's sewage treatment facility to power a fuel cell producing its electricity.[55]

As in the data center examples, where opportunistic colocation serves both parties, the construction of the Viennese metro line U2 was planned to take advantage of "ground-coupled" (or geothermal) energy—heat from the earth. Four stations utilize the constant temperature of groundwater to cool equipment rooms and to heat office spaces.[56] Switzerland's Lötschberg Base Tunnel, a 21-mile-long railway tunnel (currently the world's longest) that bisects the Swiss Alps, accommodates both passenger and freight rail. To exploit the tunnel's high potential for geothermal energy, its excess groundwater is extracted and then boosted in temperature by a heat pump,[57] allowing its moderate temperature to heat the nearby Tropenhaus Frutigen, a greenhouse and aquaculture facility that produces tropical fruit as well as sturgeon and caviar.[58]

Infrastructural Ecology in Stockholm, Sweden— Hammarby Sjöstad

Since the 1970s, central government policy making in Sweden has mobilized local governments to reduce environmental loads by coupling new technology and ecological design knowledge, with the overall goals of increasing energy efficiency and materials reuse while strengthening biodiversity. The May 1997 environmental policy of Stockholm's Municipal Council, for example, called for "a functioning eco-municipality, an eco-cycling society, and an environmental capital. . . . Our actions will be grounded on the insight that nature's resources are limited and that everything that is brought to nature must be reprocessed in a functional eco-cycle."[59]

The new Swedish neighborhood of Hammarby Sjöstad— originally conceived as part of Stockholm's unfulfilled 2004 Summer Olympics bid and later revived to address an inner-city housing shortage—has developed a unique post-industrial platform for its public services, based on a "locally as-close-as-possible eco-cycling of water, energy and other resources."[60] In its full build-out by 2016, some 25,000 residents will be housed on land repurposed from an industrial brownfield. It is a showcase of compact, mixed-use development and sustainable urbanism.

Hammarby Sjöstad was built with national and European Union subsidies funneled through Stockholm's Local Investment Programme (1998–2002), created to fund ecologically appropriate projects and project-related green jobs.[61] The goal set for Hammarby Sjöstad was a 50 percent reduction in its environmental impact compared to settlements built using 1990s technology.[62] Its primary performance metrics include reductions in CO_2 and other greenhouse-gas emission, ground-level ozone, raw resource use, and water consumption. Under the holistic approach taken by Stockholm's City Planning and City Development Administrations, this objective was realized through a joint infrastructure proposition developed among three utilities: Stockholm Energi AB (now Fortrum), Stockholm Vatten (Water), and Stockholm's Waste Management Administration. Representatives of these key municipal utilities, as well as city-planning, roads, and real estate departments were convened as a project team.

Hammarby Sjöstad's strict environmental objectives demanded innovative management solutions. These were fostered through its project office, which offered a platform for collaborative decision making and initiated a deliberately integrated planning and design process. In facilitated sessions, the utilities were encouraged to "self-organize" around the concept of redistributing residue or waste from one organization's processes for productive reuse by another. This intentional linking of multiple processes and the metabolic sharing of resources might be described as the earliest example of a full-scale infrastructural ecology.

What became known as the Hammarby Model provided a template for interactive and cooperative exchange between the energy and material flows of the locality (fig. 2-3). This transformative approach relies on an integrated and nearly closed system in which energy and resources cascade and cycle from one utility to another. This was partly achieved by creating new links among several existing utilities, both within the district and at its periphery. Waste energy (heat) drawn from the combined heat and power plant (CHP) and the sewage treatment facility is recovered to supply district heating.[63] Biogas extracted from the sewage plant is processed as fuel for both local vehicles and domestic cooking stoves. On an experimental basis, a portion of the sewage facility returns sludge for agricultural use. Mixed combustible household waste is routed for combustion in the CHP plant, where it is combined with forestry waste. Household

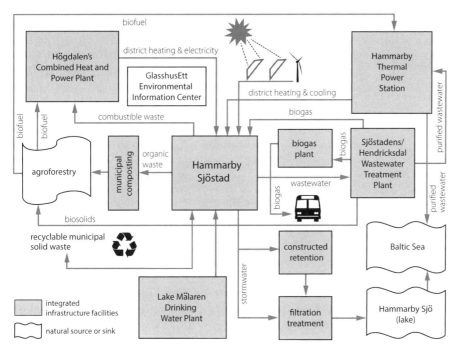

Figure 2-3. The "Hammarby Model," Hammarby Sjöstad, Sweden. (Redrawn by Hillary Brown from the original by Lena Wettrén, Bumling AB.)

and commercial organic waste (compost) reverts as fertilizer for the nearby agro-forest industry, whose woodchips return to power the CHP plant.[64] By closing loops at the most local level possible, the Hammarby Model exemplifies a nearly self-contained recovery of energy and resources.

This approach is complemented by harvesting nature's free services. Solar arrays produce local or distributed energy. Domestic hot-water systems are supplemented by fuel cells and solar thermal panels. Pollution loads are remediated by local landscapes, which purge stormwater from streets before returning it in canals to the lake along with the cleaner rainwater from courtyards and roofs.

Where targeted emissions reductions were attempted by encouraging lifestyle and behavioral changes, some measures were more successful than others.[65] Thanks to the integration of ferry and light rail services, carpooling, and a system of biofueled buses and urban rights-of-way designed to promote walking and biking, overall transportation energy per household (measuring CO_2 emission reductions) in 2008 was 48 percent below that of comparable communities.[66]

Another successful innovation is one of the town's signature features: an automated underground pneumatic waste-collection system that helps residents sort paper, metal, glass, and plastic for local industrial reuse. Source separation activities recorded on personal cards measure system use and encourage occupants to improve their waste-management behavior. The town's "GlashusEtt" is an environmental showcase and information center that helps inhabitants and international visitors recognize the necessary role behavioral change will play in reducing environmental impacts.

Hammarby Sjöstad's greatest innovation—the intentional development of a local infrastructural ecology—coupled with its efficiency and sufficiency measures, has enabled it to achieve many of its original objectives. The city of Stockholm's assessment tool, the Environmental Load Profile, has been used to assess project performance to date. This tool evaluates the full range of construction and operational activities of the development from an embodied energy and life-cycle perspective. Used prospectively, it can calculate environmental loads of design or planning alternatives. It also is benchmarking the completed project outcomes against the original targets as measured by emissions, water and nonrenewable energy use, pollutant loading, and waste. The evaluations of the first stage of Hammarby Sjöstad's performance (against its "reference case" scenario) show a 30 percent reduction in nonrenewable energy use, 41 percent in water use, 29 percent in global-warming potential, along with other pollution and GHG-reduction measures.[67]

The imaginative integration of public works showcased in Hammarby Sjöstad reflects strong and effective leadership grounded in a proactive climate of public-private cooperation. Holistic thinking and the promotion of reciprocity are the principles behind the project's realization of meaningful synergies.

Conclusion

Next-generation infrastructure can serve multiple objectives by avoiding narrowly focused solutions. Colocating or functionally conjoining different types of projects in novel ways that span scales, political jurisdictions, and sectors can serve the triple bottom line. Coupled distribution networks, piggybacked or grouped arrangements (joint trenching, PVNBs, utilidors) and vertically integrating service assets with other compatible uses can produce initial or ongoing cost economies, reduce disruption, and conserve valuable resources. By combining transit modes for convenience and efficiency in one mixed-use facility, intermodal centers can become anchor destinations and engines for urban redevelopment in their own right. The new development of Hammarby Sjöstad points the way as a deliberately considered infrastructural ecology; it's designed to systematically recover energy, water, gas or other material resources for mutual exchange within a bounded area.

Infrastructural ecology is a unifying concept for this book. As subsequent chapters further reveal, multifunctional and synergistic infrastructures can also reduce carbon intensity; beneficially combine constructed and natural systems to achieve a measure of their regeneration; achieve better integration into the local context; and adapt to the current and potential stressors of climate change.

Such future-proof solutions represent collaborative, out-of-the-box, and holistic thinking on the part of government, NGOs, communities, and/or business leaders faced with complex demands and fewer resources, including a dwindling supply of real estate. As entrepreneurial investors charging their design teams to develop multiple-objective, integrated solutions, they can effectively optimize subsystems. In this way, the actors behind the projects have collectively served to develop a new paradigm for meeting twenty-first-century imperatives.

Box 2-1. Advantages of Colocation

Colocation may yield a number of direct and indirect project benefits. These typically would include economic, environmental, and social dividends such as:

- *Site optimization*: combining several functions within a single site increases real estate productivity and reduces pressure on undeveloped sites
- *Capital savings*: shared site, infrastructure, or building components
- *Operational savings*: operating and maintenance efficiencies
- *Greenhouse-gas-emission reductions*: lower transport energy or transmissions losses
- *Material resource conservation, and recovery for reuse*
- *Environmental benefits*: reduced disruption, noise, or visual pollution
- *Public amenities / community benefits*: incorporation of additional educational, recreational, or civic uses
- *Job creation*
- *Tax-revenue production*

3. Greening Heat and Power: An Integrated Approach to Decarbonizing Energy

Humankind has depended on carbon-based fuels for millennia—but evidence has been mounting that runaway increases in carbon-intensive activity have set in motion potentially devastating climatic effects. To avoid the most extreme consequences of climate instability, it is essential for infrastructure sectors to "decarbonize"—that is, to turn from dependence on coal, oil, and natural gas toward renewable power sources (especially green ones)—and do so within a narrowing window of time.[1]

A subset of renewable power, green power not only self-replenishes over short time periods but creates a minimal amount of pollution when produced; examples include solar, moving water, wind, organic waste (biomass or bacterially digested biogas), and geothermal.[2] According to the US Environmental Protection Agency, replacing a kilowatt-hour of conventional power with green power avoids, on average, the emission of one pound of carbon dioxide.[3]

Altered planetary conditions from rising concentrations of atmospheric carbon (and other greenhouse gases) have caused mild to severe ecological degradation worldwide, affecting critical ecosystem services such as climate regulation, coastal protection, and water purification, and consequently disrupting the critical infrastructure sectors that depend on those services. Moreover, the temperature extremes, drought, storm surges, rising sea levels, and flooding associated with climate instability pose significant and increasing direct risks to infrastructural assets—energy, water, and transportation in particular. For example, during the European heat wave of 2003, estimated to have killed more than 30,000,[4] rising temperatures created unprecedented demand for air conditioning. This electric overload forced France to cut 4 gigawatts (GW) of power from nuclear plants no longer adequately cooled by river water—the equivalent of shutting down four power plants.[5] Climate instability and sea-level rise have been implicated in such high-intensity storms as Hurricane Sandy, which inflicted approximately $7.5 billion worth of damage on New York City's low-lying transportation infrastructure, about $5 billion of which was incurred by the NY Metropolitan Transportation Authority alone.[6]

While the need for climate-change mitigation cuts across all sectors of society, the infrastructure sectors, as significant producers or consumers of heat and power energy, must take special responsibility for carbon reduction. As of 2011, the electricity sector alone accounted for about 33 percent of total US greenhouse-gas emissions.[7] Here, power producers especially can be in the vanguard, mitigating emissions by retrofitting power plants to run on renewable fuels close at hand; maximizing efficiency by incorporating cogeneration, in which waste heat from electricity generation is used for heating or industrial applications; and increasing investment in new green-power technologies to meet increased demand as well as replace older, fossil-fuel power plants coming off-line.

Owners of other infrastructure systems—the water sector, information and communication technology sector (ICT), and transit systems (all large energy consumers)—can similarly lead by purchasing green power, or engaging in on-site energy production to offset grid energy use. Using localized power production (also known as *distributed generation*) would avoid the transmission losses associated with more-remote centralized energy production and improve the reliability of supply.

Increasing the availability of green power and scaling up distributed generation are key pathways to a low-carbon energy future. Notably, they will increasingly rely upon the addition of improved transmission capacity as well as digital communications and controls designed to make both central and distributed systems more reliable, efficient, and flexible— in sum, smarter.

Like the projects highlighted in the previous chapter, most of the examples explored here represent interconnected, multipurpose systems that exemplify the axiom of future-proofing: infrastructure should contribute few or no carbon emissions. The first part of the chapter examines utilities producing power and/or heat (electricity generation and/or district-wide heating), while the second covers energy-consuming utilities (the ICT and water sectors). Collectively, the examples illustrate substitution of green sources for carbon-based fuels, as well as alternative generation technologies and storage systems. A third group epitomizes more-complex, synergistic arrangements in which energy, heat, or nutrients cascade across different infrastructure assets, reducing carbon dioxide and other greenhouse gases.

Energy Producers Access Renewable Resources

On the heat- and power-production side, developers and operators of energy facilities are successfully substituting greenpower resources for carbon-based fuels at both legacy and new facilities. Examples here include those opting for on-site or adjacent resources such as biomass, landfill gas, and geothermal energy. Also included is a new solar power-plant technology that can be coupled with other land use. Chapters 5 and 6 also include examples of waste-to-energy and tidal-power production, respectively.

Many legacy generation plants can be retooled to accept fuel from renewable resources and some power producers are anxious to get out in front. As of 2012, 30 out of 50 states had adopted a Renewable Portfolio Standard (RPS) requiring that a specified proportion of electricity sales come from eligible renewable sources (typically, wind, solar, geothermal, and biomass, with some allowance for hydroelectricity).[8] California, which has one of the most rigorous set of standards, also has a bountiful agricultural waste stream, which has created opportunities for power producers to include biomass in their renewable energy portfolios.

Biomass—agricultural and forestry residues and substances derived from them—currently supplies 11 percent of the renewable electricity in United States.[9] In 2005, biomass surpassed hydropower as the leading domestic source of renewable energy until it was overtaken by wind power in 2009. It still remains underused in proportion to its availability, due to the relatively high capital cost of power-plant conversion and ongoing fossil-fuel subsidies. However, annually millions of tons of logging- and land-clearing-related wood residues remain uncollected and decay, and 39 million tons of crop residue are wasted or burned.[10]

The use of *beneficial biomass*—defined as crop residues, sustainably harvested wood and forest residues, industrial wood waste, and energy crops that do not compete with agriculture—can reduce the emission of carbon and other greenhouse gases.[11] Unlike coal, biomass contains neither impurities nor contaminants (such as sulfur and mercury). And compared with other carbon-based fuels, biomass releases less nitrogen, a contributor to acid rain and smog, and is widely available in both cultivated and by-product forms. Further, unlike solar and wind power, which are intermittent, biomass is a comparatively stable, on-call energy source. Finally, biomass is among the most employment-intensive of renewable energies, once storage and transportation have been factored in.[12]

Converting Mt. Poso Cogeneration Plant to Biomass

From 1989 to 2009, the Mt. Poso Cogeneration Plant, located 25 miles north of Bakersfield in California's southern San Joaquin Valley, relied on a blend of coal as well as coke and waste tires, both petroleum-based, to generate energy and heat. In 2012, the plant was successfully converted to 100 percent beneficial biomass, technically reducing its carbon footprint by 100 percent.[13] (Whether biomass sources are going to maintain their EPA-accorded zero-emissions claim continues to be a controversial question.) The conversion was prompted by state Executive Order S-13-08, issued in 2008, a Renewable Portfolio Standard (mandated renewable percentage) that requires investor-owned utilities—Pacific Gas & Electric, in this case—to renewably source 33 percent of their power by 2020, a 20 percent increase over 2008 levels.

When the plant's 20-year power-purchase agreement expired in 2009, Mt. Poso Cogeneration Company LLC determined that, given the mandate to increase renewable power sources, the best route to gaining reapproval for power production from the California Public Utilities Commission (PUC) would be to convert the plant to a non-carbon fuel source. Following the PUC's 2010 approval, the plant's boiler was adapted to operate exclusively with biomass, and a storage and conveyor system was installed to maintain a 30- to 45-day supply of biomass on-site. The fuel mix includes agricultural residue such as orchard prunings, nutshells and pits, as well as wood waste from construction.[14]

The Mt. Poso plant had initially been sited to capitalize on its proximity to the Mt. Poso Oil Field—a large, shallow petroleum and gas source in the southern foothills of the Sierra Nevada. The oil-recovery operation purchased both electricity and steam from the power plant; in a reciprocal arrangement, the cooled steam condensate was returned to the power plant, to be used for cooling.[15] The converted plant also benefits now from other locally available resources: thanks to the nearby presence of biomass-rich orchard, crop-agriculture, dairy, and forest regions, the plant is powered by close-at-hand waste. Moreover, in search of greater annual yields, growers have adopted techniques that result in shorter productive life cycles; the resulting acceleration in tree replacement means that agricultural wood waste is more plentiful. Nut trees, for example, are typically uprooted and replaced after 20 years instead of 30.[16]

The Mt. Poso conversion benefited from the New Markets Tax Credit program, which the federal government established in 2000 to encourage equity investment in low-income areas. The tax credit equaled 39 percent of the project's total investment over a six-year period.[17]

Improved air quality is another community benefit attributable to the conversion: the plant annually uses 335,300 tons of woody biomass that might otherwise be burned in the open, releasing carbon dioxide, or left to decay in landfills, releasing methane. The plant's upgraded emissions-control equipment also filters at least 95 percent of gas particulate releases, exceeding the strict standards of the San Joaquin Valley Air Quality Management District. Finally, wood ash, one of the plant's by-products, is used either to enrich the soil for nearby agriculture and forestry, or scattered on nearby pastures to prevent hoof disease at dairy farms.[18]

Some long-term challenges remain, including biomass's availability and seasonality, and ensuring that its cleanliness and handling characteristics are within normal operating parameters. According to Mt. Poso officials, the power producer partly addresses these issues by balancing agricultural wood waste with urban wood waste. Because the per-unit energy intensity of biomass is lower than that of carbon-based fuels, the conversion effectively lowered capacity from 50 megawatts (MW) to 44 MW.[19] On the upside, however, new jobs linked to biomass collection, processing, and transport have increased employment at the plant by more than 30 percent.[20]

Powering the University of New Hampshire with Local Landfill Gas

According to an ongoing Earth Engineering Center study, 1.5 billion tons of solid waste are disposed of annually in landfills worldwide—an amount that would yield a methane-to-biogas generation capacity of nearly 50 million tons. But only 5 million tons of methane are currently being captured; the remaining 45 million are being released into the atmosphere.[21]

One of the advantages of landfill gas (LFG) recovery for beneficial use is that much of the necessary infrastructure (e.g., gas extraction wells and collection pipes) is already in place. In addition to reducing harmful emissions and offsetting the expense of landfill regulation, such initiatives create jobs and new revenues. Municipalities, energy companies, and institutions in search of cost-effective options are tapping local landfills for methane.

Situated gracefully in the New England landscape, Durham, the flagship campus of the University of New Hampshire (UNH), is among the top-tier research institutions nationwide. An early land-grant institution (and later a sea- and space-grant institution), UNH-Durham's facilities occupy approximately 5.7 million square feet. The university's climate action plan is designed to cut CO_2 emissions by 50 percent by 2020 and by 80 percent by 2050. The plan calls for carbon neutrality by 2100. UNH took an initial step in that direction in 2006 by self-financing an on-site cogeneration plant that decreased GHG emissions by 21 percent. The plant's $28-million cost will be recovered over 20 years from energy savings.

While UNH was constructing its cogeneration plant, 13 miles away in Rochester, New Hampshire, managers at the Turnkey Recycling and Environmental Enterprise (TREE) facility, a landfill site owned by Waste Management of New Hampshire Inc. (WMI) had begun to study options for solving an operational problem. The site was taking in more than 1 million tons of solid waste each year[22]—and, deep within the 200-acre waste site, LFG produced by decomposing garbage was being mined through more than 300 extraction wells, connected by miles of collection pipes.[23] The gas was made up of about 50 percent methane, 36 percent CO_2, and smaller amounts of sulfur, nitrogen, and oxygen. Beginning in 2006 WMI had processed the gas on its own property, using some of it to fuel two generation plants that delivered 9 MW of electricity to 9,000 nearby homes.[24] But that arrangement left as much as 50 percent of the mined gas unused. To dispose of the excess, WMI was being forced to flare it on-site.[25]

In 2006, managers at TREE approached UNH and offered an unusual partnership, later dubbed the EcoLine. Under the proposed arrangement, excess LFG would be piped directly to the UNH cogeneration plant. The landfill would yield gas continuously—even indefinitely—but, even if the landfill were to close, emissions would continue for at least 20 years. A project team consisting of engineers, scientists, regulators, and representatives from supply companies worked to bring the proposal to fruition. Some four years and $49 million later, LFG had replaced commercially purchased natural gas at the UNH cogeneration plant, supplying up to 85 percent of the university's electrical and heating needs. The first university in the nation to use LFG as a primary fuel source, TREE and UNH's EcoLine is expected to reduce the campus's carbon footprint by 30 percent by 2015.[26]

Successful implementation required that several obstacles be overcome. First, because of its variable content, untreated LFG could not be used in the UNH cogeneration plant. To address this issue, UNH built its own purification facility at the landfill, where volatile organic chemicals, including sulfur and siloxane, are removed, and where a thermal oxidizer destroys the remaining contaminants. (The final yield is 70–80 percent methane.) Second, the LFG had to be safely conveyed across four townships, under rivers and streams, and through wetlands—which required multiple permits. Ultimately, the 12.6-mile-long gas pipeline was buried at least four feet below grade, although it emerges aboveground to cross two bridges.[27] Once on campus, the LFG has to be mixed with some purchased natural gas in order to meet the minimum energy content requirements of the UNH equipment.[28] Also, since LFG has lower heat content per unit of volume than does natural gas, the equipment in the cogeneration plant had to be modified to operate on this new fuel.[29]

The $49-million price tag for the project, a large portion of which paid for the pipeline and the purification plant on WMI's property, might reasonably have given the university's board of trustees pause. But the financial model showed that the combination of energy savings and revenue from other sources would allow the loans to be repaid within ten years.[30] The revenue sources, which were an important element in UNH's project financing strategy, included the sale of excess power to the grid, capacity credits from UNH's second turbine, and renewable-energy certificates for clean power production, which are sold to other power providers in the region whose mix of energy-generation sources lacks sufficient renewable energy to meet state standards.[31] These revenue sources were an important element in UNH's strategy for financing the project.

The project's overall success, including the dramatic reduction in reliance on fossil fuels, has made it a model for other institutions around the country. According to the EPA—which gave the EcoLine project its 2013 Project of the Year Award[32]—the program's annual environmental benefits are the equivalent of removing more than 12,500 vehicles from the road. For the university, another significant outcome was its ability to keep its energy dollars local.[33]

While this LFG example is rather unique at the institutional level, the overall number of US LFG-to-energy projects is increasing at the municipal and county levels, and in industrial applications. In some communities, for example, treated LFG fuels county vehicles, including school buses. In 2005, the number of LFG projects nationwide was 399; in 2010, it was 590—and supplied 14.8 billion kilowatt-hours (kWh) of energy, the equivalent of electrifying 1.07 million homes and heating 736,000.[34] Nevertheless, apart from the advantages of recovering LFG from existing landfills, there is justifiable skepticism over using LFG-to-energy as an endorsement for the ongoing construction of landfills—which, despite best practices, still produce harmful methane emissions. Ultimately, better solutions for organic-waste management lie in immediate resource recovery through composting or biogasification (the conversion of organic matter into useful biogas).[35]

Tapping Geothermal Energy from Water Bodies in Dutch Cities

Dutch cities are tapping the thermal potential of seawater and lake water, and two initiatives are paving the way.[36] In Amsterdam's expanding business sector, Nuon Energy Company eliminated the need for the conventional, energy-intensive mechanical cooling devices and cooling towers typically required by office buildings by developing a district cooling system that extracts cold water from the Nieuwe Meer, an engineered lake near the southwestern part of the city. The system produces 76 MW of cooling (equivalent to the maximum needs of about 75,000 residential units)—and, when compared with conventional cooling techniques, reduces CO_2 emissions by 75 percent. Over 25 years, the net present value of the savings averages out to €200,000 annually.[37]

The Hague, which is committed to achieving carbon neutrality by 2050, has eliminated fossil-fuel consumption in the new community of Duindorp, where a geothermal plant uses seawater drawn from the adjacent Scheveningen Harbor to meet the heating and cooling needs of 800 homes. The conditioned water is distributed to each house, where auxiliary heat pumps increase or decrease its temperature as necessary. The system results in 50 percent lower carbon emissions than conventional local power sources.[38] Another district heating and cooling project, with an anticipated annual CO_2 reduction of 4,000 tons, will rely on warm water (75°F) drawn from local wells at a depth of almost 7,000 feet to serve 4,000 new residential units plus 60,000 square feet of office space.[39]

Mining Heat: Heerlen, Holland's Minewater Project

Heerlen Municipality's Minewater Project, located in the Netherlands' southern province of Lindburg, is a unique attempt to reduce its ecological and carbon footprint by tapping local geothermal reservoirs from nearby abandoned coal mines.[40] When compared with conventional technologies, the mine-water-based district heating and cooling system constructed for the town decreased annual carbon emissions by 1,500 tons—as much as 55 percent.[41] Completed in late 2008, the project takes advantage of a former nuisance: the mine water that continues to collect when mines are no longer in use.

When a mine is active, dewatering is undertaken across a wide area to reduce the buildup of harmful waterborne chemicals. But because unused mines typically continue to amass groundwater, the caverns can become polluted reservoirs that require ongoing monitoring and dewatering to prevent widespread aquifer pollution.[42]

The accumulated water in deactivated mines can be a useful thermal-energy source, however, particularly when mining has loosened the rock structure, improving the heat-exchange potential between earth and mine water.[43] When the mine water is connected to heat pumps, it can be used either for space heating in the winter or as a heat sink for summer cooling. The deeper the water, the higher its temperature: generally, water temperature decreases by 2.5–3°C (4.5–5.4°F) for every 100 meters (328 feet) of depth. In Heerlen, for example, at the mine's deeper locations in the north, some 825 meters (2,707 feet) down, the water temperature is approximately 30°C (86°F); at about 250 meters (820 feet) below the surface, the temperature decreases to 15 or 20°C (27 or 36°F). Access to the varying temperatures offered by the mine's water levels allows for an efficient exchange between heat source and heat sink.[44]

As coal and other mineral resources are depleted, and as coal-fired energy gives way to cheaper natural gas, many industrial nations are abandoning the highly capital-intensive practice of mining. Unfortunately, neighboring municipalities often experience economic and social decline after mine closures. Heerlen, for example, which was founded to take advantage of nearby coal seams, once benefited economically from its mines, which were retired in the 1970s because of the increasing availability of (and preference for) natural gas.[45]

Throughout the world, many mine sites have fallen into disuse, while others have been put into maintenance mode to await more-favorable economic conditions for the exploitation of lower-grade resources.[46] Until recently, little consideration has been given to the giant caverns and networks of smaller cavities left behind once extraction is discontinued.

Power produced by the town's biomass-fueled, combined-heat-and-power plant pumps the extracted mine water to local energy transfer stations, where received or rejected heat (for preheating or cooling, respectively) is then exchanged with the buildings. Small internal heat pumps further amplify or reduce the water temperature at individual buildings as needed. All building systems are connected to conventional boilers for emergency backup.

Minewater meets the district heating and cooling needs for Heerlen's municipal facilities and for Heerlerheide, a new development. In Heerlerheide, the system serves the civic center, 200-plus dwellings (50 percent of which are subsidized housing), 3,800 square meters (40,903 square feet) of commercial floor space, and 16,200 square meters (174,375 square feet) of public buildings, including cultural, educational, and health-care facilities.[47] Several factors supported the adoption of the geothermal system at the district scale: the presence of mine water; the proximity of an end user (the town); the accessible variations in water temperature, which created the potential to use the water as both a heat source and a heat sink; the diversity of building and industry loads, which would help to balance demands on the system; the relatively high price of alternative sources of power; and the availability of willing investment partners.

To ensure that the heat source and heat sinks will remain balanced over time, the geothermal demand of the combined building loads needs to closely match the capacity of the mines. The necessary balance is achieved by juggling water volume, temperature, and building user loads with other potential energy sources—namely, nearby industrial processes. Two factors contribute to the system's overall high efficiency. First, differing requirements (linked to building type and occupancy schedule) reduce aggregate demand. Second, Heerlerheide's net-zero-energy buildings—with their high insulation values, passive solar heating, radiant heating and cooling, and heat-recovery systems—further reduce loads.

Minewater, a pilot project, was funded by the Dutch Ministry of Economic Affairs and subsidized by European Union (EU) Regional Development funding on the basis of its applicability to other settlements in the post-industrial coal-mining landscapes of Northern Europe. The remainder of the relatively high cost (€20.9 million) was privately financed to avoid increasing the already-high utility rates. The additional first costs associated with the geothermal approach were offset, in part, by the elimination of large-scale gas infrastructure and by the use of the same building equipment for both heating and cooling, which averted the need for separate compressors and condensers.[48]

Significantly, the project was the outcome of a unique collaboration among various partners. Led by the municipality of Heerlen, the players included the social housing association Weller Wonen and the United Kingdom's Building Research Establishment. The project also received development assistance from Germany and mine research input from France's Bureau de Recherches Géologiques et Minières.[49] The most distinctive donation, however, came from the community itself.

When coal lost market share and the mines closed in the 1970s, Heerlen experienced economic setbacks, unemployment, out-migration, and a loss of identity. But when the Minewater Project got under way, the knowledge of older coal miners turned out to be invaluable—in helping to locate the reservoirs, determining where to drill, and estimating water temperature.[50] This intergenerational involvement raised residents' morale and helped mobilize widespread support for the project.

There are an estimated one million disused mines worldwide. Underground reservoirs from mines in other parts of the world may return comparable thermal energy and offset GHGs—but, as of this writing, only a handful of projects are capitalizing on the low-grade energy contained within these abandoned properties.[51] Until the 1960s, Germany's Rhenish Massif was intensively mined for iron ore and nonferrous metals at depths of up to 1,000 meters (3,281 feet). At most of the decommissioned mines in the area, millions of cubic meters (hundreds of millions of gallons) of water offer untapped geothermal potential.[52] In the United States, a 2006 study conducted by the National Renewable Energy Lab that estimated the heat-energy potential of mine water in the Appalachian coal regions of Pennsylvania, West Virginia, and Ohio found that just 3.9 percent of the water from a single coal mine near Pittsburgh could meet the heating and cooling needs of 20,000 homes. Currently, most of this water is simply treated and discharged on the surface.[53]

Integrating Power and Agriculture: The Solar Chimney

According to a National Renewable Energy Lab study, green power generation from scaled-up technologies available today (wind, solar, tidal), if supported by a more flexible grid, could supply 80 percent of total US electricity needs by 2050.[54] But many, if not most, of these are single-purpose solutions. Imagine a 100-percent-renewable-energy plant colocated with a huge agricultural greenhouse. Since the 1980s, the structural engineering firm Schlaich Bergermann und Partner, headed by visionary German engineer Jörg Schlaich, has pursued that very goal.[55]

In his 1995 book *The Solar Chimney: Electricity from the Sun*, Schlaich made a strong case for large-scale solar-energy production based on the solar chimney concept, which he developed and prototyped. Suitable for large, sparsely inhabited locations, Schlaich has called this emerging technology a "dry hydroelectric power station for the desert."[56] His solar chimney utilizes simple physical phenomena: the solar greenhouse effect, which heats incoming air, and vertical updraft (commonly known as the "stack effect") caused by the temperature differential between air at the bottom and air at the top of this chimney.

The prime mover is solar-heated air, collected under a gigantic, low-lying transparent roof, that rises forcefully up a very tall central exhaust tower, passing through turbines at its base. The greenhouse accepts incoming short-wave solar radiation and retains the long-wave radiation (re-radiated by the ground) that heats the air to a significant temperature above the outside air. While the ground retains a certain amount of heat naturally, when covered with dark-colored, water-filled bags (utilizing water's high heat-storage capacity), the ground's capacity to store heat over longer periods is increased significantly.[57]

Between 1986 and 1998, a 50-MW prototype solar chimney operated in the town of Manzanares, Spain, about 150 km

(93 miles) south of Madrid (fig. 3-1). It was capable of running almost nine hours a day and the output level closely matched Schlaich's theoretical calculations.[58] Measurements extrapolated from this plant have since been used to predict the potential output of larger plants now under consideration.

Since the solar tower's yield remains directly proportional to the size of the greenhouse and the height of the chimney at a given solar intensity, there is no "optimum size" for the technology.[59] Theoretically, a 20-square-kilometer (7.7-square-mile) greenhouse and a 1,000-meter-high (3,281-foot) tower will support a 100-MW plant. According to Schlaich, doubling the collector area increases the capacity twofold, sufficient to electrify about 200,000 homes—while eliminating over 900,000 tons of greenhouse gases (GHGs) annually and yielding a net energy payback of two to three years.[60]

Given the extensive initial investment required, no large-scale installations have been completed, but a number have been on the drawing board: one in particular in Namibia (400 MW). The latter was expected to incorporate agriculture in the outer two-thirds of the glass shed. Studies reviewing the combined potential of agriculture and electrical-power generation suggested that with the inclusion of produce, profits could be more than double those from power sales alone.[61]

Two other such solar chimneys may be en route to commercialization: one based in the United States and another in Australia. As of May 2013, Apollo Development, LLC, of Dallas, Texas,

Figure 3-1. Aerial view of a solar updraft power plant (a later version of the one in Manzanares, Spain) (© Schlaich Bergermann Solar GmbH).

had acquired the technology-development rights to undertake a series of 200-MW solar towers in the regions around El
Paso and Laredo, Texas.[62] The projects are intended to replace
fossil-fuel-powered plants being retired for environmental and
economic reasons. Each of the solar towers has the potential to
avert the emission of 1 million tons of GHGs annually and abate
the use of 528 million gallons of potable water (which, under
conventional technology, is required for cooling).[63] A similarly
scaled 200-MW, 1-km-high (3,281-foot) tower, planned for Tuck-
anarra, in Western Australia, will drive 32 electricity-producing
turbines.[64]

Storing Energy to Increase Green Power Yields

A key problem associated with both wind- and solar-power
generation is intermittency—a drop in power when the wind
dies down or the sun doesn't shine. Storing excess power
produced during peak conditions can help. Battery storage is
expensive, but savvy producers have located renewable power
farms near naturally occurring storage reservoirs. Compressed-
air energy storage (CAES), for example, used in association with
wind power, can increase the overall economic yield of a wind-
farm by taking advantage of distinctive geological formations,
such as underground sites with voids capable of containing
compressed air. In such systems, electrical energy produced at
night (when demand and costs are lower) is used to force air
into an airtight reservoir, which acts as a storage battery. During the day, and especially at times of peak energy use, when
the compressed air is let out of the chamber, injected natural
gas is used to increase the temperature of the decompressing
air, which drives a conventional turbine generator to produce
electricity.

At the utility scale, CAES has been used since 1978—most
notably in Huntorf, Germany, where a 290-MW power station stores excess power that is produced for sale, during peak
demand, to more than 300,000 homes.[65] Like a similar installation constructed in McIntosh, Alabama, in 1991, the Huntorf
system capitalizes on the caverns left behind after industrial
extraction of potash or sodium chloride.

Salt caverns, many of them almost a half-mile deep, underlie
more than one-third of the land in North Dakota.[66] In that state,
which also has the greatest potential for wind energy in the

United States, the Electric Power and Research Institute (EPRI) is working with holders of a 5,000-acre mineral lease to explore how abandoned salt mines could offer CAES and also sequester (capture and store long term) CO_2 emissions from the state's coal-fired power plants. It has been estimated that compressed air stored in the mined-out wells has the capacity to sustain a 100-MW generator for 24 hours.[67] EPRI has found that geological structures found in up to 80 percent of the United States are suitable for CAES.

At a capital cost of $1,500 per kilowatt, CAES is relatively affordable. It is also reliable: wind energy coupled with storage technology can more dependably support peak grid-based supply, creating overall efficiency close to 75 percent (with 25 percent lost in storage and release). The CAES plants in Germany and Alabama have been operating continuously since 1978 and 1991, respectively.[68]

Energy Consumers: Other Utilities Follow Suit

To reduce their carbon footprint, other infrastructural service providers can go beyond integrating energy-efficient equipment or power-conservation measures into their operations. They can purchase green power or provide their own distributed generation. The information and communication technology (ICT) sector and the water sector have undertaken noteworthy projects to green their energy use.

Greening the Information and Communication Technology (ICT) Sector

The carbon footprint of the global computing industry is said to rival that of the aviation industry. Annual ICT emissions were 0.86 metric gigatons (Gt) carbon dioxide equivalent (CO_2e) in 2007, or just about 2 percent of global carbon emissions.[69] Under a business-as-usual scenario, this figure is expected to reach 1.43 Gt (1.58 billion tons) CO_2e by 2020.[70] Increasingly, however, forward-thinking organizations in the ICT sector are offsetting the carbon footprint of their large server loads by purchasing green power.

The corporate giant Google has taken the lead, creating its own energy-focused subsidiary to partially offset its massive carbon footprint. In 2011, before Google had swapped out fossil fuels for renewables and purchased additional carbon offsets (credits for carbon reductions undertaken elsewhere that reduce the purchaser's net carbon footprint), its carbon footprint was 1,677,423 metric tons (1.84 million tons) of carbon dioxide annually.[71] In 2010, Google entered into a 20-year power-purchase agreement for 114 MW of wind energy. A year later, it purchased another 101 MW to be sold back at wholesale price while keeping the renewable-energy credits to offset its own use of grid energy.[72] Now effectively in the energy business, Google is making long-term, very large-scale wind power purchase agreements (PPAs) directly with new producers. For example, in Iowa and Oklahoma Google's PPAs directly stimulated new renewable power ventures and have set the bar for other large users like Apple and Facebook.

Thanks in part to its burgeoning cellular communications industry, India is the world's fourth-largest emitter of CO_2, accounting for 7 percent of global emissions in 2011.[73] With half a billion cell phone users (a number expected to double by 2015[74]), India has 350,000 cell phone towers, each of which requires 3–5 kW of electrical energy to maintain transmitting capacity and cool the adjacent generators on which they depend. These generators consume 530 million gallons of diesel fuel annually.

As part of the Jawaharlal Nehru National Solar Mission, which has set a goal of installing 20,000 MW of solar capacity nationwide by 2022,[75] India's Ministry of New and Renewable Energy will require the installation of small solar panels (with battery backup) on 50 percent of all cell phone towers by 2015, which will save more than 540 million liters (143 million gallons) of diesel annually and cut about nine million tons of carbon emissions.[76] Retrofitting has been outsourced to a number of independent companies. The government is offering a 30 percent subsidy to cell phone tower companies that complete the switch to renewable power. The tower companies' remaining costs will be repaid in 7 to 12 years through avoided purchase of fossil fuel.[77] By the end of 2011 the Solar Mission had outfitted approximately 400 off-the-grid cell phone towers.[78]

A few notable examples of water-sector facilities that incorporate supplementary solar-energy systems, described below, exemplify cross-sector, conjunctive use, similar to the PV-powered communication towers mentioned above. These distributed solar energy systems contribute green power while offering some auxiliary benefits.

Reducing Water-Sector Carbon Footprints

Building-integrated photovoltaics (PVs) are an effective form of colocation, as they consume no additional space while performing dual functions. Similarly, PVs installed as floating arrays on reservoirs, irrigation canals, or water treatment plants optimize the use of existing real estate. (Stand-alone solar arrays and wind turbines are land-intensive, and the rates of return for such single-purpose installations may be disproportionately small when compared with the value of the land on which the installations are sited.[79])

Floating PV arrays are typically mounted on racks attached to plastic floats, and secured as needed by mooring lines (fig. 3-2). In addition to providing green power, the panels provide shade, reducing the water's rate of evaporation by as much as 70 percent, depending on climate; meanwhile, the thermal mass of the underlying water body cools the arrays, improving their energy output and extending their life span.[80]

Floating systems can save water across a range of locations, including waste ponds, stormwater-retention ponds, hydro-dams, and even wastewater-treatment facilities. In the United States, water agencies are starting to recognize opportunities for hybrid water and solar solutions. New Jersey's American Water, the largest publicly traded water and wastewater utility in the country, has turned the 735-million-gallon reservoir at the Canoe Brook Water Treatment Plant, in Millburn, into

Figure 3-2. Floating photovoltaic arrays, Canoe Brook Water Treatment Plant, Millburn, New Jersey. (Courtesy of American Water.)

an energy-producing platform. The plant's 538 solar modules float on a mooring system that allows them to rise and fall as the water level changes, and to withstand the severe weather, including freeze/thaw cycles, of the Northeast. Although the system offsets a relatively modest 2 percent of the facility's power needs—the equivalent of $16,000 per year— the shade from the panels, in addition to reducing evaporation, helps reduce the growth of algae and other organic matter. This is the sixth solar project that American Water has implemented.[81]

In 2012, India's Gujarat State Electricity Corporation installed solar panels over a 750-meter (2,461-foot) stretch of irrigation canals—cooling the panels, and thereby reducing evaporation and creating a 15 percent increase in efficiency. Experts have calculated that covering a mere 10 percent of the region's 85,000-km (52,817-mile) canal network would generate 2,200 MW of power while saving 2,000 crore liters of water (5.3 billion gallons) of water annually and preserving 11,000 acres of farmland that would otherwise be needed for single-purpose PV arrays.[82]

The $10-million, 2.3-MW solar-power project at the Neely Wastewater Reclamation Facility in Gilbert, Arizona, completed in 2011, sits atop wastewater recharge basins that inject cleaned wastewater into the ground for further percolation and aquifer replenishment. The PV arrays span 40 acres of what would otherwise be single-purpose real estate, that is, the dedicated percolation acreage. Solar electricity production will meet approximately 40 percent of the plant's power needs, saving about $2 million by 2031. Over 8,000 sun-tracking solar panels will generate more than 4 million kilowatt-hours (kWh) of electricity annually—enough to power more than 430 American homes.[83] Over its life span, the array will reduce CO_2 emissions by 43,000 metric tons (47,400 tons). The project, which involved no up-front capital costs for the municipality, was made possible through incentives from the local power utility, Arizona Public Service, and a third-party solar-power purchase agreement with owner/operator SPG Solar.[84]

Infrastructural Ecologies: Combining Energy Producers and Consumers

Embracing objectives similar to those that fostered the creation of circular energy and resource flows in Hammarby Sjöstad, Sweden, two additional municipal examples achieve noteworthy carbon-footprint reductions. They both reveal how conjunctive land use can promote advantageous exchanges across infrastructure sectors.

Waste Transformed into Biogas for Transit Use— Lille, France

Like the farsighted municipalities of Amsterdam, The Hague, and Heerlen, the city of Lille, France, opted to reduce its carbon intensity by closely examining its geophysical and infrastructural context for underexploited renewable resources, in this instance to provide energy for its public bus fleet. Lille Métropole Communauté Urbaine (LMCU) is a public, intermunicipal cooperative body covering 87 communes and 1.2 million inhabitants in the Nord-Pas-de-Calais region. In 1990, LMCU began to develop an integrated plan to provide low-carbon transportation by capitalizing on energy and nutrient exchanges from its own wastewater-treatment plant and solid-waste-treatment facility.

According to its 1996 Urban Mobility Plan, Lille's transportation needs were shaped by (1) a variety of demands across its constituent communes, which include urban neighborhoods, rural lands, and small villages, and (2) the city's proximity to London, Paris, and Brussels. The plan set a goal of reducing private vehicle use by 90 percent by 2015; to reach that goal, the plan recommended transportation improvements designed to double public-transit use by 2015.[85] Because the plan also required reductions in GHG emissions from public transport, LMCU began to search for a carbon-free fuel for its bus fleet, among other transit strategies. With technical and financial support from the European Commission's BIOMAXGAS program, it turned to biologically produced gases from various waste sources.

In Europe in general and in Lille in particular, interest in biogas technologies began in the 1990s, with an eye to reducing GHG emissions. Biogas (also known as biomethane), a high-quality fuel derived from various types of waste, can be used for process energy (energy consumed by industry), combined heat and power, combustion in vehicles, and injection into the national grid.[86] Biogas is produced when organic matter decomposes into CO_2, water, and methane in the presence of bacteria; this process, known as *biodigestion*, can occur aerobically, in the presence of oxygen, or anaerobically, in the absence of oxygen. Because biogas can be readily sourced from a variety of plant materials or other organic matter, including wastewater and industrial, forest, and agricultural waste, it is considered a renewable energy source. The production of biogas also leaves residuals that can be used as fertilizer.

The Marquette wastewater-treatment plant, located in a Lille suburb, treats about one-third of the population's wastewater, producing about 15,000 cubic meters (530,000 cubic feet) of sewage gas (biomethane) daily.[87] While 80 percent of this output was recovered for process energy and heat for the plant, the rest was flamed or wasted. Recognizing a potential resource, Lille launched a pilot program in 1990 to recover, clean, and upgrade (compress) the remaining biogas to 95 percent methane in order to fuel a portion of the city's converted public bus fleet. Methane is chemically similar to natural gas, and Lille's first methane-powered buses were soon operational, with notable improvements in acceleration and drivability as well as reductions in ozone, hydrocarbon, nitrogen oxide, and particulate emissions. Noise levels from the buses also diminished by as much as 60 percent.[88] Based on these successes, the city cast about for other sources of clean fuel, with the goal of expanding the program first to 100 buses and ultimately to its entire fleet.

The answer was found by looking across municipal departments to the city's waste sector, where a crisis had been unfolding. After a 1998 study revealed that milk from cows grazing near solid-waste incinerators was heavily contaminated by dioxin, the three plants that had been burning the city's solid waste had to be shut down. In lieu of incineration, the city chose instead to construct an organic waste recovery (ORC) facility. Completed in 2007, that facility offered Lille Métropole another source of clean fuel (fig. 3-3).[89]

The ORC receives approximately 700,000 tons of waste produced annually by Lille's 87 communes. In addition to domestic waste, agricultural residue and wastes from food processing are added to the presorted organic household material for combined processing. The material arrives at the ORC via eco-friendly barge transport; the combined organic materials then spend roughly a month in oxygen-free digesters that separate biogas from sludge, or semi-solid waste. Some of the recovered biogas (methane, CO_2, and water vapor) is used directly for heating the facility. The rest is further purified, water-washed

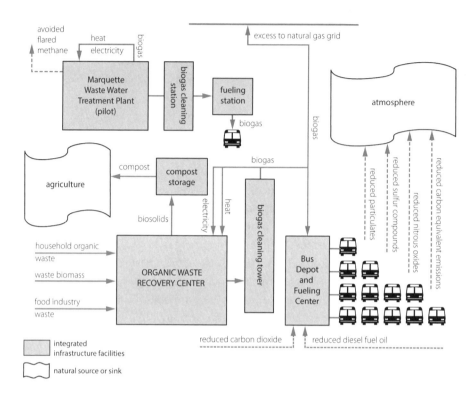

Figure 3-3. Lille Métropole Organic Waste Recovery Center and Transfer Center, Lille, France. (Figure by Hillary Brown.)

(using collected rainwater), concentrated, and stored as 4 million cubic meters (141 million cubic feet) of fuel—sufficient for powering 100 buses.[90] Since all biogas derived from decayed plant material was originally photosynthesized, the fuel is considered carbon neutral.

The separated sludge is mixed with chipped wood waste and is heat-processed further to yield approximately 34,000 tons of compost, which is then returned by barge to agricultural areas.[91] A lingering difficulty was solved when Lille Métropole colocated the new bus depot immediately adjacent to the ORC. Before the colocation, the buses had needed to refuel at the sewage-treatment works, adding miles to their routes.

The program eliminated the use of an estimated 5 million gallons of diesel oil annually and reduced two major sources of GHG emissions—first by substituting renewable energy for fossil fuel, and second by averting the release of methane accompanying the processing of wastewater and solid waste. When compared with emissions from diesel-fueled vehicles,

CO_2 equivalent emissions were reduced by more than 75 percent, suspended particulate matter by 97 percent, sulfur compounds by 99 percent, and nitrous oxides by 70 percent.[92]

The program owes its success to a number of factors, including the political and technical support of the EU. The combined cost of bus adaptation and the refueling infrastructure, which was more than €2 million, was met through EU, national, and subnational grants.[93] A bus manufacturer (Renault) and a gas producer (Gas de France) contributed expertise. Ultimately, however, the critical factor was the commitment of local and regional authorities to effect an ecologically integrated solution to transportation, wastewater treatment, and solid waste processing.

Hydrogen Power Revives an Island Economy— Lolland, Denmark

Scandinavia, a region far advanced in its deployment of low-carbon and carbon-free technologies, offers perhaps the most innovative example of infrastructural ecology. The fourth largest of Denmark's 400-odd islands, Lolland has historically been known for growing sugar beets. Today, the island is being celebrated for its commitment to carbon neutrality and renewable energy as an engine of economic development. Vestenskov, one of Lolland's villages, is well on its way to becoming the first fully hydrogen-powered community in Europe. Its transformation is the outcome of a 2008 partnership, funded by the Danish Energy Authority, between the Municipality of Lolland (which covers about half the island, incorporating seven different villages, including Vestenskov and Naksov, in 2007) and Baltic Sea Solutions, a regional nonprofit sustainable-development organization founded in 2005.[94]

In the mid-1990s, the villages of Lolland were attempting to rebound from an economy weakened by shipyard closings, which had accelerated the decline of an already sparse population. In 1998 the largest village, the former shipyard community of Nakskov, decided to capitalize on the island's unique resources. It envisioned leveraging renewable energy—specifically, an integrated mix of low-carbon strategies—to encourage private development.

It planned to do this by transforming the degraded harbor sites into the Nakskov Industry and Environment Park, a facility designed to attract renewable-energy and agro-industries.[95] The Nakskov governing board modestly increased local taxes to fund the project (a surprising move, given the waning economy); however, the hope was that the investment would pay off for the community. One outgrowth of the park was the 2007 creation of Lolland Community Testing Facilities (CTF), which was conceived as an international platform for piloting renewable-energy technology and products through full-scale local applications. The goal of the CTF partners—the Danish Energy Authority (DEA), Baltic Sea Solutions, several private industry firms, and 20 universities—was not only to test new technologies in isolation, but also to create synergies among them. As an economic driver, the program would spawn new businesses, create jobs, and amplify research. Significantly, CTF engaged in participatory public meetings to ensure that its community and private investments would support local job creation, resulting in a heightened sense of the villages' shared ownership of the project.[96]

Denmark's substantial subsidies for the renewable-energy industry are helping the nation to reach its goal of meeting its entire electrical demand through wind power by 2025.[97] Between 1999 and 2009, wind-power production on Lolland increased twelvefold, thanks to more than 500 land- and sea-based turbines (many of which were constructed as demonstration projects), which currently produce annually about 1,000 GWh. The addition of planned offshore wind farms will expand production to approximately 1,500 GWh, 50 percent more electrical energy than the island can consume.

In 2007, CTF developed a plan to couple wind power with a hydrogen-production project—both to store excess wind power and to address its principal liability: intermittency. The plan gave rise to the Lolland Hydrogen Community (fig. 3-4), a multiphase demonstration project developed by the municipality of Lolland, Baltic Sea Solutions, and IRD Fuel Cells through research dollars and subsidies provided by the DEA. The project, sited in the village of Vestenskov, would use residential fuel cells to produce combined heat and power, and would be the EU's first full-scale hydrogen-powered community. An electrolyser plant, built in the nearby Nakskov Industrial and Energy Park, uses an electrical current (from excess wind power) to split water into hydrogen and oxygen. The hydrogen is then piped, via a hydrogen distribution network, to the Vestenskov households that are the testing sites for the distributed heat-

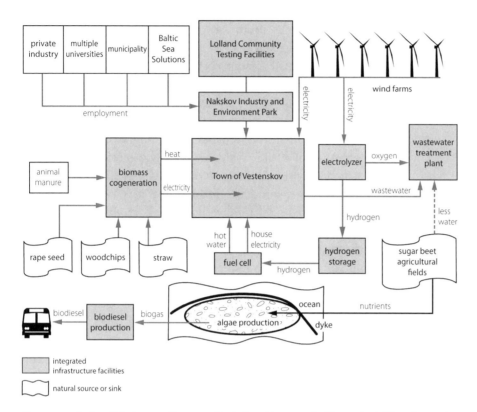

Figure 3-4. Lolland Hydrogen Community, Lolland, Denmark. (Figure by Hillary Brown.)

and-power arrangement. At each home, individual fuel cells—
which work electrochemically (without combustion) and have
zero carbon emissions—use hydrogen to produce electricity
and heat on demand, yielding domestic hot water as a by-product. This combined heat and power production approaches 90
percent efficiency.[98]

As noted earlier, CTF was interested in modeling how it
could capitalize on local synergies, an interest shared by the
municipality of Lolland, which plans to maximize the utility
of each of CTF's projects to support its long-term goal of sustainable redevelopment.[99] Lolland's development of an infrastructural ecology was also furthered by the application of a
dynamic modeling tool, developed and customized for Lolland
by the US Millennium Institute, a nonprofit sustainable-development organization. The tool analyzed economic, social, and
environmental factors to assess the potential for synergies
across sectors. For example, because most of its renewable-
energy sources are intermittent, Lolland maximized efficiency

by integrating them: the surplus nighttime wind power that would otherwise sell at lower rates is used to produce and store hydrogen. Instead of simply being vented, the oxygen produced by electrolysis is piped to the local wastewater-treatment plant in order to improve the efficiency of its purification processes. Because of its rural and agricultural base, Lolland has also committed to biomass-derived district heating, which relies on the plentiful availability of straw, wood chips, wood pellets, and gasified sugar-beet waste. Animal manure is sold to a new biogas plant, which produces an additional 101 GWh.[100]

These synergies improve both the cost efficiency and the ecological performance of Vestenkov's power, heat, and waste infrastructure—and the savings are being used to help underwrite ongoing renewable-energy investments.[101] Another environmentally adroit source of savings is the diversion of some of the excess, nutrient-rich surface water from agricultural fields to water impoundments that have been formed by the erection of new dual-functioning dikes. While these protect against rising sea levels, they also provide contained areas for the cultivation of algae used to produce biodiesel fuels. Significantly, the production of biodiesel in these community-held areas has created additional income streams for local farm communities, helping to alleviate the tax increases initially required to fund redevelopment.[102]

Thanks to its demonstration projects and local business-redevelopment efforts, Lolland has earned additional EU funding designed for depressed areas that are trying to overcome economic difficulties. With its academic, industry, and non-profit partners and a locally based holding and venture-capital company created to further its energy initiatives, Lolland is positioned to stand as an exemplar in Denmark's production of export earnings.

The island's ongoing trial of hydrogen as an energy carrier is now in a third phase that will examine economies of scale. From both a financial and an energy-performance perspective, quantifiable results are still preliminary. Moreover, even assuming the success of the trial, the marketability of hydrogen remains an issue. Although in many ways an attractive, low-carbon substitute for fossil fuels, hydrogen doesn't occur in nature in a usable form, which means that energy is required to produce it. There are also many challenges associated with safe, efficient, and cost-effective storage and delivery.

Three aspects of the breakthrough in Lolland are especially noteworthy here: first, the synergies that were revealed by research and put into place across the energy, wastewater, and agricultural sectors; second, the embrace of an emerging industry—in which local governments, community residents, and area farmers participated—as means of redressing unemployment; and third, the simultaneous anticipation of and response to climate change. (The third aspect will be discussed in greater detail in chapter 6.)

Conclusion

Lolland's entrepreneurial venture is a robust infrastructural ecology—an advanced, public-private, community-based, and municipal-scaled green-energy system, organized around an integrated infrastructure network of power, water, waste, and agriculture.[103] While comparable research resources and top-down national investment may not be readily replicable in other municipal undertakings, there is much that forward-thinking public officials and utilities can do to advance next-generation, integrated energy systems.

Public and private gas and electric utilities can start by attuning themselves to untapped local resources. They can consider co-firing or altogether replacing coal (or other fossil fuel) with locally available beneficial biomass waste. (Both would require equipment modifications and storage capacity.) They can consider deep-water or below-grade assets such as geothermal energy for heating or energy storage—with the potential to boost yields. They can consider landfill-gas-to-energy projects, next-generation waste-to-energy facilities (detailed in chapter 5), or the use of methane gas and other sewage treatment by-products as renewable energy sources. Cogeneration, particularly with renewable resources, compounds the energy yield while lowering carbon emissions. At an even more entrepreneurial level, power providers in sunny climates might acquire underused expanses of land capable, in the near future, of cohosting a solar tower and food production facility.

Similarly, both public and private utilities can begin to better control their own energy destiny and lower their carbon footprints by establishing on-site or integrated renewables, as in Lille, France. Mounting PV panels or arrays on transmission towers, facility roofs, or other underutilized properties, or floating them on water storage or wastewater collection areas can also reduce water loss while protecting standing water quality.

Through the right partnerships, careful spatial planning, and state-of-the-art strategies for technical integration, including connectivity to the grid, next-generation infrastructure will make optimal use of simple colocation to extract collateral benefits from shared energy and resources. Many of these options, however, will require advocating and enabling policy frameworks (at the federal, state, or local levels) to support new investment cycles needed to reach the full potential of low-carbon energy sources.

Two projections—one short-term, the other longer-term—give rise to some optimism. The International Energy Agency (IEA) estimates that by 2035, wind and solar together could be supplying 10 percent of global electricity, an increase from 1.5 percent in 2012.[104] In the United States, projections made by the Department of Energy's National Renewable Energy Lab suggest that renewable electricity generated by commercially available technology could, in combination with a more flexible electric system, supply 80 percent of total US generation by 2050 while "meeting electricity demand on an hourly basis in every region of the United States."[105] The infrastructure sectors have both the obligation and the opportunities to play a leading role.

4. Advancing Soft-Path Water Infrastructure: Combined Constructed and Natural Systems

In the mid-1980s, a development boom in the southwestern parts of Staten Island, New York City's least-populous borough, triggered overflows from combined storm and sanitary sewers, causing flooding and degraded water quality. Instead of installing a traditional gray infrastructure drainage system, the city's Department of Environmental Protection (DEP) responded with a unique, multipurpose solution tailored to the area's hydrologic patterns. Natural wetlands and drainage corridors—known as "blue belts"—were upgraded to handle the additional functions of storing and filtering stormwater.

The Blue Belt plan involved acquiring 10,000 acres of marshlands and augmenting them with reengineered streams, ponds, stilling basins that dissipate rapidly flowing water's energy, sand filters, and other water-control elements. This constructed drainage system was inseparably entwined with the area's self-regulating ecosystems. At a savings of about $80 million (in 2009) over conventional large sewer mains, these enhanced natural features convey, store, and filter stormwater, reduce peak discharges, and improve water quality, while protecting scenic vistas and wildlife habitat.[1]

As epitomized by the Blue Belt, the soft-path water paradigm described in this chapter entails the use of localized, low-impact water-treatment systems.[2] Like green infrastructure, soft-path systems capture, store, treat, and re-utilize stormwater runoff at or near the site of use, improving groundwater, soil, and air quality; biodiversity; and even carbon sequestration and climate modification.[3] As spatially diffuse natural systems, their enhanced landscapes and water features preserve open space while fostering recreational, scenic, and educational uses. Soft-path systems, distinguished here from green infrastructure, may also serve beneficial cross-sector functions as revealed in the examples featured in this and other chapters: treatment of wastewater, recovery of nutrients (e.g., phosphates) and biosolids for fertilizer or energy production; and utilization of recovered waste heat or treated water for beneficial uses. Soft-path processes stand in sharp contrast to the centralized, single-purpose, "hard-path" waterworks (filtration and wastewater treatment) typically used across the developed world. In the United States alone, approximately 161,000 public water-supply systems collect, treat, and deliver potable water, often pumping it great distances.[4] More than 21,000 publicly owned wastewater treatment works provide sanitary or combined storm and sanitary treatment services.[5] Both types of facilities are expensive to construct and to operate: 70 percent of their operating energy goes to moving and treating water and wastewater, which represents nearly 4 percent of the entire nation's electrical demand. (Sludge digestion alone contributes over 0.5 percent of total US emissions of CO_2, nitrous oxides, and methane.[6]) As currently engineered, these single-purpose facilities are considered noxious by neighboring communities.

Finally, many are threatened by climate perturbations, including intense storms and rising water levels.

Since the mid-1970s, wastewater engineers have been interested in the use of a variety of biological systems to treat wastewater naturally, under controlled (or bioengineered) conditions. Water treatments that rely on native ecological functions can supplement, reduce reliance on, or (as demonstrated by the Staten Island Bluebelt) even entirely replace energy- and chemical-intense traditional "gray infrastructure" with "green infrastructure" by mimicking a locality's original hydrology.

Natural stormwater and wastewater treatments rely on the movement of water through streambeds, plant material, and/or soil, where living organisms remove sediments and metabolize ("bioremediate") impurities, filtering and adsorbing pollutant molecules such as phosphates and nitrogen. With treatment at or as close to the source as possible, the *water balance* (equilibrium between inflows and outflows necessary for assured water availability) for a locality is improved over the performance of centralized systems.[7]

Soft-path systems can also help reduce peak plant in-flows and avert the need for wastewater treatment-system expansion. In addition to reducing carbon emissions by avoiding conventional construction and carbon-fueled operations, the biomass and soil that are inherent in soft-path systems act as "carbon sinks" for natural sequestration of atmospheric CO_2 in the soil and plant matter. Finally, soft-path infrastructure improves resiliency against climate change through protection of our water commons, in terms of sufficiency and quality.

Although relatively low in first costs and operating costs when compared with gray infrastructure, soft-path measures require substantial financial investment if they are to be implemented at the scales required to safeguard urban waterways.[8] And, like any other water-treatment system, they require upkeep to function properly. In the long run, however, increasing use of decentralized, low-impact treatment alternatives can provide substantial savings, which can then be passed on to water ratepayers.

From the micro to the macro scale in the realm of stormwater and wastewater treatment, the examples in this chapter provide a window on the transition from hard- to soft-path approaches, highlighting the third principle of post-industrial infrastructure: integration of human-engineered systems with natural systems. To a significant extent, stormwater and wastewater treatment recapitulates the natural purification processes of wetlands, the vital yet fragile outlets of watersheds, where rivers drain into large bodies of water. Improving water quality through slow movement across textured and vegetated terrain is the organizing principle for the pioneering designs, based on natural processes, that are the focus of this chapter. Among the examples are smaller-scale, transformative interventions sited in urban rights-of-way (ROWs) or other marginal spaces; municipal-scale applications that reduce and treat stormwater (and even wastewater) flows. As described at the end of this chapter, even our freshwater supply systems are improved by the preservation of large urban watersheds and drainage areas that perform the collection, infiltration, and storage of potable water that can reduce or even avoid the need for costly water-filtration-plant construction.

Localized Interventions That Add Up: Greening Public Rights-of-Way

Since the 1990s low-impact development (LID), a set of tools and techniques for stormwater treatment that rely on natural ecosystem services while satisfying regulatory standards, has been largely regarded at the federal, state, and local levels as a desirable alternative to centralized stormwater management. Because water districts may have differing permitting requirements, however, barriers remain to widespread implementation. Pilot applications, here and abroad, as well as the research proving their effectiveness, have helped to remove many of the technical barriers. Numerous municipalities and counties have targeted roads and public ROWs as testing grounds for LID—because of both their ubiquity and their harmful effects on hydrologic functions (box 4-1). The science of road ecology further studies many of the adverse effects of interactions between natural systems and road networks, including constraints on wildlife and aquatic systems.

As of 2008, the linear extent of the US paved roadway network was 6,506,204 miles—nearly double the length of any other road network worldwide.[9] In fact, the nation's dedicated "vehicular habitat" (paved roads, parking lots, and driveways) constitutes about two-thirds of all impervious surfaces in the country—and, at more than 43,000 square miles, boasts a footprint approximately the size of the state of Ohio.[10]

Box 4-1. Pilot Projects and Guidelines

Demonstration projects across the United States are introducing working landscapes within spatially and materially reconfigured streets, parking lots, and other paved areas. Among the showcases for program initiatives and policy are the Green Streets program of Portland, Oregon; the *San Mateo County Sustainable Green Streets and Parking Lots Design Guidebook*; *Low-Impact Development: A Design Manual for Urban Areas*, produced by Fayetteville, Arkansas; and Chicago's Streetscape and Sustainable Design Program. Long the purview of civil and traffic engineering, the conventional, single-function ROW is being reimagined to do double or even triple duty through the incorporation of multiple functions: traffic calming, new bicycle lanes, enhanced pedestrian zones, continuous tree trenches, stormwater management, and enriched and diversified tree canopies and ground-level plantings.

One of the early policy guides, New York City's *High-Performance Infrastructure Guidelines: Best Practices for the Public Right-of-Way*, published in 2005 by the city's nonprofit partner, the Design Trust for Public Space, helped advance the adoption of environmental strategies for public ROWs and underscored the crucial need for interagency collaboration in the interests of integrating best practices for streetscapes—including stormwater management, porous pavements, improved access to utilities, and multifunctional landscapes—into the design, construction, and refurbishment of ROWs.

The manual was developed for a particular scale: New York City's 20,000 paved-lane-miles, which make up an area nearly double the size of Manhattan. Designed to support the compound use of greened ROWs, the guide merged practical performance goals with concern for the human experience of the urban environment.

Following the 2007 rollout of the city's PlaNYC, an action-oriented, integrated framework of what were originally 127 initiatives designed to manage the city's growth, sustainability, and climate-change adaptation agenda, Mayor Bloomberg continued to raise the bar for environmental performance across numerous agencies. The city's Departments of Parks (High Performance Parks for the Twenty-First Century), Environmental Protection (NYC Green Infrastructure Plan, Wetlands Strategy, and Sustainable Stormwater Plan), and Transportation (2009 Street Design Manual) all recognize the role of urban streets and open spaces in the critical shift away from single-purpose grey to multifunctional green construction. Many pilot projects developed under these guiding documents are currently being implemented and evaluated.

Chicago's nearly 2,000 miles of narrow, paved alleyways and service streets bisecting the city's long blocks are targeted for retrofit. Typically unsewered, these imperviously paved alleys will receive light-colored porous or permeable pavement to relieve the storm-sewer loads, recharge local water tables, and reduce localized flooding and the urban heat-island effect.[1] As of 2010 more than 100 Green Alleys have been implemented.[2]

---

1. City of Chicago, "Green Alley Program," City of Chicago's Official website, 2010–13, www.cityofchicago.org/city/en/depts/cdot/provdrs/street/svcs/green_alleys.html.

2. Ibid.

Paved, single-purpose byways generate compound deficits: they accumulate toxic mixtures of atmospheric particulate matter, rubber debris from tires and brake linings, agricultural chemicals, hydrocarbons, and bacteria and other harmful microorganisms, and they convey these and other pollutants to receiving waterways. They prevent the infiltration of aquifer-replenishing stormwater, increase localized flooding, and foster the buildup of polluted air. Paved areas create urban heat islands and even alter the weather patterns around cities. Finally, paved surfaces take a toll on wildlife and ecosystems by breaking up habitat.

In demonstration projects, sections of ROWs may be reengineered to promote infiltration, storage of excess water, and pollutant remediation. New ROW profiles combine traffic-safety measures (e.g., bike paths, medians) with soft-path working landscapes made up of both biotic and abiotic components, such as green medians, vegetated bioswales (drainage ditches with mixed plantings), interconnected street-tree trenches, detention basins, and pervious pavements.[11] Once in place, these features moderate climate stresses, remediate waste, circulate nutrients, and remove water pollutants. When joined with other marginal patches of landscape (e.g., highway edges, transmission easements, landscaped plazas, rail corridors), the enriched ROWs foster ecosystem connectivity and biodiversity. Along with wetlands, parks, cemeteries, campuses, and urban river corridors, green ROWs return the benefits of nature to urban environments.

Street Edge Alternatives: Radical Reconfigurations in the Right-of-Way

Seattle's pilot program, the Street Edge Alternatives Project (SEA Streets) is among the more inventive multipurpose ROW interventions. Developed by planners from Seattle Public Utilities (SPU) in consultation with local community groups, the project addresses local and bioregional water quality and quantity and includes vehicular and pedestrian safety measures and amenities—all at a savings over conventional drainage systems.

Given that local waters are home to the region's prized salmon, overarching goals included the restoration of streams and the protection of nearby aquatic habitat. The objectives for the streetscape included reducing the volume and flow rate of

ROW runoff, and eliminating pollutants—oil, heavy metals, pet waste, chemical fertilizers, and pesticides—that would otherwise make their way downstream.

SPU chose a typical residential street in a low-density urban environment in northwest Seattle for its two-block-long, 2.3-acre drainage test site. Completed in the spring of 2001, the ROW features a serpentine layout that slows traffic (fig. 4-1). Because the site's predevelopment natural landscape has been closely simulated, the ROW handles stormwater without the need for traditional piped drainage. Instead, runoff is directed into "bioswales"—vegetated ditches engineered for collection, conveyance, treatment, and infiltration of stormwater—placed on either side the roadbed; these ditches are lined with soil, river rocks, and salmon-friendly plants (sedges, rushes, grasses). More than 100 new evergreen trees and 1,100 shrubs line the front yards. These plantings, plus the bioswales, afford visual interest and privacy while "evapotranspiring"[12] the collected stormwater.[13]

Figure 4-1. Street Edge Alternatives (SEA Streets) project, Seattle, Washington. (Courtesy of Seattle Municipal Archives, no. 155416.)

In lieu of raised curbs, two-foot-wide bands of porous, light-colored concrete pavement smoothly abut the pervious asphalt of the driving lane, effectively adding enough width to the roadway, which had been dramatically reduced from 25 to 14 feet, to satisfy municipal regulations, which require sufficient street width for fire trucks to be able to pass. A single meandering sidewalk, combined with clustered and angled parking, allows more room for working landscape while encouraging neighborly interactions.

The homeowners and the SPU jointly maintain the ROW. Two years of continuous monitoring revealed that the SEA Street reduced the total volume of stormwater leaving the street by 99 percent. During peak rainfall months, the ROW reduced discharge to creeks by a factor of 4.7 when compared wih conventional Seattle streets. The SPU further estimates that infrastructure based on natural drainage systems costs 25 percent less than traditional roadside systems, primarily because reducing runoff at the source decreases the need for additional pipes and holding tanks.[14]

Today, the quality-of-life improvements associated with the pilot attract many visitors even as they boost local environmental stewardship. With SEA Street as a model and its *Right-of-Way Improvements Manual* as a guide, SPU hopes to widely replicate bioswale-based storm drainage, achieve water-quality objectives, institute traffic calming, and improve the appearance of neighborhoods across the northern part of the city.

Upgrading Urban Wastelands: Transforming Queens Plaza to "Dutch Kills Green"

SEA Street demonstrates the efficacy and benefits of supplanting gray with green in the ROW. Similar strategies are being successfully applied to marginal strips and poorly maintained or abandoned spaces (what might be called "infrastructural brownfields"), including bridge abutments and areas around or under elevated byways. The revitalization of Queens Plaza, in Long Island City, is one result of such transformative efforts.

A formerly anarchic interchange and derelict public space—consisting of multilane vehicular approaches to the Queensboro Bridge across the East River, a congregation of elevated subway lines, and an asphalt sea of commuter parking—this gateway from Queens to Manhattan is now unified by a raised and planted landscape that defines a new, 1.5-acre public space. As one of the first projects created in accordance with New York City's *High-Performance Infrastructure Guidelines* (box 4-1), what is now known as Dutch Kills Green is the product of an unprecedented level of collaboration among numerous local government agencies committed to developing a unique, multifunctional public work.

The new park's raised landform supports a densely planted canopy of almost 500 ironwood and other hardy trees, along with shrubs and native grasses capable of standing up to urban pollutants.[15] Berms, trees, and other features provide windbreaks and filter sunlight while helping to dampen ambient noise and the cacophony of overhead trains. Working features in the Green perform vital functions: stormwater diverted from the combined sewer system is now collected and filtered by constructed subsurface wetlands, then used to irrigate the park and the median plantings.

The rehabilitation of the plaza was necessary to support a burgeoning residential and cultural district—one that had been recently upzoned for high-density mixed-use development. A local group now called the Dutch Kills Civic Association took the initiative—and, with the cooperation of the city's planning department, lobbied to have the Queens Plaza upgrade included in the existing appropriations for nearby capital improvements. The $45 million improved landscape and streetscape, tracking the 1.3-mile approach to the bridge, unites residents with the existing park at the East River's edge. Timed crosswalks, as well as the realignment of roadways with medians, help to calm traffic. A planned lighting scheme will animate the steelwork of the elevated structures, illuminating the public space at night and creating a sense of enclosure for the park.

Completed in 2012, the redesigned plaza disentangled and regulated the movements of pedestrians and bicyclists, and rationalized vehicular and rail circulation. It has provided aesthetic and social coherence to the complex while remediating the adverse environmental conditions that remain (fig. 4-2). In all, it is an appropriate complement to a truly "post-industrial" neighborhood—one that has, in fact, already lost much of its industrial base.

Figure 4-2. View of Dutch Kills
Green, Queens, New York. (Cour-
tesy of Michael Singer Studio;
Photo: Sam Oberter.)

The artistic and ecological sensibilities of the design team members combined to devise some of the park's remedial, soft-path strategies—the most notable of which is the selection of unusual construction materials. When the project was in the planning stages, the city's park standards precluded the use of pervious pavers, but the team was able to circumvent regulations by relying on the "artistic license" granted to Michael Singer, the environmental sculptor who was hired through the city's Percent for Art Program. Singer's customized concrete paving stones direct surface water into wetlands and planted areas; notches in the edges of the patterned pavers promote water infiltration in situ, demonstrating a soft-path approach to stormwater management. Singer's artistry also comes into play in the unusual design of the park benches.

In another unorthodox use of materials, landscape architect Margie Ruddick covered the numerous traffic medians with rows of upended, broken chunks of concrete salvaged from the site.[16] Although their loose spacing facilitates stormwater infiltration and helps with noise reduction, the main purpose of these intimidating gray shards is to discourage random pedestrian crossings. To the discerning, they also present an ecological allegory in which artificial urban surfaces have been deconstructed to reestablish a natural cycle.

The convergence of multiple spaces and infrastructure systems rendered the redesign of Queens Plaza particularly challenging. For the leaders of the city's planning team, the work demanded extraordinary levels of interagency collaboration among representatives from the Metropolitan Transportation Authority (the elevated structure and access), Parks & Recreation (plantings and paving), the state and city Departments of Transportation, DEP, and the city's Department of Design and Construction. Innovative measures—including a rain garden, the use of hydrodynamic separators that use the physics of flowing water to catch sediments and other pollutants, and the installation of permeable pavers—were controversial and involved compromise. Other features and plantings that would have entailed complex, costly, or unconventional maintenance were ruled out.

At one juncture it became necessary for the Mayor's Office of Capital Project Development to assemble every consultant and member of city staff involved in the project, in order to coordinate a myriad of design and operational details—everything from light-pole placement to utility lines, tree spacing, timing of traffic signals, and maintenance of vehicle-passage areas. Resolution was achieved through a facilitated, hours-long forum conducted at City Hall. According to senior planner Penny Lee, it was "this 'all-agency' format that made the project go forward."[17] In the course of the planning and development process, participating agencies began to recognize that investment in the services of one sector could support the core mission of another; for example, incorporating green infrastructure reduced the DEP's stormwater-treatment burden. Ultimately, the collaborative process was essential to the bioengineered landscape that transformed the urban experience at the plaza.

A Hybrid Treatment Plant and Park—Sherbourne Common, Toronto

Across parts of many older cities in North America, legacy treatment facilities deal with the inflow of both sewage and stormwater for treatment before discharge into local water bodies. During major storms the total load may exceed plant capacity, and some of this combined sewer overflow (CSO) may be released untreated. In the United States alone, more than 700 communities cope with the impacts of CSO-released pollutants.[18] Waterfront cities, such as Chicago and Toronto, which extract their drinking water from nearby lakes, are particularly mindful of risks to water quality, and acutely aware of the imperative to address non-point-source pollution—the sediments, nitrogen, phosphorus, animal waste, oil, benzene, and other harmful substances discharged in runoff from impermeable surfaces.

In Toronto, an urban revitalization project on its waterfront has the collection, treatment, and conveyance of stormwater as a central organizing concept. When fully realized, Toronto's transformation and revitalization of its urban waterfront—a formerly derelict industrial district abutting the city's urban core—will consist of miles of wetlands and promenades, along with newly developed public parks on the edge of Lake Ontario. Totaling more than 2,000 acres, the waterfront—one of the largest urban redevelopment projects in North America—is being spearheaded by Toronto's Waterfront Revitalization Corporation (now known as Waterfront Toronto). The district known as East Bayfront now centers on a new waterfront park, Sherbourne Common, which bisects former industrial frontage.[19] Soon to be bounded by new institutional, commercial, and residential structures, the north end of the site is scaled for quiet activities and children's play, while the south section, overlooking Lake Ontario, has been designed to accommodate concerts, festivals, and other citywide and regional events.[20]

From the gardens and playgrounds in the northern section to the multipurpose pond in the southern section—which serves as a "splash pad" in summer and a skating rink in winter—water is integrated into the public attractions. The principal unifying feature, crisscrossed by pedestrian bridges and roadways, is a long channel that conveys cleaned water to the lake.

The park's articulated treatment train offers an elegant narrative—and a playbook of mixed ecological and artificial processes. The site's runoff is collected in tanks beneath the adjacent East Bayfront Park boardwalk for initial processing in a constructed wetland. After conveyance to an underground purification station, in lieu of chemical chlorine treatment, the water is subjected to high-intensity ultraviolet light to eliminate bacteria—a step that is necessary because the park's water features encourage human contact.[21] After disinfection, the treated water reemerges aboveground and is oxygenated as it cascades from the height of one of three sculptural pillars (fig. 4-3). After entering a raised pool, it passes through a

Figure 4-3. Sherbourne Common with integrated water feature, Toronto, Canada. (Courtesy of Waterfront Toronto.)

planted biofiltration bed and overflows into the long north-south channel that is the central feature of the project. Passing under several pedestrian bridges, it travels the length of the park before discharging into Lake Ontario. (Some of the water is diverted before reaching the lake, so that it can be used to irrigate the park.)

Waterfront Toronto, the agency charged with the redevelopment, advocated at the city's parks and health departments for the design team's unorthodox approach in merging biological and artificial treatment methods—the former affording the public amenity of natural processes, the latter, an additional factor of safety. The solutions used at Sherbourne Common are meant to inform the design of future waterfront parks. Although colocation of the treatment center added to the project's initial cost, James Roche, Waterfront Toronto's project lead, has noted that the design has already returned value: the public delights in the park's urban watercourse and vivid exposition of the transformative power of landscape.[22]

Stormwater Parks and Progressive Regulations— Philadelphia

The Schuylkill and Delaware Rivers, the source of Philadelphia's drinking water, come together within the confines of the city. Across a 64-square-mile area that houses 75 percent of the city's residents, 60 percent of the city's sewer system is combined with storm drainage. With 164 CSO points, severe storm events that can happen up to 85 times a year will release excess sewage into the Schuylkill, Delaware, and other waterways.[23] Since 1999 Philadelphia has engaged in integrated stormwater management in order to reduce runoff and thereby extend the useful service life of the city's current stormwater infrastructure. Among the strategies used to eliminate CSOs is the conversion of vacant lots into stormwater parks, which incorporate small-scale treatment and detention structures. Community groups participated in the development of the park designs, which include seating, play areas, murals, and landscaping.

Since 2007 Philadelphia has used its water and stormwater billing system to make green infrastructure standard practice for on-site stormwater management in public- and private-sector developments. Customers pay parcel-based rates that reflect the site's percentage of impervious covering, but they also receive credit for green infrastructure measures that meet specific standards. Given the extent of the measures committed to during the program's first-year rollout, the city foresaw that these and other low-impact measures will, when fully phased in by 2014, manage 1-inch storms (that is, 1 inch of stormwater falling on a site within a 24-hour period) and reduce CSO inputs by 25 billion gallons, at a reduced treatment cost to the city of $170 million.[24]

In 2011, the city signed a letter of agreement with the US EPA's approval for a 25-year, $2-billion Green City, Clean Waters initiative, which is further designed to solve CSO-induced water-quality problems. The program will rely on combined public and private financing to retrofit nearly 10,000 acres of public and private property with a wide range of green infrastructure measures designed to yield sufficient natural hydrologic absorption processes to manage 1-inch storms. One of the most progressive and comprehensive of municipal measures nationwide, the initiative could potentially save billions of dollars in capital and operating costs while simultaneously creating significant public benefits, including savings in health-care costs, greater recreational use of urban waterways, increased property values, restoration of ecosystem services, and energy savings from localized cooling.[25]

Engineered Wetlands for Wastewater Treatment—Arcata, California

The Arcata Wastewater Treatment Plant and Wildlife Sanctuary, near California's Humboldt Bay, is one of the earliest examples in the United States of a constructed wetlands system employed to treat municipal wastewater (fig. 4-4). The facility's history demonstrates how a progressive local body, asserting control of its own resources, not only rejuvenated and enhanced wetlands to treat the town's wastewater naturally, saving significant capital and operating costs, but also opened the same acreage to multiple use as wildlife habitat and for passive recreation and educational opportunities for the community. The plant is still in operation and continues to be a productive influence on the community.

Figure 4-4. Aerial view, Arcata Wastewater Treatment Plant and Wildlife Sanctuary, Arcata, California. (Courtesy of Terrence McNally.)

In 1958, in order to meet secondary treatment standards for the quality of the water discharged into Humboldt Bay,[26] the town of Arcata added 55 acres of oxidation ponds to its original treatment system.[27] These water bodies contain partially treated wastewater, fostering algae and bacterial growth for further decomposition. In 1968, the town chlorinated the ponds for further disinfection. With the advent of more stringent federal standards by the mid-1970s, the town had a choice: either upgrade the existing system or opt into the state- and regionally proposed $25-million centralized processing plant slated to handle wastewater for the entire region. The then-mayor and his public works director hoped to pursue a local solution.

Arcata, a city with a population of 12,850 in 1980, has long been home to many ecologically proactive citizens—in particular, students and professors at nearby Humboldt University. In its efforts to maintain a decentralized approach, the city's Wastewater Treatment Task Force (city and university officials) relied on experimental advances undertaken by the university's environmental engineering program, which included the successful release of partially treated wastewater for aquaculture nourishment (a natural cleaning process) en route to discharge into the bay.[28] Further university trials persuaded the task force that the addition of 30 to 40 acres of artificially constructed surface freshwater wetlands could sufficiently purify partly treated municipal wastewater while improving the biological productivity of the wetlands. Foreseeing the potential economic benefits, Arcata's public works director, Frank Klopp, and the task force proactively enlisted buy-in from both the state's and the region's water-quality control boards and funding assistance from the state's Coastal Conservancy. In 1983, the Arcata City Council moved ahead with the first phase of this innovative project; it opened in 1985, at a cost of less than $700,000.[29] Klopp's estimates were borne out: enhancing the acquired acreage as new wetlands for water treatment would incur about half the cost of buying into the centralized system and a third of the operating cost.[30] To increase capacity over the next two decades, the city acquired and repurposed nearby pastureland, a lumber-mill pond, and a closed sanitary landfill—more than 100 additional acres of freshwater and saltwater marsh close to the plant.

The wetland acreage was divided into staged treatment marshes and enhancement marshes, both free-water-surface

(FWS) constructed wetlands that receive and process partially treated wastewater from the oxidation ponds. The treatment marshes consist of thickly overgrown canopies of cattails and hardstem bulrush—plants whose roots and stems filter suspended solids, while bacteria remove dissolved organic material (effluent from the oxidation pond). After leaving the treatment marshes, the water is further disinfected by chlorination treatment; it then enters the denser enhancement marshes for tertiary treatment, where the remaining organic content (as measured by biological oxygen demand, or BOD, and including nutrient content) is further reduced.[31] At this stage, reeds take up phosphates and nitrates while their long shadows prevent algae from proliferating. After dechlorination with sulfur dioxide, the water flows through an adjacent, 6.9-hectare (17-acre) lake before exiting into the bay.

Routine maintenance for constructed wetlands consists of periodically harvesting vegetation and detritus to remove phosphorus and nitrates captured by the plants, controlling the depth of the water, cleaning inlets and outlets, and managing collected solids.[32]

It was the unique partnership among the public, private, and academic sectors that achieved this landmark transformation and captured critical associated benefits. The city enjoys low-carbon, low-maintenance, naturalized wastewater treatment, accomplished through sedimentation, filtration, oxidation, and adsorption. Former brownfields, remediated as constructed wetlands, restored public access to the waterfront. Together with nearby ponds and estuaries, the resulting assemblage of aquatic vegetation provides enriched habitat for permanent and migratory bird wildlife (some 270 species across the 300 acres).[33] The complex, now known as the Arcata Marsh and Wildlife Sanctuary, annually attracts some 150,000 visitors, who enjoy scenic vistas and miles of walking trails.

The approach also yielded important self-reinforcing benefits. First, the city's decision to reject the centralized system and pursue a local alternative has fostered community pride in the town-gown partnership and has forged further broad identification with conservation goals. Also, as over 200,000 people visit the sanctuary every year, their positive experiences further help "evangelize" this alternative treatment mode. Second, Humboldt University students and faculty gained from applied research opportunities while providing expertise for the city.

Third, the hybrid approach had long-term land-use consequences. Whereas signing on to the planned regional plant could have easily opened the way for unfettered development and sprawl, instead, wetland annexation—coupled with the city's subsequent acquisition of a community forest—established a barrier that has preserved the landscape's scenic and cultural integrity.[34] Arcata's example suggests that other communities planning to extend existing treatment plants or build new plants could blend biological systems with constructed ones. According to the EPA, surface-flow constructed wetlands work best in smaller municipalities, where land costs may be lower and skilled operators for the more technically complex engineered plants may be scarce.[35] They are especially beneficial as a means of restoring ecological health in communities where wetlands have been lost or degraded.

Colocated wastewater treatment plants and wetlands can be found elsewhere in California and in other parts of the United States, including Orlando and Lakeland, Florida, and Beaumont, Texas, where the wetlands cover over 900 acres. Wetlands also perform wildlife-enhancement functions, with emergent vegetation attractive to varied regional waterfowl, mammals, and reptiles in, for example, Show Low, Arizona, and Grand Strand, South Carolina, in the Carolina Bays. FSW wetlands have also been used to treat municipal landfill leachate in Fenton, New York, and industrial effluent in Columbus, Mississippi, and Mandan, North Dakota; and to remove metals and recharge groundwater in Tres Rios, Arizona.[36] By demonstrating how constructed systems can nest elegantly with natural ones, the decentralized approaches used in Arcata and elsewhere are fostering the integration of infrastructural functions into the landscape. Significantly, they are also transforming public perceptions of waste as a potential resource.

The Transformative Return of Wadi Hanifah—Riyadh, Saudi Arabia

The examples described so far in this chapter have focused on green infrastructure networks that attain water balance and regulate water quality in temperate climates—areas with adequate rainfall. The following example explores the use of similar practices in one of the most water-scarce countries in the world, where soft-path technologies are used to restore water balance within desert drainages; to rehabilitate ancient wetlands for recreational, cultural, and agricultural purposes; and, most important, to sanitize urban wastewater for beneficial non-potable use. This Saudi project successfully renewed a major but long-degraded watercourse, the Wadi Hanifah, which drains over 4,500 square kilometers in the west and north of the rapidly urbanizing city of Riyadh, the modern capital of Saudi Arabia and home to nearly 5 million people, and the project successfully forestalled Riyadh's need to construct a chemical- and energy-intensive treatment plant.

Despite the scant rainfall of this fragile desert environment, balance had historically been maintained between the wadi's supply and the population's needs.[37] In the 1970s, however, with growth fueled by an oil-dominated economy, Riyadh began importing costly supplies of desalinated water. The infusion of new water resulted in rising groundwater that then picked up septic seepage, industry discharges, and other pollutants; ultimately, the wadi was transformed from a seasonal stream into a polluted, permanently flowing watercourse.[38]

Planners hired by the Arriyadh Development Authority (ADA) pointed out the profligacy of Riyadh's water cycle: imported urban water (one barrel of which cost as much as a barrel of oil) was flowing away to waste in the desert.[39] In 2001, ADA staff, working with a team of planners, landscape architects, and engineers, developed a bold plan designed to repurpose the wadi. The basis for a decade-long work program, the plan featured hydrologic, recreational, and tourism goals, as well as guidelines to control future development in the wadi basin.

The wadi was carefully regraded to achieve a consistent slope, and its channel was widened, in order to attenuate the flood peak, eliminate standing water, and increase surface area (permitting greater oxygenation and thereby improving water quality).[40] Rows of large boulders spaced at intervals form weirs, providing additional aeration. Finally, a roughened stone lining and coarse-bedded shallows increase water turbulence—which, in turn, aerates it, fostering the growth of microorganisms that metabolize toxicants and excess nutrients.

Final remediation occurs downstream from the weirs, where 134 bioremediation cells—arranged in a herringbone pattern and filled with riparian plants—create the food web that is required for final water cleaning. The stone surfaces and artificial substrates of the cells accumulate algae and other aquatic microbial material (fig. 4-5). Aerating pumps increase the water's oxygenation. Tilapia nurtured on the algae complete the feeding chain—the last stop in a serial process that "bio-accumulates" the water's nutrients and metabolizes odor-producing nitrogen compounds.[41] The facility anticipates an eventual monthly harvest of about a ton of tilapia.[42] Remarkably, the capital cost of this in-situ natural treatment was roughly one-third that of a mechanical plant.[43]

The scale of this bioremediation complex is unique. Water-balance returns are high: by restoring the stream to pristine condition, the ADA recycles Riyadh's regular urban outflow—currently some 400,000 cubic meters (about 105 million gallons) daily, enough to satisfy one-third of the city's total non-potable water needs. By 2025, that number is expected to increase to more than 1 million cubic meters (264 million gallons).[44] Ongoing monitoring ensures that the facility performs at or beyond expectations.[45]

Figure 4-5. Wadi Hanifah bioremediation cells, Riyadh, Saudi Arabia (© Arriyadh Development Authority).

The government distributes the treated water at no cost to farmers, supporting increased agricultural yields. Some is used by oil refineries; significantly, however, the remaining water is pumped back to the city in order to irrigate public gardens and parks, a dividend that has supported a boom in lush riparian real estate. The wadi restoration added nine major waterside parks and six lakes, welcome amenities in a city that had lacked significant public open space. Some of the newly landscaped parks, with trees, shrubs, and grasses, extend along sub-wadis into adjacent residential areas.[46] With such improvements in place, property values along the wadi corridor have increased tenfold.[47]

The recovered water supports 4,500 date palms and 35,000 shade trees planted along the wadi's banks.[48] Indigenous vegetation has also been reestablished in the wadi bed: evergreen shrubs, acacia, and tamarisk in the dryer northern sections, and reeds, marsh herbs, and bushes for wildlife attraction in the southern sections.[49] Ecological health has been further nurtured through the reintroduction of indigenous animals and the establishment of a plant nursery to expand the greening of the wadi.[50]

Constructed and natural elements fuse seamlessly throughout the project. The wadi's banks are filled with pedestrians; its working features—explained by signs along terraces, bridges, and rebuilt trails—have lured back a once-wary public.[51] In carefully arranged coves along the banks of the wadi, families can enjoy privacy while picnicking and enjoying the water. The stepped banks of the watercourse invite access to the swiftly moving stream. Twenty-five miles of gravel-and-stone walking trails extend the five miles of paved pedestrian promenades that are dramatically illuminated during the cooler evening hours to encourage public use.

The project economics were compelling: with desalinated water priced at over $5 per cubic meter (about 264 gallons), recycling 400,000 cubic meters (about 105 million gallons) of water a day would create a very short payback period.[52] The most costly part of the reconfiguration was the relocation of the roadbed and utility infrastructure—overhead and underground, respectively, that ran along the streambed. (A dedicated channel now conceals utilities and protects them from flooding; formerly haphazard roadway infrastructure along the wadi was also minimized to reduce traffic and environmental impacts.)

In addition to realizing significant cost savings, the reha-bilitation and repurposing of a degraded natural system has generated intensive public use, justifying the investment many times over. Wadi Hanifah is a model "high-thought / low-tech"[53] approach—one that is desperately needed to influence twenty-first-century public works not only in the developed world but also in the developing world, where water quality is a critical concern.

In the future, the ADA hopes to foster new private-sector investment in tourism, leisure developments, and mixed-use shopping districts in the vicinity of the wadi.[54] Other cultural and environmental improvements are also under consideration, including an interpretive center focusing on the socio-historical aspects of the stewardship and use of the Wadi Hanifah. Addi-tional recreation areas are also planned.

A successful fusion of civic artistry and engineering logic to achieve vital ecological ends, the "Great Park of Riyadh" was essential to meeting the demands of the city's growing pop-ulation. Rejuvenated as a healthy natural drainage course for Riyadh and the surrounding region, the wadi has helped to restore vital water balance in the desert by conserving water and reducing the energy and cost for potable-water production. In 2010, in recognition of the project's response to the needs and aspirations of Islamic societies everywhere, it received the prestigious Aga Khan Award. As cities worldwide seek to reclaim their water bodies from industrial-era contamination and blight, designers are acknowledging and celebrating the vital import of naturalized water and riverine biology in an urbanizing world.

Creative Solutions to New Needs: New York City's Croton Water Filtration Treatment Plant

Like Riyadh, New York City had succeeded for decades in avoid-ing construction of a conventional treatment plant (in this case for water *supply*), despite having one of the most exten-sive municipal water systems in the world. The city's water-shed—three upstate areas totaling 2,000 square miles, and encompassing nineteen reservoirs and three controlled lakes—supplies a downstate population of 9 million with 1.1 billion gallons a day. This vast, networked system has yielded naturally

filtered potable water since its initial construction in the nine-
teenth century.

For most of the watershed's history, various management
strategies have been used to ensure that the water conveyed
to the city by means of 6,200 miles of water pipes, tunnels, and
aqueducts continued to be of high quality. By the early 1990s,
however, as a consequence of suburban growth and commercial development, the watershed areas and particularly Croton
watershed—the one closest to New York City—had begun to
suffer the effects of pollutants from septic systems, lawn care,
and agricultural and paved-surface runoff.[55]

In 1996, the City finally faced enforcement action from the
EPA and the New York State Department of Health for noncom-
pliance with federal drinking-water standards (Safe Drinking
Water Act Amendments, 1986). The City had to choose between
building and operating an expensive new water-filtration for
the system (at what would then have been a cost of $6–8 bil-
lion) or upgrading the protection of all its watersheds by other
means. Presented with compelling economic and ecological
arguments in favor of a natural approach, the City selected that
option, and in January 1997 the New York City Watershed Memorandum of Agreement was signed by New York City, New York
State, the communities in New York City's watershed, the US
EPA and five environmental organizations for large-scale land
acquisition and the use of extensive hydrological protection
measures.[56] The City's case for a natural approach was made,
in part, through the valuation of ecosystem services—specifically, the natural system's capacity for filtration and decontami-
nation. Also identified, but not priced, were further gains from
watershed protection, including the aesthetic and recreational
(primarily hunting) benefits of conserving open space, and the
benefits to marine and terrestrial habitat. The avoidance of
chlorination and other chemical disinfectants was also among
the noted benefits.[57]

Over a 10-year period beginning in 1997, the City agreed to
commit $250 million to watershed improvements overall, and
an additional $10 million to Croton; these funds, along with $7.5
million from the state, were used to acquire lands that would
serve as buffer zones along rivers and around reservoirs. The
City's efforts also benefited from additional local land-use regulations, from partnerships with community groups, and from

assistance of agricultural councils that agreed to control nutrients from agricultural runoff.[58] The City made further funds available to upstate municipalities subsidizing upgrades of septic systems and local wastewater-treatment plants within the watersheds and improving buffer zones along streams. Finally, the City purchased conservation easements for the protection of riparian buffers.

Despite the City's commitment of hundreds of millions of dollars to programs intended to forestall the construction of a water-treatment plant, the Croton system's exemption from mechanical filtration was ultimately doomed. Because water aesthetics (odor, taste, and color) were seasonally affected by the presence of organic matter during drought or peak use,[59] the Croton system frequently had to be shut down, undermining the redundancy—and, consequently, the reliability—of the entire network.[60] In November 1998 and again in 2002, pursuant to a consent decree released by a federal court, New York City began to evaluate sites for the construction of a water-filtration treatment plant. It ultimately found one—in the Bronx, on a golf course within Van Cortlandt Park.

That the City was ultimately compelled to use mechanized filtration to support the natural functions of one part of its system does not diminish the value of the unprecedented experimental measures it had historically—and successfully—used to avoid conventional treatment. Large swaths of the watershed are still protected by natural means[61]—and the City has ensured that such measures are mirrored and enshrined in the new Croton Filtration Treatment Plant, a multifunction complex scheduled to be completed in 2014.

The Croton plant—which will greatly augment but not replace the watershed's natural filtration—will be the first of its kind in New York City and one of the largest in the nation, with a nine-acre footprint and a depth equivalent to six stories below grade. When it is completed, this facility will treat up to 290 million gallons of water per day.[62] The plant's single above-grade story, capped by the country's largest high-performance green roof, will not only serve as a new driving range for the existing golf course but will also be used to host a variety of public and community functions. Most notably, the iconic design effectively recapitulates the functioning of the Croton watershed, at a micro scale, through the design's integration of landscape and topography with the human-engineered system.[63]

From the outset, the facility was designed to retain the hydrologic integrity of the site (fig. 4-6). Its nine acres of impervious concrete, placed in otherwise permeable soil and rock formations, displaces groundwater accumulating beneath the complex. The plant is designed to relieve the resulting groundwater pressure without simply discharging it as "excess" into the combined sewer system; instead, the flows are impounded on-site. First, the collected groundwater (warmed geothermally) is circulated through heat exchangers in order to help offset the building's energy costs; the groundwater is then stored in underground basins, which also capture the large volumes of roof rainwater. Finally, the groundwater is mixed with stormwater runoff from on-site roads and parking lots, and the combined streams are pumped to the site's rooftop high point.[64] The water then cascades downward through a series of ten

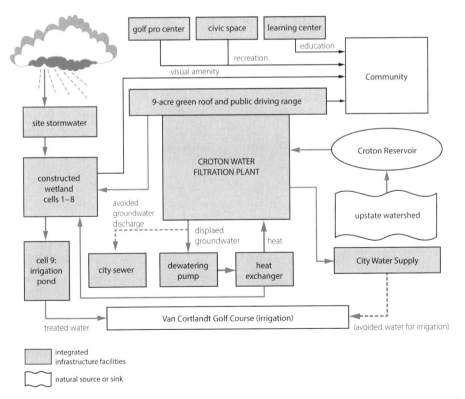

Figure 4-6. The Croton Water Filtration Plant, Bronx, New York. (Figure by Hillary Brown.)

planted pools that make up the working wetland ringing the facility.[65] Stocked with plants that are native or adapted to the region, this mixed surface and subsurface wetland "polishes" the water by removing suspended sediments. Built-in weirs and landscaped rock formations help aerate the stream, adding dissolved oxygen.[66] Microbes break down petroleum products, while plants take up dissolved nutrients. The cleansed water is stored at the base of the cascade for use in building mainte-nance and golf-course irrigation—replacing the 280,000 gal-lons of potable water that would otherwise be required, during each summer month, to irrigate the golf course.[67]

The creative integration of building form and ecosystem ser-vices also solved security concerns that were heightened after the 9/11 attacks in 2001. In addition to eliminating the need for unsightly security fencing, the encircling wetlands double as a protective moat, surrounding the facility. Elsewhere, land-scaped elements such as swales, runnels, and berms contribute to making the perimeter both secure and handsome (see also fig. 5-1).

While costly by any standard, the $3.1-billion complex nonetheless provides compound value to the public, returning essential social assets to the community while improving the hydrology of its campus—paired benefits that will be discussed further in the next chapter. Ultimately, by demonstrating how investment in municipal utilities can improve urban water quality while enhancing local ecosystems and civic space, the plant sets a high bar for future infrastructural projects.

Conclusion

For next-generation infrastructure, the integrating framework for water treatment must be a comprehensive consideration of the natural hydrologic cycle. Just as low-carbon energy strate-gies employ local renewable-energy flows to supplement the energy cycle, so can low-impact water management strategies exploit local water flows and natural landscapes to optimize hydrologic cycles.

From precautionary protection of watersheds to down-stream cycles of cleaning, storage, and reuse, the examples in this chapter demonstrate how reduced-impact water ser-vices—reliant upon bioengineering and conjoined with adaptive landscapes—can be gracefully woven into the urban fabric. The Croton Water Filtration plant mimics the hydrologic functions performed by healthy watersheds. A rejuvenated urban watercourse in Riyadh, designed as a water-treatment train, has become a major public amenity. And at the Arcata Wastewater Treatment Plant and Wildlife Sanctuary, a series of constructed wetlands annexed to increase the capacity of the facility obviated the need for the city to opt into centralized water-treatment services. Sherbourne Common, Dutch Kills Green, and other successful projects piloting green infrastructure are diverting urban pollutants from receiving waters and using landforms and water features to unify and ornament public space, as well as to becalm and rejuvenate it.

The strategies and design sensibilities illustrated in this chapter epitomize the new ecological design paradigms that are emerging in urban infrastructure. These alternative models champion an integrated perspective that demands interdisciplinary collaboration. Solutions are attentive to patterns of both regional and local hydrology, and decentralized technologies achieve a lighter footprint by treating and managing water at or near the site of use. Significantly, citizens will begin to associate visual and recreational amenities of soft-path systems with improved overall water quality in the urban domain, and they will appreciate the enhancement of land values, protection or improvement of biodiversity, and the improvement of the microclimate. Finally, artful visions have paved the way for innovation as artists have capitalized on the leniency accorded them to invoke unconventional solutions to environmental problems. Despite the existence of successful models, there is as yet no clear-cut route by which local entities can move from the hard to the soft path. Compartmentalized funding and regulation of water-quality management still present obstacles to a more holistic, systems-oriented approach. And, because of the sunk costs invested in conventional treatment and delivery infrastructure, whatever funding is available will likely be used to maintain aging central plants and increasingly fragile distribution networks. As a result, in a world where competition for water resources is increasing, a likely outcome is that green infrastructural systems will be implemented at smaller, more diffuse scales as expansions of or enhancements to existing systems.

Notwithstanding these barriers, the shift evidenced in these projects confirms that local governments are increasingly sensitive to the long-term financial benefits of soft-path approaches, coupled with their ecological imperatives and the ways in which such imperatives align with various agencies' missions. The principle of urban sustainability, invoked as an argument in support of each of these projects, is a powerful unifying force—as is the cost-effectiveness of alternative measures. Public bodies today are laying the groundwork for the hybrid complexes of the future: new engineering models based on interconnected and synergistic infrastructure. Many such systems also reflect a heightened awareness of, and an inclination to prepare for, the advancing era of climate instability and the challenges it will create for urban hydrology.[68]

5. Destigmatizing Infrastructure: Design of Community-Friendly Facilities

In 1999, when New York City advanced plans to construct the Croton Water Filtration Treatment Plant in Van Cortlandt Park in the Bronx, it faced strong resistance from the surrounding community, largely comprised of minority and low-income residents. But the plan had powerful supporters, including downstate construction unions that lobbied heavily in anticipation of construction contracts and upstate developers who believed the plant would reduce pressure to protect upstate watershed areas.

In alliance with environmentalists and other citizens' groups, residents protested—and later litigated—against the plant's large footprint that would take away parkland and the potential effects of the construction-related noise, traffic, and pollution on the 26,000 people who lived within a half-mile radius of the plant.[1] The litigation briefly delayed construction but was ultimately unsuccessful. Mayor Bloomberg and Bronx officials brokered an agreement that promised $43 million in capital improvements to Van Cortlandt Park, plus a windfall of $243 million for other Bronx parks over four years. The deal also promised local employment related to the plant, ensured mitigation measures (such as pollution controls on construction vehicles and the muffling of blasting noise), and included community monitoring and oversight of the project. The restoration and return of precious community parkland was one of the city's key concessions.

To honor the agreement—and under pressure from the Public Design Commission—the City retained a world-class design team—which, as described in the previous chapter, creatively integrated a closed-loop water management scheme into the design.[2] The project is ringed by a moat with bioengineered planting and stone walls that also reprise the heroic design legacy of New York's renowned historic water-supply infrastructure. In addition to a new clubhouse and pro shop, the project includes other amenities, such as a learning center and community civic space (fig. 5-1).[3] The litigation—and these eventual trade-offs—exemplify the complexities and challenges of infrastructure placement in an urbanizing world.

Even when they are not sited in residential areas, environmentally intrusive assets—such as waste-transfer stations; water-treatment plants; electrical-transmission towers, and gas-fired power plants—are likely to engender controversy, if not outright opposition. Such resistance was first seen in the 1950s, when nuclear power plants were initially commercialized. Siting processes became increasingly complex in the 1970s due to mounting public awareness of environmental and public health concerns. In the 1980s, as the environmental justice movement burgeoned, community resistance became more tactical, often involving lawsuits. By the 1990s, in the face of increasingly stringent permitting and review processes and growing public concern about diminished quality of life, the utility sector had

Figure 5-1. Croton Water Filtration Plant's above-ground buildings, Bronx, New York (© Grimshaw Architects).

begun to recognize the need for greater public participation in siting decisions and in the monitoring of operations.[4]

As in the case of the Croton plant in the Bronx, communities that host infrastructural facilities often face significant burdens and risks. These include diminished quality of life from disruptive construction and ongoing operations, potential exposure to environmental hazards, and loss of property value. Recognition of the need to address these burdens and risks, real or perceived, has given rise to the fourth principle governing post-industrial infrastructure: sensitivity to social and environmental context. In practical terms, such sensitivity is expressed through proactive local engagement—deliberative processes that are open to all members of the community.

This chapter explores both participatory and smart-design approaches that are intended to ensure that public-utility facilities are viewed, if not as highly advantageous assets, then at least as considerably more benign presences. More broadly, the chapter explores what new opportunities might emerge—specifically, tangible social or economic dividends—as infrastructural assets are more fully and beneficially integrated into the fabric of the community. Finally, the chapter explores mechanisms that can be used to proactively engage, persuade, and empower stakeholders.

The first hallmark of community-friendly infrastructure is the provision of physical and environmental improvements that exceed public health codes and regulatory requirements through creative design solutions. The use of sophisticated iconography, environmental messaging, and artful urban design are notable advances beyond conventionally engineered infrastructure complexes. The second characteristic is collaborative decision making as a means of ensuring that quality of life will be protected or restored, and that social and economic benefits will be incorporated into project planning: what might be called "extra-functional" or accessory spaces that range from community meeting rooms, to conference centers, to interpretive centers designed to deliver education focused on the mission of the facility. The third characteristic is co-development, which means that the entire venture, from initial planning through construction and operation, exemplifies joint and deliberative environmental, social, and economic engagement. Each project explored in this chapter exemplifies at least one of these characteristics that can help neutralize community anxiety and make meaningful contributions to the affected locality.

Hard-Won Improvements to the Newtown Creek Wastewater Treatment Plant—Brooklyn, New York

All three of the approaches outlined above are featured in the example of the Newtown Creek Wastewater Treatment Plant, but this came about only after persistent community pressure on the New York City Department of Environmental Protection (DEP). It stands in contrast to the projects that follow where adjustments were done proactively, anticipating community concern.

How much risk—including intrusion, displacement, pollution, and disruption—may be assigned to any one community, while benefits accrue to a much wider public? This is the question of *fair share* as it relates to infrastructure placement. Concerns about fair share are particularly germane to communities that abut waterfronts, which have traditionally been home to wastewater treatment, power generation, incinerators, and solid-waste-handling facilities, as well as to polluting and hazardous-materials-handling industries. As neighborhoods strive to revive the scenic and recreational potential of urban waterways, conflict over priorities may intensify—as was the case in Brooklyn's Greenpoint community, where the expansion of a wastewater-treatment plant sparked conflict over fair share, land use, and waterfront access. Positive outcomes were achieved only through long-term community activism and extensive local consultation.

Draining into New York City's East River, Newtown Creek separates the boroughs of Brooklyn and Queens. Along its four miles of bulkhead-lined banks lies the oldest continuously industrialized district in the country, hosting over 50 manufacturing uses, including oil refineries, petrochemical plants, fertilizer factories, glue factories, sawmills, lumber yards, and coal yards.[5] The legacy of pollution includes a decades-old, 100-acre underground oil plume, and a more recent spill that polluted a further 55 acres of commercial and residential property along the waterway.[6] Overflows from combined sewer and stormwater systems have caused additional damage to the creek, and heavy traffic on the bordering Brooklyn/Queens Expressway contributes mobile-source air and water pollution.[7] Finally, since its opening in 1972 the city's wastewater-treatment plant was found to be noncompliant with federal secondary-treatment standards imposed under the Clean Water Act passed that same year.[8] The last of the New York City Department of Environmental Protection (DEP) plants to be upgraded, it remained noncompliant until 2012.[9]

In the ethnically diverse, historically working-class Greenpoint community, residents had long endured the persistent smell of oil in their basements, as well as odors from the chronically underperforming sewage-treatment plant. According to environmental planner Kate Zidar, these environmental insults provided the foundation for a highly vocal and active community, and the development of "a savvy community constituency"[10] that first challenged the then-named Newtown Creek Water Pollution Control Plant (NCWPCP) for noncompliant sewage discharges in the late 1980s, and later unsuccessfully resisted the city's proposed expansion of the plant. In 1996, under the city's land-use review procedure, community activists established the Newtown Creek Monitoring Committee (NCMC), an oversight body focused on the plant's expansion.[11]

DEP's prolonged failure to comply with state permitting requirements set the stage for the establishment of an environmental benefits program (EBP). Under the EBP, which was established in 1990 under three consecutive consent orders issued by the New York State Department of Environmental Conservation (DEC), DEP was required to partner with the community to comprehensively address environmental problems; as part of that effort, funding from its $850,000 noncompliance fine was earmarked for Greenpoint improvements, specifically to work with the NCMC and the community at large to assess environmental problems and implement specific projects reducing pollution and protecting the community from further environmental damage.[12] As part of the EBP, the NCMC gained a designated "environmental watchperson" to monitor odor, construction noise, truck traffic, garbage, debris, and other disruptions, for which the DEP would be held accountable. According to NCMC community liaison Christine Holowacz, the community eventually developed a productive working relationship with DEP; partly as a result of this relationship, the NCMC was often DEP's best advocate in the community.

In 1999, the elegant, silver-skinned architecture of the new addition to the plant received one of the City's coveted Public Design Commission design awards. Both aesthetic enhancements and new public spaces had been secured through New York's Percent for Art program, which requires that 1 percent of City-funded construction budgets for its facilities go to associated artwork. And perhaps most importantly, the community gained through the proposed art project what it had long been denied: access to its waterfront (fig. 5-2). Instead of anodyne building adornments, the selected artist, environmental sculptor George Trakas, created a creekside public right-of-way now called the Newtown Creek Nature Walk. Trakas incorporated boat moorings as well as steps that cascade into the creek, a gesture that allows direct contact with the water and embodies the community's ongoing guardianship of the waterway.

In 2010, a new public destination was added to the wastewater-treatment plant and nature walk: the Newtown Creek Wastewater Treatment Plant Visitor Center. Here, DEP commissioned exhibits that chronicle the stewardship of the daily

Figure 5-2. Newtown Creek Nature Walk, Brooklyn, New York (© Maggie Trakas).

"upstate-to-downstate" hydrological cycle, through which 2,000 square miles of watershed provide a billion gallons of drinking water to city residents each day, and DEP discharges 1.3 billion gallons of treated wastewater into New York's harbors.[13]

As of this writing, further improvements to the plant and park are in the planning stages. For the former, the City has taken an environmental leap forward with plans to partner with a private utility to build a "digester gas-purification plant." Scheduled to begin construction by the end of 2013, the City will harvest and clean anaerobic gas from the treatment plant's sludge, which had previously been flared. The resulting gas-to-grid distribution system will produce enough power to heat 2,500 homes while averting the annual release of 16,650 metric tons (18,353 short tons) of greenhouse gases (GHGs).[14]

With its visitor center, shapely digesters, and nature walk, Newtown Creek Wastewater Treatment Plant's campus suggests possible futures of more-benign if not harmonious associations between infrastructural installations and civic contexts. Even more transformative solutions may accompany post-industrial complexes: using their composite skills, teams of engineers, urban designers, landscape architects, and artists are finding ways to reinvest otherwise intrusive facilities with inventive new uses, thus coupling amenity with utility.

Post-Industrial Visions for Waste-to-Energy Facilities

Despite being relatively well accepted in many Northern European countries, waste-incineration plants that recover energy are among the most controversial facilities in the United States. Among the factors that have made WTE or energy-from-waste (EfW) plants, as they are known in Europe, both desirable and feasible are high fuel costs; a scarcity of real estate available for landfills; strict (and stringently enforced) pollution controls;[15] and the opportunity to reduce carbon footprints.[16]

In 2008, Denmark, Germany, the Netherlands, and Sweden collectively landfilled less than 2.25 percent of their solid waste and incinerated more than 45 percent in WTE facilities, a function of advanced recycling policies.[17] In 2009, the United States landfilled 54.3 percent of its solid waste and incinerated a mere 12 percent in waste-to-energy or WTE facilities.[18] Among the reasons for the disparity is the fact that the US public associates WTE with harmful emissions, including mercury, dioxin, and furans.[19] (Some also believe it will "encourage" the production of waste.) In reality, improved technologies control emissions: from 1990 to 2000, for example, state-of-the-art WTE facilities reduced their dioxin emissions from 4,260 to 12 grams (150 to 0.4 ounces) TEQ (toxic equivalent).[20]

With the promulgation of stricter operational regulations in 1995, the US Environmental Protection Agency (EPA) designated WTE as renewable energy, based on the fact that it requires no new fuel sources other than the waste that would otherwise be landfilled. In 2007, the United States had 87 waste-to-energy plants that generated approximately 2,720 megawatts (MW), or about 0.4 percent, of total US power generation.[21] According to the EPA, US WTE plants produce electricity with less environmental impact than almost any other source.[22] And, as of 2009, when WTE was compared with even the most aggressive landfill-gas-to-energy practices (recovery of landfill methane gas for energy production), it had between 17 and 65 percent fewer GHG emissions.[23] Moreover, landfilling produces persistent harmful emissions, including methane, mercury, and volatile organic compounds, and it contaminates water sources with chemical leachates.

The Isséane Recycling Center and Energy from Waste Plant—Paris, France

Discreetly sited in the town of Issy-les-Moulineaux on a brownfield along the Seine, less than two miles upriver from the Eiffel Tower, the Isséane Energy from Waste Plant is one of a bold new breed of such plants located in dense urban environments. Completed in 2008 and serving more than 1 million residents, it features an unusually modest profile for a structure of its size. In addition to its strict emissions controls, the plant used a number of ameliorative strategies to guarantee local acceptance.

From the earliest planning stages, the two primary goals for the facility were to reduce environmental and visual impact and to protect human well-being. Isséane is based on the "proximity principle," which calls for waste to be treated as closely as possible to where it is generated—in this case, no farther than six miles. Colocating the MSW recycling facility with the WTE plant eliminates emissions from trucks that would otherwise be transporting materials between two facilities.

The plant was conceived and developed by SYCTOM, the largest public authority responsible for waste disposal in France, as a syndicate of 85 local governments in greater Paris. In December 2000, SYCTOM and the town of Issy-les-Moulineaux signed an environmental-quality charter governing construction and a 40-year operating agreement. In addition to enumerating environmental health and safety objectives, the charter established a committee to monitor achievement of those objectives. At the same time, a group of local residents (known as *sentinels*) were charged with alerting plant operators to any observed noise, smell, dust, or other disturbances. Other concessions to the town included assigning priority to persons with disabilities in the facility workforce.[24]

At the recycling side of the plant, some 55,000 metric tons (60,627 short tons) of combined wastes annually are mechanically and manually sorted (fig. 5-3). Member communities receive an income stream that depends on the amount of sorted tonnage they contribute.[25] The energy-production side of the facility incinerates 460,000 metric tons (507,063 short tons) of domestic waste each year. The resulting waste heat,

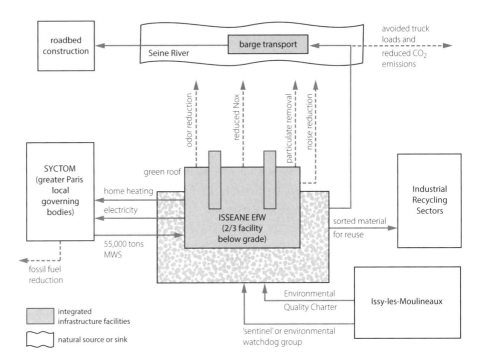

Figure 5-3. Isséane: Issy-les-Moulineaux Household Waste Sorting and Energy Production Center, Paris, France. (Figure by Hillary Brown.)

converted to high-pressure steam, drives turbines that produce 52 MW of renewable power, averting the use of approximately 110,000 tons of fossil fuels, along with the associated GHG emissions. Surplus steam is routed to Paris's urban heating association, which supplies 79,000 homes. The plant's liquid effluents are chemically treated on-site and released into the sewerage system. Some 8,000 tons of slag and residual metals are collected each year; the slag, used in roadbed construction, is diverted from the facility by barge, thereby averting 26 20-ton truck shipments per day and avoiding 23 tons of CO_2 emissions annually.[26]

Among the most effective strategies used to reduce the plant's visual impact is its modest profile: with just two stories visible above grade, the facility looks like an office structure, with handsome glass and wood cladding topped by a living roof.[27] Only the slightly elevated tops of the emissions stacks betray the building's real identity. In addition to reducing the bulk of the facility, situating the four remaining levels below grade cuts down on noise: garbage trucks descend nearly 100 feet to the basement levels. (Above grade, extra soundproofing muffles noise.) The daylit sorting center is concealed below a courtyard garden. A state-of-the-art process removes 99 percent of the particulates from the plant's combustion gases, and nitrous oxides are chemically converted into water and nitrogen; dioxins have been measured at nearly one-tenth of acceptable limits.[28]

Dubbed a "green factory" by SYCTOM, Isséane routinely hosts visiting waste-management experts from around the world. Progressive, anticipatory strategies for community participation, reliance on an environmental charter, and the avoidance of an industrial-looking eyesore—not to mention the regulation of noise, odors, and harmful emissions—have made this infrastructural design a success worthy of emulation.

Elegance and Amenities at the Naka Facility— Hiroshima, Japan

Because of lack of space in its densely urbanized areas, Japan burns more of its trash than any other developed nation. But by the 1990s routine incineration had created hazardously high dioxin levels. With updated pollution controls resulting in 97 percent reduction in dioxins—and in response to the unsustainability of the nation's energy model, under which fossil fuel imports satisfy more than 80 percent of energy needs—Japan has shifted its focus to WTE technologies.[29] Currently 21 colossal WTE plants provide electric and thermal energy to citizens of Tokyo.[30]

Hiroshima is engaged in proactive measures designed to address the haphazard reconstruction that occurred after World War II. Mindful of the approaching centennial of the city's destruction, Hiroshima established the 2045 City of Peace and Creativity initiative. As part of this effort, the city has commissioned distinguished public works by the country's most celebrated architects, tasking them with providing "excellent urban scenery through fusion design"[31]—*fusion design* being what the Japanese call collaboration among architects, civil engineers, landscape architects, industrial hygienists, and others.

In response to a growing waste problem, the mayor of Hiroshima and the city's Urban Development Bureau undertook the enlargement of an existing incineration facility. The design of the new Hiroshima Naka Waste Incineration Plant was a particularly sensitive issue—first because of the plant's location at the terminus of both a major artery (the city's celebrated boulevard, Yoshijima Street) and a visual corridor connected to the Hiroshima Peace Memorial Museum, and second because the architect wanted the building to restore the city's connection to the sea.

Architect Yoshio Taniguchi approached the infrastructural redesign as he would that any of the world-class museums for which he is best known. The graceful composition of what is affectionately known as Taniguchi's "Museum of Garbage" pays special homage to visitors. The incinerator's elegantly boxed volume is bisected by a 400-foot-long, glass-enclosed corridor, called the "Ecorium," where nearly 200,000 visitors a year look down upon the colossal inner workings of the plant as if into a glass vitrine in a museum (fig. 5-4). Below, on the plant's floor, silvery cylindrical gas-vacuum towers dwarf an ornamental *allée* of trees. All is daylit, airy, and spotless. The visitor's path, a literal extension of Yoshijima Street, terminates outdoors on a platform cantilevered over a newly incorporated public park with a splendid harbor view.

Figure 5-4. View from the "Ecorium," Naka Waste-to-Energy Plant, Hiroshima, Japan. (Photo by Kenta Mabuchi.)

By means of this gateway-to-the-sea corridor, with its inter-active exhibits on refuse processing, the mayor and architect intended to highlight the interrelationship of material, energy, and water as municipal services.[32] Visitors first encounter the 400 tons of incoming daily dross from an overlook six floors above the waste pit. As they continue along the visitors' path, they follow the combustion process by which steam-driven turbines produce 12.5 MW of electricity to run the plant (surplus power is sold to the city's electric utility, supplying 20,000 homes).

Steam condensate from the plant's cogeneration heats a swimming pool and a fitness center, as well as a health clinic for elderly people—noteworthy dividends that helped to win community acceptance of the plant.[33] In addition to its digni-fied design and adroit integration into the urban landscape, Naka exemplifies the concept of "coupled" and "synergistic" infrastructure ecology with its incorporation of diverse func-tions (including cascading energy and heat), a visitors' gallery, and other community uses.

A Combined Heat and Power Facility—Copenhagen, Denmark

Naka is just one example of public authorities awarding com-missions to architects or artists in order to transmute poten-tially offending facilities. With its festooned onion domes, spires, and profusion of playful ornaments and colored-glass openings, Friedrich Hundertwasser's fanciful Maishima Incineration Plant and Sewage Treatment Facility, constructed in Osaka, Japan, in 2001, continues to be a major tourist attraction.[34]

If it is true that unorthodox or polemical forms can disarm the public and gain approval for what would otherwise be contested public-works projects, surely Copenhagen's Amager Bakke Combined Heat and Power EfW facility has advanced the art (fig. 5-5). Something of a wolf in sheep's clothing, the €470-million (approximately $81-million) project broke ground in March 2013. When it is completed, in 2017, it will replace a 40-year-old facility, using a diversionary tactic that promises not only to delight but also to achieve what its designer calls "hedonistic sustainability."[35] Visitors to the top of the plant's stack, after first being afforded a view of the operations within, will ski down the facility's 1,500-meter (about 5,000-foot) flank on manufactured snow, choosing among slopes with three

Figure 5-5. Rendering of the Amager Bakke Combined Heat and Power Waste-to-Energy Plant, with ski slope, Copenhagen, Denmark. (Courtesy Bjarke Ingels Group.)

different grades.[36] (The visitors center within will also accommodate educational groups and tourists, and will serve as the backdrop for special events.)

The plant is being carefully integrated into an industrial area just outside the central city, located on the grounds of a new "terrain park" (landscape accommodating skiers, snow-bikers, etc.) that also features sailing, rock climbing, and other recreational opportunities. The Amager Bakke plant will transform incinerated waste from five municipalities into heat for 97 percent of Copenhagen's homes and electrical power for 50,000 households.[37] Like other examples of eco-industrial infrastructure, the plant will provide environmental mitigation measures: its façades are to be tessellated with greenery-filled planters that will manage stormwater and improve air quality. The plant will also feature an environmentally progressive "billboard": upon the cumulative release of one ton of CO_2, a single smoke ring will rise from the plant's stack.

Creative Compensations and Community Reparations

Sophisticated iconography, environmental messaging, and art-ful urban design are notable advances beyond conventionally engineered infrastructure complexes. Other enhancements that may help neutralize community anxiety include the incor-poration of what might be called "extra-functional" spaces into public utility structures—accessory spaces that range from community meeting rooms, to conference centers, to inter-pretive centers designed to deliver environmental education focused on the mission of the facility.

Elevating Water Treatment—Wilsonville, Oregon

As water demand from a burgeoning population outstripped local well supply, the town of Wilsonville, Oregon, looked to the adjacent Willamette River—historically polluted by agricul-tural effluent and logging activities—as a sustainable, poten-tially reliable new source of drinking water. Today, through an approach that involves extracting and treating river water (through advanced sedimentation and filtration processes), the Willamette Water Treatment Plant provides potable water that surpasses federal standards.

Sensitive to prospective community concerns, the Willamette City Council and public works department adopted a nuanced planning approach. In addition to holding public consultation about the project, it assembled an integrated design team. Working together, this team of architects, landscape architects, and plant engineers configured a facility joined to a new land-scaped parkland and a watercourse that runs the length of the site, from the upstream intake of river water to the system's outflow at a terminus overlooking the river (fig. 5-6). A path parallels the streambed and abuts a monolithic concrete wall that divides the park from the plant. Intermittent wall open-ings reveal the plant's inner workings, and signage explains the steps in the treatment process. Stormwater collected from the site, as well as from other areas, is pumped up to run down the watercourse, filling the streambed. Gaining clarity as it flows over rocks and through pools and waterfalls, the stream reminds visitors of the ways in which the plant's mechanical and chemical operations simulate nature's purifi-cation processes.[38]

Figure 5-6. Willamette River Water Treatment Plant from downstream, Wilsonville, Oregon
(© Nic Lehoux).

The site's modest amenities—sheltered picnic tables, rock perches, bridges, and viewing platforms—allow visitors contact with the water, while the sound of the waterfalls muffles noise from the adjacent freeway. Meadowed parkland separates the plant from the parallel riverbank and provides a pedestrian connection to the river, linking the waterway and the adjacent neighborhoods to other community open space. By integrating educational and recreational elements, this award-winning plant demystifies the sourcing and purification of potable water.

Solving for Pattern at the Phoenix Waste Transfer Station

Some of the most ardent campaigns against infrastructural facilities have been waged against proposed solid-waste plants and waste-transfer stations—facilities that are infamous for the truck traffic they generate, as well as for noise, unpleasant odors, and potentially harmful environmental releases.

The energy crisis of the 1970s, coupled with federally required closures of unsanitary landfills, made the incineration of municipal solid waste (MSW) the preferred waste-removal option. The percentage of MSW being combusted increased up to 15 percent in the late 1980s, and by the 1990s the majority of these plants began recovering energy. Simultaneously, however, newly recognized threats posed by mercury, dioxins, and other residuals led to the shutdown of many plants unable to meet EPA's 1990 mandated air-pollution-control systems. This loss, coupled with the emergence of the environmental justice movement and the advent of new recycling and zero-waste policies, effectively set back the American WTE industry.[39] Since that time, municipalities have largely depended on local landfills, typically sited at the outskirts of cities and towns. As these landfills have reached capacity, they have been displaced by transfer stations—specialized operations that consolidate local waste for long-haul shipment to more-remote (out-of-state, or even foreign) disposal sites.

In Phoenix, Arizona, during the 1980s, the transfer station—that pariah of public works—was itself the subject of considerable reinvention. When the fast-growing city had nearly exhausted its landfill capacity, the public works department did not seek a far-flung location for a new transfer station; instead, it chose a nearby brownfield site, setting aside 147 acres (one square mile) to receive the city's prodigious waste: each day, about 550 trucks would deliver 3,500 tons of refuse; once salvageable materials had been recycled, the remainder would be diverted to another landfill site located 20 miles to the north.[40] In choosing to establish the new transfer station next to a closing landfill, the department had the foresight to create a neighborhood-friendly model that would pave the way for the placement of future such facilities in the vicinity of residential enclaves.

In its effort to address an increasingly sprawl-obscured setting and restore a modicum of both the natural and the cultural landscape through the creation of recognizable, community-oriented public works, the Phoenix Arts Commission found important partners in the Phoenix Public Works Department and in the city's Public Arts program. The latter requires the allocation of 1 percent of a project's construction budget to support the integration of specially commissioned art into public works, with the overall objective of making these "working zones . . . powerful, vivid and compelling."[41] Since 1986 participating artists have worked to transform the city's canals, freeways, waterworks, and pedestrian landscapes into humane, appealing environments.

In late 1989 two artists, Michael Singer and Linnea Glatt, initiated the adroit interventions that ultimately produced the 27th Avenue Waste Transfer Station and Recycling Center (fig. 5-7). Singer and Glatt won early favor with the public works department by exposing problems with—and offering remedies for—the engineering team's off-the-shelf plan. Given license to rethink the site and the program, the artists reconfigured and reoriented the facility not only to obtain good solar access, but also to improve orientation so that the administrative and visitors' wing was no longer downwind of odors. Singer and Glatt also rationalized circulation by creating a one-way loop around the site, reducing the impact of truck traffic and affording separate access for workers and preferential views to visitors.[42] Ultimately, the $18-million, 25-acre complex became a local amenity, even as it created a necessary buffer between the community and the former landfill.

Singer and Glatt's context-specific approach can be described as "solving for pattern"[43]—that is, resolving multiple problems elegantly and economically. The site was re-graded to elevate the facility above flash-flood levels; the void left by that excavation was then filled by a stormwater-retention pond. Ringed by mountain views and adorned by vegetated terraces and courtyards, the facility is largely screened from the view of neighbors by berms. A new community park was placed directly adjacent to the self-haul area of the plant, where residents can also deposit compost and yard waste and gain access to the Salvation Army drop-off station.

Public works officials and public art curators alike championed the artists' collaborative approach to problem solving. In particular, Singer and Glatt helped the design team engage in an open public dialogue that acknowledged community concerns while promoting a higher undertaking: reducing wasteful consumption patterns and encouraging alternative behaviors, including composting and materials recovery. "Environmental rehabilitation" serves as the organizing theme for the whole campus. Affiliated environmental nonprofits (various recycling partners and the headquarters of Keep Phoenix Beautiful) share space in the administrative wing. Additional amenities include a library, exhibit space, and multipurpose community rooms.[44]

Tourists enjoy dramatic vistas from the entrance overpass as they watch trucks enter below, making garbage mountains from their payloads. Inside, facility operations are framed by windows in a gallery above and explained by interpretive exhibits. At a public amphitheater (fig. 5-7)—which one critic called an "operating theater for environmental therapy"[45]—spectators reencounter their collective dross as they take in the trash-sorting choreography of men and machines from behind glass. By dramatizing the ordinarily quotidian processes for metabolizing waste, the designers challenge patterns of social behavior.

The plant's comprehensive recycling program today processes some 127,000 tons of commingled residential solid waste (newspaper, mixed paper, aluminum, scrap metal, glass, plastics, and cardboard) from the approximately 90 percent of area residents who participate in the city's voluntary recycling program.[46] About 1,500 citizens drop off other disposable waste at the transfer station each weekend,[47] and more than 5,000 schoolchildren tour the facility each year.

Figure 5-7. Public amphitheater, 27th Avenue Waste Transfer Station and Recycling Center, Phoenix, Arizona (© Michael Singer Studio, photo: David Stansbury).

Besides training the public eye on the grimier realities of solid waste disposal through the lenses of higher art, the ecologically inclined artists also saw opportunities to establish infrastructural symbiosis: the treated effluent from a nearby wastewater plant is combined with stormwater from the site and used to wash down trucks, equipment, and the site itself; a constructed wetland filtration process cleanses the water before it flows into the nearby Salt River; solar hot-water panels double as shade structures along the visitors' entryway; and methane extracted and piped from the adjacent closed landfill is diverted to a small cogeneration facility at the site. Even including these closed-loop enrichments, the facility came in significantly below the original budget through smart trade-offs such as eliminating superfluous cosmetic treatment of concrete panels.[48]

This artful way station for urban refuse has inspired many subsequent commissions both in Phoenix and elsewhere. Since his success in Phoenix, Singer has continued to apply ecological solutions while importing aesthetic considerations into technical infrastructural processes. His studio champions stakeholder involvement as a means of both transcending the blight of conventional infrastructural development and creating a genuine rapport with communities. His work and perspectives have been commemorated in a joint publication with the Environmental Defense Fund—*Infrastructure and Community: How Can We Live with What Sustains Us?*[49]

Diverse Synergies—Svartsengi Resource Park, Iceland

Along the Mid-Atlantic Ridge, where the continents of Eurasia and North America collide, the light-blue waters of the Blue Lagoon geothermal spa are a major attraction for visitors coming from nearby Reykjavik, Iceland's capital. At this scenic spot, a light mist hovers over bathers enjoying the pond's 100°F seawater, which laps gently against the surrounding dark hillocks. In the background, columns of steam rise from world's largest geothermal power plant.

The privately owned Svartsengi power plant sits atop a porous lava field, the remnant of a 1226 volcanic eruption in the geothermally active Reykjanes peninsula, which lies along Iceland's southwestern coast. Underground steam fields supply geothermally heated brine; brought to the surface by a dozen wells, the brine produces district heating and electricity. Svartsengi is one of many Icelandic power-generating enterprises that collectively produce some 4,400 GWh (gigawatt-hours) of electricity annually, while heating almost 90 percent of all Icelandic homes. Combined with hydropower, these low-carbon power stations account for 82 percent[50] of the country's primary energy.[51]

The oil embargoes of the late 1970s pushed Iceland in the direction of petroleum independence. Today Iceland capitalizes on direct and indirect geothermal energy, which meets the nation's power and heating needs most months of the year, including supporting hot water for swimming pools (371 GWh), greenhouse heating (207 GWh), space heating (5,290 GWh), fish-farming (528 GWh), and industrial processes (505 GWh).[52] As a consequence of the transition to hydropower and geothermal energy sources, GHG emissions in the Reykjavik area dropped from 270,000 to 12,000 tons between 1960 and 2000.[53]

Geothermal plants avoid many of the environmental impacts associated with their fossil-fuel counterparts.[54] They emit only trace amounts of nitrogen oxide, little or no sulfur dioxide, and small amounts of carbon dioxide and methane. The primary pollutant now routinely abated at many geothermal plants is hydrogen sulfide, which is found in many subsurface reservoirs.[55] Unlike coal or WTE counterparts, geothermal plants produce insubstantial amounts of residual waste (apart from the construction waste associated with drilling wells).[56]

The Svartsengi combined heat and electricity plant (fig. 5-8) consists of five separate units that straddle the deep reservoirs where seawater, mixed with groundwater, comes in contact with magma intrusions at depths of about 2 kilometers (about 1.2 miles). The plant extracts this reservoir fluid (brine) using deep wells. The brine ascends to the surface as high-pressure steam at about 240°C (about 464°F), driving ten turbines with a production capability of approximately 76.5 MW of electricity and 150 MW of thermal energy for the complex.[57] Heat exchangers transfer some of the excess thermal energy from the condensed steam to freshwater, which is then routed to nine nearby towns for district heating. The same heated water is also piped to melt snow at the nearby Keflavik International Airport. Leftover brine condensate produced by the Svartsengi plant is disposed of in an adjacent surface pond now known as the Blue Lagoon.

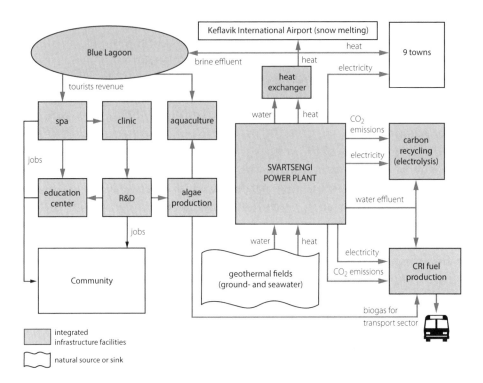

Figure 5-8. Svartsengi Resource Park, Grindavík, Iceland. (Figure by Hillary Brown.)

Over time, minerals (mostly silica) precipitating from the brine have formed a waterproof coating in the otherwise porous lava; this coating, coupled with algae, gives the pond its bluish-green cast. Because of the water's high temperature, which kills common bacteria, as well as its mineral content and the fact that the geothermal seawater is continuously renewed by the power plant over the course of a 40-hour cycle, the lagoon is not only hygienic for bathing but also provides relief from psoriasis and other skin ailments. The benign waters of the lagoon, its qualities discovered by locals, have been used therapeutically since the plant began operating in 1976.

The power plant has spawned several ancillary uses within what has been named the Svartsengi "Resource Park," a name chosen to connote its special ecology and multiple economic and social uses. The park was the vision of HS Orka hf, the privately held utility that developed the geothermal plant and is partly owned by nearby communities. The park's mission includes both judicious use of its many resources and, at the same time, careful maintenance of its ecological balance through education as well as research and development.

The park's spin-offs, which have generated more than 180 jobs, are colocated entities lured by the site's unique resources. The famous Blue Lagoon Spa features a 15-room clinic, a dermatology research and development center, and a number of other amenities (swimming pools, steam baths, geothermal waterfalls, and a restaurant). The spa alone attracts more than 400,000 tourists and patients annually and generates over $21 million in annual revenue.[58]

The Eldborg Education Center, operated through a partnership between the Blue Lagoon Spa and the power company, offers on-site conference and meeting facilities, as well as an educational center focused on the area's geology and geothermal activity. Along with the dermatology research and development center, a mineral and biotech unit researches medicinal properties of the brine and algae. Other key projects are algae cultivation for fish food (aquaculture) and fish-drying facilities.[59]

A recent addition to the infrastructural ecology of the geothermal plant and Resource Park is the cultivation of microalgae for the production of next-generation biofuels, a project supported by the National Energy Fund. This colocation increases the use of geothermal-energy by-products in both the transportation sector and the power-intensive industrial sector.[60] A collaboration among the Blue Lagoon Spa, HS Orka hf, the government of Iceland, and Carbon Recycling International (CRI), an American-Icelandic company, the venture uses plant electricity to separate hydrogen from water. The hydrogen is then combined with the plant's effluent CO_2 emissions to form a synthesis gas.[61] This gas is compressed, cooled, and liquefied as crude methanol, which can then be upgraded to fuel-grade gas when combined with gasoline or biodiesel.[62] Since opening in 2013, CRI, located near the Svartsengi campus, has converted approximately 3 million tons of CO_2 emissions into 2 million tons of methanol. Distributed through existing transportation-fuel infrastructure and used in conventional engines, the gas yields better fuel efficiency and lower pollution.[63] This renewable transport fuel—the first derived from non-biological material—was introduced to the Icelandic market in 2011; in 2013 CRI made its first shipment to the Netherlands.[64]

The successor company to HS Orka hf, Svartsengi's original owner and operator, is an unusually progressive firm that views its power-supplying infrastructure as a seamless extension of local resources: geothermal reservoirs, local groundwater, and seawater working in a reciprocal, integrated system. The firm remains mindful of both the "macro" and the "micro" history of the area, as well as its climate, spiritual and cultural traditions, political system, educational and health care systems, and tourist culture.[65] Thanks to an astutely integrated stewardship of local biogeophysical phenomena, the complex has flourished.

How transferable is geothermal technology to the United States? Recent assessments show that nine western states have sufficient geothermal resources to meet more than 20 percent of US electricity needs.[66] Nevertheless, these resources produce less than 1 percent of US electricity, much of it in energy-hungry California.[67] According to a 2006 Massachusetts Institute of Technology (MIT) study, if enhanced geothermal systems (which access deep hydrothermal capacity) were to be deployed in the continental United States, they could provide some 100 GW of electricity of cost-competitive energy within the next 50 years, with a combined public-private investment between $800 million and $1 billion over a 15-year period.[68] To date, the primary barrier in the United States to accessing this indigenous resource has been limited support for R&D in geothermal technology, compared with Europe and Australia, where this renewable source is becoming commercialized.[69]

If the United States were poised to creatively capitalize on geothermal energy obtained from US reserves, along the lines of the Icelandic entrepreneurs, the nation might similarly access multiple yields. Geothermal plants, with their low environmental impact, can be readily colocated with most agricultural and recreational uses. In addition, eco-infrastructural development served by thermal energy could be developed in many areas, even those remote from large population centers. Finally, a look ahead suggests that, as in Iceland, useful minerals such as silica, lithium, and zinc can, with sufficient R&D, be productively extracted from geothermal fluids. The technology that makes mineral extraction possible would provide the added co-benefit of reducing the environmental impact of conventional mineral mining.

Developing the Bolivia-Brazil Gasbol:
A Megacommunity in Action

When it comes to community-friendly infrastructure development, the highest principle is good governance, which ensures
the absolute protection of community rights and the satisfac-
tion of community needs. And the more drastic the intervention and the higher the risk, the greater the need for structured,
negotiated stakeholder exchanges, as well as implementation
oversight.

Developed by Petrobras, a joint public-private Brazilian
enterprise, the $2.15-billion Bolivia-to-Brazil gas pipeline known
as Gasbol exemplifies the progressive management of sensitive social and environmental concerns. Unlike other projects
described in this chapter, the binational Gasbol is spatially diffuse, and its affected populations are neither urbanized nor
local but diverse and widespread. The pipeline traverses almost
2,000 miles of varied terrain, two nations, numerous states and
cities, and more than 100 small, remote villages. It runs through
some of the world's most fragile ecosystems, and it crosses
lands occupied by indigenous peoples. Moreover, even though
the project involves the transport of fossil fuel, it nonetheless
achieves significant carbon- and urban-pollution reductions by
switching Brazil from dirty sulfur fuel oil and wood to cleaner
gas.[70]

A challenging undertaking in virtually every respect—politically, environmentally, and socially—the Gasbol project involved
a vast number of participants, including the federal governments of Bolivia and Brazil and their often independent-minded
states and townships; landowners; a number of multilateral
lending agencies, among them the World Bank, the Inter-Ameri-
can Development Bank, and several private equity partners; local
and global environmental advocates and organizations; universities; indigenous community representatives; an environmental committee; and a range of nongovernmental development
organizations. The project's multi-sectoral, inclusive governance
and proactive management approach, both of which relied on
continuous dialogue and consensus building, is particularly
suited to large and complex infrastructural projects.

Among Petrobras's notable accomplishments were the
reduction of the project's environmental footprint and impacts

on cultural heritage, and the mitigation of social impacts through the skillful engagement of a "megacommunity"—a purposeful, action-oriented collaboration between government, business, and civil society that builds common ground and capitalizes on the advantages of each sector to solve large-scale problems of unprecedented complexity, achievements that none could accomplish alone.[71] The megacommunity approach adopted by the project developers was specifically designed to embrace a large and diverse consortium of interests and to expedite construction, which took just eighteen months. Communications and outreach helped to reduce conflict, for example, by ensuring that the pipeline avoided archaeologically and ecologically sensitive areas and that construction camps were not set up in the immediate vicinity of indigenous areas or small towns. Through a series of public meetings and community workshops—attended by as many as 900 people in total—Petrobras, acting as the management hub of this overall approach, maximized transparency and accountability to all stakeholders and worked with affected populations to develop strategies for returning benefits to communities.[72]

Gasbol faced daunting ecological challenges. The route of the pipeline penetrated environmentally sensitive and legally protected lands, as well as biodiversity hot spots, including Gran Chaco National Park in Bolivia, the Pantanal wetlands (a World Heritage reserve that straddles both countries), and Brazil's forested Mata Atlantia. After extensive ecological assessments, Petrobras factored environmental benefits into its cost-benefit analysis, assigning an environmental premium to the substitution of clean-burning natural gas for more polluting fuels.[73] Petrobras then implemented a $36-million innovative environmental and social management plan (over and above World Bank conventions),[74] one previously unprecedented in Latin America.

Petrobras's first strategy was to avoid collateral damage. The route was altered to reduce environmental impacts. The easement for the buried gas line was also carefully colocated with existing agricultural and animal husbandry land uses. Wherever feasible, access roads utilized existing roadways. The gas line was also tunneled beneath important river crossings. To a great extent, the project mitigated the many disturbances normally triggered by construction: habitat fragmentation; air, water, and soil pollution; damage from erosion and deforestation; and disruption of hydrologic patterns.[75] Mitigation efforts included drilling under 13 rivers in order to minimize riparian damage. Noise control and restricted work schedules protected wildlife, especially migrating bird species. Trees were selectively felled in the right-of-way to reduce impacts in the area. To avoid the use of pesticides, especially in areas with indigenous populations, semidomesticated birds were used to help control pests. And to revegetate the easement after the pipeline was completed, indigenous people were engaged to sow, harvest, and maintain native plant species.[76] In Bolivia, the easements remain closed, to prevent any traffic. Finally, Petrobras provided an ecological compensation package ($1.0 million to Bolivia and $7.5 million to Brazil) to protect and manage more than a dozen national and state parks.[77]

In addition to stakeholders being involved in decisions about environmental protection measures, community-based committees and civil-society organizations were consulted in the local distribution of compensatory benefits provided as consideration for disruption caused by the pipeline. With the facilitation of a dedicated ombudsman, these groups participated in meetings and hearings. "Social auditing"—ongoing monitoring that engaged residents of local communities and civil-society representatives—was yet another innovation designed to protect individual and community rights along the pipeline right-of-way.[78] Brazilian and Bolivian communities (non-indigenous peoples) adversely affected received a total of $4.4 million to establish new schools, town halls, community health facilities, libraries, and other local infrastructure (water, sewerage, electricity, and road improvements).[79] Some of these communities additionally received training and technical assistance in agriculture.[80] More significantly, at a cost of $3.7 million in Bolivia alone, indigenous peoples were granted secure land rights through titling programs covering some 1.5 million hectares (3.7 million acres).[81] Finally, the project employed an innovative arrangement called the Indigenous People's Development Plan, whereby indigenous populations were employed in certain mitigation efforts. The achievements in the realms of mitigation, compensation, and monitoring—all negotiated across vast distances—demanded good relationships among all the working groups. Petrobras's project-management team ensured that the necessary high levels of communication, cooperation, and integration were maintained.

Widely regarded as an archetype for inclusive governance achieved through a megacommunity, Gasbol moved beyond a bilateral model to create a multilateral networked structure.[82] Gasbol has garnered multiple awards for mainstreaming not only environmental but also social concerns into the practices of the energy sector. It has already become a benchmark against which future large, complex international infrastructural efforts may be measured.

Conclusion

If the projects described in this chapter have a single lesson, it is that next-generation infrastructure must move beyond mitigation toward provision of tangible amenities, and must embrace the community as a valued and essential partner in facility development. Particularly in light of mistakes made in the past, intrusive or unwelcome ventures will be evaluated by the transparency, frequency, and seriousness of consultations with stakeholders. Approaches based on local engagement can not only achieve community acceptance but can also repair or even boost trust and reciprocity. In addition to building social capital, inclusionary practices can create community pride in environmental protection and regeneration. In the case of Newtown Creek, for example, the community's proactive participation created a strong link between social restitution and environmental remediation.

The exemplary projects featured here reveal a variety of characteristics that can foster community acceptance: (1) context-sensitive design excellence (Isséane Waste-to-Energy and the Naka facility) and rebranding (Amager Bakke); (2) respect for local ecology and economic resources (Svartsengi, the Willamette Water Filtration plant, and Phoenix's 27th Avenue Waste Transfer Station and Recycling Center); (3) the inclusion of recreational, civic, or educational amenities (Phoenix, Willamette, Naka, Croton, and Amager Bakke); (4) proactive strategies such as transparent processes, jointly developed charters, co-management agreements, compensation programs, and the provision of local employment (Croton, Isséane, and Gasbol).

The successful ventures described in this and earlier chapters have fostered an inclusive, cross-sector approach that enabled the people, the project, and the place to *co-evolve*. Through collaborative ventures, engaged local entities were able to self-organize and thereby to build greater economic, ecological, and social capital. Svartsengi, for instance, used a tri-sector approach (public-private and nonprofit) to capitalize on context-specific resources and to invest in cultural and educational, as well as health and recreational, spin-offs to become a world-class attraction. These successful utility-sector approaches to collective leadership point the way to tackling the global challenges of rebuilding and expanding infrastructural services. Moreover, such collaborations can more readily lead to and support facilities that are designed to be multipurpose—diversified and in some cases significantly synergized—infrastructural ecologies.

6. Creating Resilient Coastlines and Waterways: Hard and Soft Constructions

For 400 years the 287-hectare (about 710-acre) Abbotts Hall Farm, situated on the United Kingdom's East Anglian coast, had been protected by a 4-kilometer-long (2.5-mile) seawall. By 2002, flooding of the Essex tidal estuary had breached this hard infrastructure many times. When OURCOAST, an integrated coastal management program sponsored by the European Commission, did a cost-benefit analysis on alternatives for repairing the wall, the results showed that the seawall should no longer be maintained; instead, it should be "deconstructed" in five locations, creating an 80-hectare (about 200-acre) "soft and flexible'" coastal defense zone. At the Abbotts Hall Farm of today, mudflats, salt marshes, and freshwater wetlands are used to absorb tidal and wave energies and to sustain an enlarged habitat that helps support commercial fisheries. The area has also become home to salt-tolerant crops, it acts as a carbon sink, and it provides a haven for wildlife—all at a cost savings of £500,000 ($805,550) over hard solutions.[1]

Perturbations to critical infrastructure systems—among the signatures of a destabilizing climate—are occurring worldwide. Scientific studies have deduced that climate warming is unequivocally occurring, and trends observed since the 1960s implicate increasing anthropogenic releases of heat-trapping gases.[2] Climate instability will have both direct and indirect impacts on infrastructure, and no sector will be spared the effects of heat waves, drought, increasingly intense and frequent storms, and the inexorable advance of rising seas. Sea-level projections—based on thermal expansion and ice melt—from the International Panel on Climate Change (IPCC) anticipate a rise of between 7 and 23 inches this century, which will be accompanied by significantly worsening flooding and storm surges.[3] The increasing likelihood of disturbances to constructed systems will demand skillful policy adjustments across infrastructure sectors. At best, climate impacts may render vulnerable assets less reliable; at worst, they may trigger catastrophic failure.

On the world stage, climate-change treaties and protocols have largely focused on mitigation—specifically, reductions in greenhouse-gas (GHG) emissions.[4] But there is increasing recognition that adaptation measures, which focus on protecting people and assets from harm, are critical elements in the response to climate change. This chapter considers initiatives that embody the final axiom of next-generation assets: "Infrastructure should be resilient and adapt to foreseeable changes brought about by an unstable global climate" as it relates to river and coastal communities. Here, *resilience* refers to the ability of assets or systems to anticipate, absorb, adapt, and/or rapidly recover from a disruptive event.[5] Natural ecosystems have demonstrated the ability to absorb shock, readjust, and produc-

Box 6-1. Climate Change Impacts in the United States

As a result of climate change, the United States will face hardships across all latitudes and on both land and sea. Along the Alaskan shore, for example, rising seas already threaten 180 communities—among them Newtok, a Yupik village on the west coast so heavily damaged by erosion that it is retreating inland at a cost of $2 million per household.[1]

Throughout the country, the frequency of 3-inch-plus storms (3 inches of precipitation in a 24-hour period) has more than doubled between 1961 and 2012.[2] The Mississippi Delta and the adjacent Gulf states have been particularly hard hit. As the Texas and Gulf Coasts host much of the US oil- and gas-shipping industry, several thousand offshore oil-drilling platforms are vulnerable to extreme weather events. In 2004, Hurricane Ivan damaged 24 platforms and 168 pipelines. In 2005, Hurricanes Katrina and Rita harmed more than 100 platforms—including a prized $250-million Chevron platform that had to be sunk to the seafloor—along with almost 600 pipelines, shutting down nine refineries and reducing Gulf Coast oil production by 20 percent.[3] In the next 50–100 years, the combined effects of land subsidence (natural sinking)[4] and rising seas will yield a 4- to 6-foot rise in sea level along the Texas and Gulf Coast, permanently flooding an estimated 2,400 miles of major roadways and 246 miles of freight-rail lines, and affecting more than 72 percent of freight and non-freight facilities at the region's ports.[5]

Crippled for months by the release of raw sewage that resulted from Hurricane Sandy in 2012, New York and New Jersey's wastewater infrastructure will require $1.1 billion for repairs alone, excluding mitigation measures such as moving equipment to higher levels and constructing levees to prevent facilities from flooding.[6] The storm also put 8 million electric-utility customers in the dark, which had a cascading effect on water services and heating. Gasoline supply networks were also paralyzed. According to MTA officials, New York City's transportation infrastructure suffered $7.5 billion in damage, almost $5 billion in the subway system alone.[7]

In the Midwest, floods and increased tornado activity have become the traumatic inland counterparts of coastal hurricanes. The Great Flood of 1993 affected 500 miles of the Mississippi and Missouri River system; caused catastrophic flooding in Jefferson City;[8] and halted major east-west traffic from St. Louis to Kansas City, Missouri, and as far north as Chicago—disrupting one-quarter of all US freight for about six weeks.[9] In August 2011, in an area

Box 6-1. Climate Change Impacts in the United States (continued)

130 miles south of St. Louis, days of pounding by deadly storms and tornados led to flooding along the Black River. When a levee along the river in Poplar Bluffs, Missouri, failed in at least four locations, 7,000 people had to be evacuated.[10]

1. Kristen Feifel and Rachel M. Gregg, "Relocating the Village of Newtok, Alaska, Due to Coastal Erosion," Climate Adaptation Knowledge Exchange, July 3, 2010, www.cakex.org/case-studies/1588 (accessed December 1, 2012).

2. Stephen Saunders, Dan Findlay, and Tom Easley, "Doubled Trouble: More Midwestern Extreme Storms" (New York: Rocky Mountain Climate Organization & Natural Resource Defense Council, 2012), 4, www.rockymountainclimate.org/images/DoubledTroubleHigh.pdf (accessed June 12, 2012).

3. United States Global Change Research Program, "Energy Supply and Use," in Global Climate Change Impacts in the U.S. (New York: Cambridge University Press, 2009), 57, www.globalchange.gov (accessed November 24, 2012).

4. Subsidence is attributable to both anthropogenic activities (drainage, soil oxidation, and groundwater withdrawals) as well as natural (compaction and tectonic down-warping activity).

5. M. J. Savonis, V. R. Burkett, J. R. Potter, T. W. Doyle, R. Hagelman, S. B. Hartley, R. C. Hyman, R. S. Kafalenos, B. D. Keim, K. J. Leonard, M. Sheppard, C. Tebaldi, and J. E. Tump, "What Are the Key Conclusions of this Study?" in Impacts of Climate Change and Variability on Transportation Systems and Infrastructure: Gulf Coast Study, Phase I (report by the US Climate Change Science Program and the Subcommittee on Global Change Research, ed. M. J. Savonis, V. R. Burkett, and J. R. Potter [Department of Transportation: Washington, DC, 2008]), 6–4.

6. Michael Schwirtz. "Sewage Flows after Storm Expose Flaws in System," New York Times, November 29, 2012.

7. See: http://m.npr.org/news/front/166672858.

8. US Global Change Research Program, Global Climate Change Impacts in the United States, ed. T. R. Karl, J. M. Melillo, and T. C. Peterson (New York: Cambridge University Press, 2009), 120.

9. National Research Council, Potential Impacts of Climate Change on U.S. Transportation: Special Report 290 (Washington, DC: Transportation Research Board, 2008), 81–82, http://onlinepubs.trb.org/onlinepubs/sr/sr290.pdf (accessed April 5, 2010).

10. CNN Wire News Staff, "Missouri Levee Fails, Prompting More Evacuations," CCN, April 26, 2011, www.cnn.com/2011/US/04/26/missouri.levee.failure/index.html (accessed April 27, 2011).

tively reorganize around a new state.[6] Resilient constructed systems, which are often modeled on natural ones, are designed to have a similar capacity.[7]

The projects explored in this chapter focus on improving resilience to coastal and river flooding. According to the Union of Concerned Scientists, sea level is rising—and at an accelerated rate. This is caused by global warming's melting of glaciers, ice caps, and ice sheets.[8] At the same time, increased temperatures are producing changes in weather patterns and increasing drought and evaporation—conditions that will demand enhancement of existing water resources. Infrastructural adaptations to water stress and scarcity will be addressed in the next chapter.

Coastal Flooding Adaptations: Hardening the Coast

Ten percent of the world's population lives on the 2 percent of the earth's land area designated as "low-elevation coastal zones."[9] These settlements are at the greatest risk of damage from sea-level rise and storm surges, as well as seawall breaches, erosion, loss of wetlands, and an influx of sediments. Because critical urban systems such as power stations, wastewater treatment and solid-waste management plants, and pumping stations have historically been sited along rivers or on or near coasts, they, along with their associated substations, gas pipelines, and landfills, are subject to inundation. Tunnels and coastal airports, also typically located on oceanfront sites, are subject to flooding, and bridges are vulnerable to river scouring (water currents abrading bridge abutments), which can undermine their structural integrity. Finally, widespread interdependencies mean that inundation in one infrastructural sector can trigger shutdowns in others: for example, transportation failures can prevent fuel from reaching power stations, and brownouts can impair or halt operations at water filtration and wastewater-treatment plants. Low-lying nations are the most vulnerable to the risks associated with cascading failures.

In the Netherlands and Japan, the prospect of major flooding in urban areas has led to sophisticated water-management policies. Both countries are contemplating even greater adaptive measures. In the Netherlands, the greatest threat comes from the fact that 27 percent of the country's landmass—home to 60 percent of the population and the source of about 70 percent of the nation's gross national product—is below sea level.[10] Among the changes already detected in the Netherlands are higher river discharges, caused by more-intense winter rains; soil subsidence; increasing salinity in the water table;

and growing demands for water during heat-induced droughts. Japan's primary concerns are that higher temperatures will cause lower rice yields, and that storm surges will threaten its 1.3 million coastal residents.

Structurally and Mechanically Refusing the Sea in the Netherlands

Living within one of the great deltas of the world, where the Rhine, Meuse, Waal, and Schelde Rivers join the North Sea, the Dutch have perfected the art of hydraulic engineering as a defensive response to inundation and storm surge. The area defined by the rivers' outflows is home to the Netherlands' 16.6 million people, as well as to some of the most productive wetlands and agricultural soil to be found anywhere. By manipulating an integrated system of dikes, dunes, pumps, ditches, and canals, the Dutch have drained indigenous bogs, mudflats, and lakes, transforming them into productive *polders*—reclaimed, low-lying farmland. With a line of primary defenses stretching more than 3,500 kilometers (2,175 miles), the nation has largely managed intermittent flooding.[11]

The requisite skills were gained through necessity over centuries of inventing ways to protect the Netherlands from the sea. In February 1953, a fierce storm drove a 6-foot wall of water over the dikes in the province of Zeeland, taking 1,800 lives, inundating nearly 2,000 square kilometers (about 770 square miles), and necessitating widespread evacuations. Losses sustained then are estimated today at €1 billion.[12] In the decades since those catastrophic floods, the Dutch government has developed unique water-management policies—now overseen by the Center for Water Management, part of the Ministry of Infrastructure and the Environment.

The government's initial response to the 1953 flood was the Delta Works, a multi-billion-dollar complex of coastal-defense projects executed over a period of 25 years. Sea closures—each made up of dams, locks, and surge barriers—enclosed three of the main estuaries, armoring the Netherlands' far western flank with a concentric series of "dike rings" and reducing the exposure of 720 kilometers (about 450 miles) of interior coastline.

The Delta Works program followed a prescribed logic, arriving at acceptable protection levels by assigning system components ratios that indicated the risk of failure over time. For sea flooding, the ratios ranged from 1:10,000 years to 1:4,000 years; for freshwater flooding, the ratio was 1:1,250 years. In addition to providing flood protection, Delta Works facilitates inland shipping by keeping the Nieuwe Waterweg and Wester-schelde waterways open between the ports of Rotterdam and Antwerp.[13] The dikes along these waterways have been raised and fortified—and, notably, are occasionally combined with road infrastructure, to improve transportation between key port cities.

Environmental and practical concerns—including high costs—have drawn the Netherlands' coastal adaptation efforts away from the use of large engineered systems. The Ooster-scheldekering, one of the last pieces of the Delta Works to be built and a unique, prodigious piece of engineering, is part of the outer ring of defenses that effectively protect the Ooster-schelde (Eastern Scheldt) from the sea. The structure was origi-nally intended to be a dam, but the environmental and fishing community's resistance to the potential alteration of the area's saltwater ecosystems led to a successful compromise in this instance: a storm-surge barrier that includes large sluice gates ordinarily left open to the sea, but which can be raised between 20 and 40 feet during extreme weather to make the structure watertight. (The gates have been fully closed 24 times between 1986 and 2011.)[14]

Completed in October 1986, this €2.5-billion undertaking consists of three units slung between two sandbars, spanning across a 5½-mile waterway. The surge barrier's opening is nearly 2 miles long, and the openings in its 63 steel gates allow the inflow and outflow of the seawater that sustains the estuary's ecology. In keeping with the national affinity for multipurpose land uses, a roadway sits atop the water-securing infrastruc-ture, connecting two otherwise remote islands to each other.[15]

Behind the Oosterscheldekering the tides still fluctuate, nourishing the estuary's unique natural habitat—a breeding ground for fish, a migration spot for birds, and the locus of the region's most prominent economic activity: the cultivation of mussels, cockles, and oysters. On the estuary side of the barrier, reinforcing stone was deposited during construction to reduce erosion and strengthen the barrier against the force of the sea. The use of different types of stone has attracted a variety of seaweeds, sponges, anemones, and starfish—part of the rich diet of the many wildlife species that are indigenous to the area.[16]

The dramatic landscape created by the seawall attracts human visitors as well, and the artificial island built as a foundation for the barrier has been enhanced by educational and recreational uses. Now known as Neeltje Jans, the island features recreational areas including a public park that hosts exhibitions about local history and ecology, a series of open aquaria showcasing local species, and a water park where fishing vessels formerly used in the Oosterschelde are on display.

Elevating Land Mass as Super Levees in Japan

In Japan, where rivers flow through low-lying cities and urbanization has drastically reduced absorptive surfaces, multipurpose flood-control infrastructure has gained considerable traction. For example, in an approach that allows the government to share construction costs, parks and stadiums have been designed for intermittent use as water-retention basins.

Since the early 1990s Japan has been constructing "super levees"—gently sloping embankments with earthquake-resistant foundations and widths almost 30 times their height. Currently in place along the Edo, Tama, Yamota, and Yodo Rivers, among others, the levees provide flood control while improving river ecology. Under normal conditions, their inner slopes permit colocated uses: public facilities such as roads, parks, and riverside amenities.[17]

Shifting from Resistance to Resilience

The use of highly fortified structures of levees and barrages to reinforce the shoreline represents one set of solutions to rising sea levels. They may or may not prove the right solutions for coastal areas due to cost, feasibility, or the concern that these barriers simply shunt surging water to another location, one that is unprotected. A different solution is one that appreciates the shoreline as a landscape in flux, allowing for periodic flooding or reliance on "soft" buffers—wetlands, reefs, and other ecologically appropriate materials—that have an ecologically sound, protective value.

Dual-Functioning Rural Floodplains: The Netherlands' "Room for the River"

During the winter of 1995, severe rainfalls in northern France and southern Germany led to mass evacuations downstream as the Netherland's receiving waters (Rhine, Meuse) overtopped their banks, causing widespread loss of livestock. Technocratic control of the canalized and locked rivers was judged by the government to be inadequate in the face of future threats. Since that time, given the increasing volumes of river discharge, adaptation strategies designed to achieve resilience through a soft-path approach have become the core approach to national water management in the Netherlands, as well as upstream participation in France, Germany, and Switzerland.

According to the Royal Netherlands Meteorological Institute, by 2050 rising temperatures will produce milder winters and hotter, dryer summers, and winter precipitation may increase by as much as 14 percent. Such changes could increase inland-river discharge volumes by as much as 40 percent in winter, while reducing summer flows by as much as 30 percent.[18] Another concern is that hot, dry summers will lower water levels in the polders, causing peat dikes to shrink and collapse, and leading to the salinization of groundwater and freshwater inlets, which would imperil drinking and irrigation water.[19] The institute's recommendation is to "live with water"—that is, to periodically surrender or sacrifice space to water, rather than trying to hold it back. This would also allow for safely impounding river water in winter to store for summer use. Without sufficient space, land subsidence and rising sea levels will make river drainage difficult, and major inflows will cause breaches in riverine protection systems and loss of life and property. In other words, simply excluding river water cannot guarantee safety.

The goal of the Room for the River campaign is to ensure that new or altered land-use designs are physically compatible with water storage, especially in the vicinity of major river bottlenecks. First introduced in August 2000 and published in a December 2000 report from the Dutch Ministry of Transport, Public Works, and Water Management, the program incorporates new adaptive management strategies designed to reach from the national to the local level, and to involve civil society.[20]

Under the initiative, water management and spatial planning are administratively yoked in an arrangement that will affect urban and rural redevelopment, zoning plans, and new infrastructure.

By 2015, more than 30 riverine locations will have been considerably altered by a variety of measures that will allow rivers to flood safely and thus temporarily occupy shared space. Among the plans are the following measures: creating storage areas, either by excavating existing floodplains or widening them (by moving dikes further inland); removing obstacles to water flow such as berms; creating new, high-water drainage channels to discharge river water via alternate routes; and, most significantly, establishing large, sacrificial retention areas (a measure known as *de-poldering*). Agricultural or other land uses that will recover from the occasional inevitable inundation will be located in such retention areas. Room for the River emphasizes ecosystem-based water management, which is designed to achieve resiliency by reestablishing natural processes.

At a cost of €111 million, the de-poldering of the Overdiep, a 550-hectare (about 1,260-acre) dike-protected area along the Meuse River, will protect Den Bosch, a city of 140,000, from flooding.[21] Scheduled for completion in 2015, the project will also lower the high-water level in the Overdiep, as well as in areas upstream of the polder, by about 27 centimeters (11 inches).[22] Because the design assumes that river water will inundate the polder once every 25 years, a number of land uses currently in the floodplain—16 dairy and crop farms, a large pig farm, a marina, and a military exercise ground—were permitted to remain. Homes and other buildings, however, were transferred to large mounds situated adjacent to the relocated dike.

In an ambitious effort currently being undertaken by the City of Nijmegen, a 350-meter inland dike is being relocated, and a new, 200-meter-wide (656-foot), 3-kilometer-long (1.9-mile) channel is being constructed to divert part of the Waal River in the event of high water. This new channel splits to form an island park in the city center. According to the plans developed by local stakeholders, the redesign will feature floating restaurants, a new marina on the channel, and a nature refuge.[23]

Dual-Functioning Urban Infrastructure

The above-described innovative approaches used to manage river water in the Netherlands have their counterparts in heavily urbanized areas, which are also encouraged to "make room for the river." Low-lying infrastructure and the density of existing development render urban interventions much more complex, however. Among the adaptive measures that have already been undertaken are the following: re-excavation of filled-in areas; the creation of new canals; elimination of some paved areas; subsidies to encourage the construction of residential green roofs; separation of storm drainage from sewer drainage; and in-filling with new water-storage facilities and underground reservoirs.[24] To optimize the use of every square meter of land, new urban infrastructure is assigned two or more roles, wherever possible.

Two prototypes illustrate adaptive, multifunctional approaches to floodwater accommodation.[25] The first, completed in 2011, is an underground, multistory garage with reinforced walls that doubles as a water-storage facility; in addition to being the largest such facility in the country, the structure is topped by the Museumpark, Rotterdam's newest park. Designed to accommodate 1,150 vehicles, the garage can also retain up to 10,000 cubic meters (about 2.6 million gallons) of water (equivalent to four Olympic-sized swimming pools). The second prototype, also in Rotterdam but as yet unbuilt, is a combination plaza and sports field designed to sit slightly below grade, allowing it to double as a water-storage receptacle after heavy rains. The shallow basin, which can retain just under 1,000 cubic meters (about 264,000 gallons) of water, will help reduce street flooding and relieve pressure on drainage systems.

The project, known as WaterSquare Bloemhof, will be in dry mode 90 percent of the time. Initial or light rainwater will be discharged to the sewers as part of the "first flush" (first rains that remove accumulated dirt and dust). In the event of a downpour, however, a control will trigger the drains to close and water will be diverted to the plaza, passing through a purification filter. Impounded, it will transform the plaza into a children's water park, animated by water features, including small spouts, ponds, and streams.

Once these pilot projects have been evaluated, the city hopes to install similar adaptations elsewhere that can double as playgrounds, public squares, skate parks, or ball courts. As a low-lying port city, Rotterdam faces special vulnerabilities—and, as these initiatives show, is continuously striving for resilience in the face of climate change.[26]

An Integrated Water-Management System for Greater New Orleans

Despite its seat within a perfect storm of natural and man-made vicissitudes, the city of New Orleans will assuredly long endure. Its urbanized area sits predominantly below sea level and within a major river delta that is undergoing subsidence. Much of the lakefront area is built on backfilled marshland. The city has been a bull's-eye for increasingly destructive hurricanes. The effects of rising sea level (3–10 millimeters, or 0.1–0.4 inches, annually) and significant loss of wetlands compound the effects of the sinking coastline: 117 square miles were lost to Hurricane Katrina in 2005, and current projections call for an overall loss of 1,500 square miles by 2050.[27]

While improvements have been made to its conventional levees and other engineered coastal flooding defenses, the metropolitan region is now the subject of the 2013 "Greater New Orleans Water Plan" (GNOWP), developed under a $2.5-million federal grant, which aims to control the city's destructive *internal* flooding caused by frequent storms and high rainfall levels. It offers a transformational vision for "living with water." Its proposed strategies are gleaned from a series of conferences and intensive multi-stakeholder workshops initiated in 2008 by local architect David Waggonner and cosponsored by the American Planning Association and the Royal Netherlands Embassy, known as the "Dutch Dialogues."[28]

A new paradigm is proposed, partly amending New Orleans's time-honored but energy-intensive and costly pumping of run-off through drainage piping to outfall canals ($50 million annually).[29] Further to the city's detriment, these existing concrete drainage channels cut across the urban grid, creating continuous and unsightly barriers between neighborhoods. Instead, the GNOWP advocates for increased tolerance of stormwater *where it falls*. It proposes to gracefully store it and gainfully use it within the urban fabric. This integrated water-management strategy has three components: (1) *detaining* water temporarily through swales and rain gardens adjacent to roadbeds, and through porous pavement; (2) further *storing* water in existing and new surface-water bodies that form part of the drainage system, but are envisioned to become recreational and scenic amenities at different scales throughout the city; and (3) *optimizing draining* capacity through reconfiguring and redirecting some of the drainage systems.[30]

Akin to the Dutch tradition, the resultant "water city" would tightly couple streetscape and landscape (naturalized waterways, green boulevards) as water-management systems. In one example, the existing concrete-lined drainage canals (fig. 6-1A) would be reconfigured as continuous multipurpose parkland, affording recreation and contact with water while remaining capable of managing high drainage flows (fig. 6-1B).

Figure 6-1A and 6-1B. Orleans Parish: (A) existing outfall canal, and (B) proposed new canal, New Orleans, Louisiana. (Courtesy of Waggonner and Ball Architects.)

The plan, pieces of which are undergoing pilot studies, will likely be funded through a combination of federal hazard-mitigation grants, foundation grants, and perhaps a drainage fee similar to that imposed in Philadelphia (see p. 82).[31] GNOWP represents a uniquely innovative whole-systems approach to an urban watershed.

Kovalam, India, Artificial Reef—A Three-for-One Natural Solution to Beach Erosion

The community of Kovalam, on India's south Kerala coast—famous for its exquisite, crescent-shaped beaches—has constructed an artificial offshore reef that successfully emulates one of nature's approaches to stabilizing and replenishing beaches. Long a fishing hamlet and a major destination for European vacationers, this Edenic coastal spot had suffered severe erosion, particularly during the heavy storms and cyclones of the monsoon season. Since the 1950s, the stabilizing silt and clay deposits that had once been delivered by the area's rivers had been retained behind dams. As a consequence, the loose, sandy shore had eroded, despite relatively small increases in sea level.[32] About half of India's coastline is hardened by costly seawalls or groins; in Kovalam, however, concrete seawalls along the heavily trafficked beaches had only exacerbated the undermining and scouring of the beach. According to the project consultants, about 1,380 km (857 mi.)—23 percent of India's coastline—faces similar threats: it is retreating at a rate of about 450 hectares (1,112 acres) annually.

Undertaken jointly by the Kerala government's departments of tourism and harbor engineering, and based on an evolving understanding of natural processes, Kovalam's infrastructural solution—a "soft-engineered" offshore structure—was built in four sections. Giant capsules, each about the size and shape of two buses and made from ultraviolet- and abrasion-resistant geotextiles, strong synthetic fabrics used in civil engineering, were pumped full of approximately 4,000 cubic meters (about 5,230 cubic yards) of locally dredged sand. The 28 megacontainers were then placed end to end and positioned asymmetrically, toward one end of the bay, to help realign the incoming waves so they would be parallel to the beach, correcting the earlier misalignment which caused sand to drift down the coast.[33]

By turning the current north and thus eliminating the currents that had been passing sand to the south, the capsules caused new sand to accumulate behind the artificial reef, visibly broadening the beach. Naturally occurring algae accumulation on the reef has supported colonization by fish of all kinds and has also strengthened biodiversity in other ways. From the perspective of tourism, the major attraction has been the creation of a new surfing spot: breakers arriving at the reef are transformed into shapely waves, offering surfers a dramatic ride along the full length of the reef.[34]

Designed to work in accord with natural patterns that dissipate wave energy before it reaches the beach, multipurpose reefs (MPRs) modify near-shore currents by refracting the angle at which the waves hit the shore, causing sand to be transported into the area shadowed from wave action behind the submerged reef, thereby widening and stabilizing the beach.[35] The size, location, orientation, depth, and other characteristics of artificial reefs are typically developed through computer models that simulate wave refraction and sediment transport. MPRs have become increasingly appealing to coastal managers considering moving coastal fortifications offshore and underwater, and Kovalam's success has been duplicated in several locations around the world.[36]

Knowledge of an artificial reef's potential to improve habitat dates back to at least 500 B.C.E., when Egyptian fishermen observed that sunken ships were ideal nursery grounds, attracting large colonies of fish.[37] In addition to supporting local fishing industries, today's artificial MPRs serve the recreational needs of divers and snorkelers. For example, the Gold Coast Reef of Queensland, Australia—a prime snorkeling site that is an MPR—features 270 identified species of marine life.[38] In Japan, artificial reefs have been constructed for sea-urchin fisheries.[39]

Because of a lack of independent studies and only a handful of anecdotal successes, little is known about the long-term impacts of MPRs, which are still in a relatively early stage of development. Some MPRs have already drawn criticism, and one study has recorded some adverse effects, including the degradation of refurbished beaches over time.[40] Another issue is whether MPRs actually increase the fish population or simply attract fish from other ocean locations (and thereby contribute to overfishing). The answer is not conclusive; nevertheless, reef building does appear to have potential as part of a multipronged solution. Certainly, placing MPRs in the breaker zone improves opportunities for surfing and provides positive returns: according to one study, the Gold Coast Reef showed returns on investment of 60:1 as a consequence of increased tourism, protection from erosion, higher property values, and new income for the community.[41]

In Kovalam, members of the local fishing industry, along with some civil-society groups, remain skeptical about the MPRs and are specifically concerned that the Kerala government used federal tsunami rehabilitation funds to construct the reef to encourage tourism, thereby draining funds that were needed by more vulnerable communities.[42] Although more extensive monitoring and research on outcomes are in order, multifunctional coastal-protection measures, used in the context of holistic management approaches and without resorting to "armoring," can possibly sustain real dividends: not only increasing coastal resilience to climate change, but rebuilding beaches, strengthening marine life, and improving waves for surfing—all paybacks that underscore the effectiveness of alignment with natural patterns and processes.

Toward Low-Carbon Coastal Infrastructure: Mitigation and Adaptation

Mitigation and adaptation currently make up the two primary approaches to a destabilizing climate, but the relationship between the two has changed over time. Before 2007 the IPCC was focused primarily on lowering carbon intensities (mitigation); since then, however, the organization has begun to discuss protections against climate impacts that are already under way (adaptation). This book argues that next-generation infrastructure should, wherever possible, target both. The concluding examples in this chapter strive for that sweet spot where one aspect of a strategy mitigates and the other adapts.

The Sihwa Lake Tidal Power Station Turns the Tide

In 1994, the Korea Water Resources Corporation (Kowaco), a public authority, constructed a dike across Banwol Bay, on the country's western coast, bordering the Yellow Sea. The intent of the 12.7-kilometer-long (7.9-mile-long) embankment was to provide flood control and, over time, to transform a tidal estuary into a freshwater reservoir—Lake Sihwa, a 56-square-kilo-meter (22-square-mile) freshwater lake, which Kowaco would use to supply water for irrigation and industry. According to a 2012 report by the Organisation for Economic Co-operation and Development (OECD), among the OECD's 34 member countries, South Korea faces the greatest risk of water shortages. The two principal reasons are climate-change-induced drops in precipi-tation, and contamination of the water table by agricultural and other non-point-source pollution.[43] As part of the same project, which is not far from metropolitan Seoul, Kowaco also redeveloped 173 square kilometers (67 square miles) of land for agricultural and industrial development.

By 2000, however, in response to sharp criticism from envi-ronmentalists, Kowaco had to scrap its original plan to use the lake as a source of agricultural water. Once the lake was cut off from cleansing tidal currents, industrial wastes from nearby factories and increasing amounts of sewage (from a rapid influx of population) caused rapid deterioration of water qual-ity. In 2004, to restore water quality and ecological integrity in the basin, Kowaco abandoned its freshwater reservoir scheme and reintroduced seawater to flush out contamination.

This environmental restitution was, first and foremost, a governmental response to a water-procurement project gone awry. Conveniently, however, Kowaco was able to convert the liability into an opportunity to create an imposing, nonpolluting renewable-energy project. In an initiative completed in August 2011, the embankment was repurposed as the Sihwa Lake Tidal Power Station, the largest tidal-energy power station in the world. Not only is Sihwa a large source of hydroelectric power, but the barrage acts as an efficient water-filtering system, rein-vigorating the basin twice daily with salt water issued from its turbines, and thereby helping to restore marine life and fishing-based livelihoods.[44] The Korean expression for what the project has accomplished is "to catch two pigeons with one bean"—three pigeons, actually, since the barrage embankment became the foundation for a new four-lane highway that crosses the bay, radically shortening the travel distance between the tour-ist island of Daebu-do and the major port of Incheon.

South Korea's growing water demands parallel its escalat-ing energy needs. With virtually no oil, gas, or coal reserves of its own, South Korea is the fourth-largest importer of Iranian oil; it is also the 12th-largest emitter of greenhouse gases.[45] In the 1970s, to foster greater energy security, the South Korean government encouraged the construction of nuclear power plants; by 2006 the state-owned power company was operating 20 reactors with a combined generating capacity of 16,840 megawatts.[46] But South Korea shifted course in 2002 when it ratified the Kyoto Protocol. (It subsequently adopted a nationwide Renewable Portfolio Standard to reach a goal of 8 percent renewable energy by 2020.) With the need to make a major leap forward, South Korea turned an eye to the Yellow Sea, whose tides—with a mean range of 18 feet and a spring tidal range of 26 feet—are among the most powerful in the world. Sihwa Lake Power Plant, developed jointly by Kowaco, Korean Midland Power, and Lunar Energy, was a perfect example of adaptive reuse: in addition to repurposing an existing asset, it helped to mitigate the damage caused by the original, poorly planned intervention.

Tidal power plants convert the intermittent kinetic energy of incoming and/or outgoing tides into electricity by forcing rising water through turbines that drive generators embedded in the barrage (dam). Because water is 840 times denser than air, underwater turbines with blades comparable in size to those of wind turbines have far greater outputs. Sihwa is a single-effect (or one-way) tidal power-generating system, whereby the plant uses only the incoming tide to fill the basin of the former lake, thereby preventing tidal flooding. During tidal inflow, ten 25.4-MW submerged turbines generate electricity. During ebb tide, the system is in "sluicing mode," and separate sluice gates located to one side of the turbines open to release seawater into the ocean. The circulation of seawater (some 60 billion tons annually) flushes the lake, improving conditions for fisheries. The plant produces 552 GWh annually, sufficient to power the electrical needs of half a million people, or some 200,000 homes, in nearby Ansan City.[47] The plant will also reduce annual oil imports by approximately 862,000 barrels (worth $43 million), averting the release of 315,000 tons of CO_2.[48]

Building on the environmental lessons it had learned, Kowaco created Reed Wetland Park, an artificial wetland within Sihwa Lake where perennial marsh plants continue to purify incoming polluted water. Like many such multipurpose colocations, the park also serves as an ecotourism project: it features an educational pavilion, and its wildflower and bird-watching trails function as refuges for wildlife and citizens alike.

The Korea Electric Power Corporation, in which the state has a majority ownership, has conducted studies to investigate taking further advantage of tidal power along the Yellow Sea coast, which contains many large and small bays and exceptionally strong tidal currents. The results showed that 10 possible sites could collectively yield 6.5 gigawatts (GW) of power.[49] Although this attractive technology performs compound duties—providing both flood control and reliable renewable power—a number of considerations hinder large-scale replication. First, when compared with conventional, land-based thermal-power plants and other renewable-energy sources, water-based construction has higher first costs. Second, because productivity naturally fluctuates during the day, tidal power cannot be used as a primary power-generation technology; it must be connected to the grid. Finally, many optimal sites for tidal power plants coincide with fragile estuarine ecosystems that provide prime habitat for fisheries, shorebirds, and migratory marine animals; as a result, the plants could significantly unbalance the local ecology.

Controversy over the Severn, UK, Tidal Barrage

The chapter's last example, which is still under consideration, raises significant questions about the trade-offs among climate-change mitigation, renewable energy, and long-term environmental conservation. France's Rance Tidal Power Station—the world's first, completed in 1966, and now the second largest, after Sihwa—has recovered its high development costs and is delivering electricity at €0.18 per kilowatt-hour (kWh), versus €0.25 for nuclear power generation.[50] Despite this initial success, and that of subsequently built barrages such as the Jiangxia Tidal Power Station, south of Hangzhou in China, and the Annapolis Royal Generation Station in Nova Scotia, the proposed construction of a 10-mile barrage across the Severn Estuary, which separates England from Wales, is generating contentious debate over the environmental impacts of barrage construction. The Severn's 45-foot tidal range has drawn several successive barrage proposals since the 1980s, all of which have been defeated because of possible economic and environmental drawbacks. Under the current proposal, the barrage would enclose a sweeping, 77-square-mile intertidal area, habitat for migrating waterfowl.

As of this writing, the UK government is evaluating a privately financed, multifunctional tidal barrage (dam-like structure used to capture tidal energy), proposed by Corlan Hafren Limited, a private, independently funded tidal-energy business, which could provide up to 16.5 terawatt-hours (TWh) of low-carbon energy annually—the energy equivalent of three to four nuclear power stations, or more than 3,000 wind turbines. Corlan Hafren maintains that the barrage could satisfy 5 percent of the nation's current demand, with an annual carbon savings in excess of 1 million tons,[51] helping to advance the UK's legally binding commitment to an 80 percent reduction in GHG emissions by 2050, a carbon budget enacted under its Climate Change Act 2008. The £25- to £30-billion proposal calls for 1,026 bi-directional, low-head turbines generating power from both flood and ebb tides.[52] According to the proposal, the turbines will emulate the estuary's natural pattern, preserving local fish and invertebrate ecology while minimizing effects on banks and river tributaries.

As envisioned, the Severn barrage's additional functions would include the protection of cities and agricultural land—approximately 90,000 properties—against inundation that might otherwise eventually cost the nation billions of pounds in flood damage. Corlan Hafren suggests that restraining the estuary's currently turbulent waters will enhance biodiversity and allow the estuary to accommodate greater marine leisure and commercial activities. The design could also integrate a highly desirable third highway across the Severn, as well as a rail link between Wales and southwest England. Environmental mitigation plans call for at least 50 square kilometers of compensatory new intertidal wetlands outside the estuary.

Critics cite the loss of mudflat habitat, which currently supports a water-bird population of some 73,000 waders and wildfowl; uncertainties about the effects on fish; the potential for silt build-up in the dammed estuary; the risk of excessive shipping traffic at the locks; and, perhaps of greatest concern, the risk that displaced seawater will cause flooding in south Wales, Devon, and Ireland. All these questions call for more research. Debate continues among Welsh and English members of Parliament regarding the project's ecological acceptability and financial feasibility.

Despite these legitimate concerns, interest in tidal energy continues to grow. It has been estimated that the world's current electricity demand might be satisfied by a mere 0.2 percent of globally available tidal and wave energy.[53] Technological improvements, including smaller-scale tidal barrages—may surmount some of the environmental and economic obstacles. But large-scale, climate-adapted, low-carbon projects will inevitably raise thorny questions, answers to which are not yet readily knowable, even with some of the most sophisticated modeling tools. Will the environmental impacts rise to the level of significant harm? If so, are there potential mitigations or adaptations that would be acceptable? In particular, how do the potential impacts stack up against the potential dividends, for both marine and avian environments, that may result from carbon mitigation, including reduced risk from catastrophic oil spills, deforestation, and ocean acidification? Avoiding narrow traps and expanding analyses to embrace large spatial and temporal scales is essential to a whole-systems approach; nevertheless, they do add significant complexity to cost-benefit equations.

Conclusion

The effects of climate change on coastal and river urban infrastructure are already visible and will become more pronounced with the anticipated increase in extreme weather events. The requisite responses depend on timely, climate-sensitive design modifications for existing assets, and updated codes and standards for new assets. Although improved forecasts of climate change will help shape policy, the "no-regrets test" offers a valuable tool for identifying those adaptations that will offer genuine economic, environmental, and social benefits even if climate-change scenarios are not borne out. Such an approach would inevitably lead to multifunctional infrastructure investments—such as those at Oosterschelde, along Japan's riverbanks, at New Orleans's Lafitte Greenway / St. John Bayou, in Rotterdam, and at Sihwa, South Korea. Investing in multi-yield, multi-service systems will help to ensure long-term utility in the face of uncertainty.

Envision for a moment a potential high-profile scenario: a decision to construct a series of barrages to protect New York Harbor from future catastrophic storms. Although many would consider such a decision imprudent and inappropriate—on the basis of cost, feasibility, and adverse impacts on social justice and the environment, among other reasons—the no-regrets test would mandate the inclusion of a number of adaptive, mitigative, and beneficial features, including railways, roads, and integrated tunnel crossings at the closures; new bridges providing pedestrian and bicycle access to barrier islands; the colocation of utility tunnels; and, ultimately, the construction of tidal turbines.

Optimizing climate-change adaptation calls for several courses of action. First, we must recognize that threats from climate change cross public-works silos and jurisdictional boundaries; thus, adaptations need to be considered at the whole-systems level. Proper assessment of trends (acute events, long-term weather patterns, population pressures, and competing uses) can be helpful in such efforts by yielding new opportunities for multifunctional structures and synergies. Second, we must better leverage the adaptive capacity of natural capital—ecosystems that include salt marshes, mangroves, and other wetlands or planted shore buffers, as well as reefs—while recognizing that such features also add scenic and recreational value. We then need to better integrate land-use and infrastructure planning. For planning departments and zoning regulators, this means not only restricting land use in areas subject to coastal or inland flooding but, more importantly, optimizing flood control and land value by establishing compatible uses that can apply under various conditions. Examples include urban landscapes or cultivated lands that can be used for temporary floodwater storage; transportation tunnels adapted for stormwater storage; railway or road embankments that serve as flood defenses; and barrages that serve as transportation and utility connections. Finally, wherever possible, we need to combine adaptation and mitigation. For example, distributed energy generation, through micro-hydropower (small hydrogeneration from naturally flowing streams) or tidal power, can simultaneously render the grid more robust and provide flood control. In sum, we must understand the things we can adapt to, accept and admit to those we cannot, and achieve the wisdom to know the difference.

7. Combating Water Stress and Scarcity: Augmented Sources and Improved Storage

The effects of climate instability on water resources for irrigation and drinking are less apparently dramatic than sea-level rise and storm surges, but just as sinister. According to experts, there are already a billion individuals dependent upon groundwater sources that are "simply not there as renewable-water supplies."[1] Now planetary warming, in part caused by anthropogenic increases in CO_2, is altering precipitation patterns; increasing surface water temperatures, pollution, and atmospheric water-vapor content; and reducing ice- and snowpack, groundwater-recharge rates, and soil moisture. Rising sea levels may also cause saltwater intrusion into coastal groundwater aquifers. At the watershed scale, terrestrial and aquatic agro-ecosystems throughout the world will be increasingly vulnerable to alterations in the precipitation and storage cycles.[2] These changes, which are projected to continue, are already straining water resources and increasing irrigation demand.[3]

The previous chapter described a range of multifunctional, socially beneficial solutions that have been used to address threats to coastal and riparian regions. To continue to meet agricultural, energy-production, industrial, and domestic needs in the face of both climate change and population growth, freshwater procurement and management practices must engage in similar adaptations.

The volume of Lake Chad, a major water source for four African nations—Niger, Chad, Nigeria, and Cameroon—has decreased by 95 percent since the 1970s. In China, the combination of excessive irrigation and decreasing precipitation have led the Huanghe River to run dry more than 30 times since 1972. Much of northern China, including the city of Beijing, has endured long-standing water shortages, which ultimately required the construction, in 2008, of a $2-billion, 191-mile waterway to transport water northward from the country's less populated southern regions.[4] In addition to experiencing direct climate stresses, nations are also coping with increasing cross-sector vulnerabilities; for example, in 2001 the combination of severe drought and heavy reliance on hydroelectric systems (which are less dependable during drought) strained power production in São Paulo, Brazil, to the point where industrial energy use became subject to quotas.[5]

In the United States, the freshwater supplies that have been largely taken for granted are no longer immune to declining water tables, reservoir depletion, cessation of river flows, and desertification of grazing and agricultural lands. In most river basins in the West, snowpack—historically the largest source of water—has decreased substantially. Between 1945 and the late 1990s, snow volume dropped approximately 16 percent in the Rockies, 22 percent in the interior, and 29 percent in the Cascades.[6] In the Southwest, where water is a limiting resource (where appropriation exceeds availability), earlier snowmelt and the increasing severity of sustained drought have decreased soil moisture, lowering plant productivity and leading to greater incidence of wildfires.[7]

In the Los Angeles basin, saltwater from the Pacific Ocean is finding its way into aquifers, displacing groundwater resources for the nearly 10 million residents of the region. In Monterey County, 300,000 acre-feet of freshwater storage are presumed to have been lost: two-thirds of it to saltwater intrusion, and the rest to unsustainable rates of withdrawal from aquifers.[8] In the Florida Panhandle, rising sea levels are compounding excessive groundwater extraction, threatening both freshwater supplies and wastewater treatment. Inland water quality is also vulnerable to both major storms and long-term meteorological changes: after torrential rains, the inflow of suspended sediment has stained New York City's upstate reservoirs brown for days.[9]

In light of increasing water stress and scarcity, developed and developing nations alike are evaluating water supply strategies and technologies.[10] Existing water infrastructure was developed in the context of particular historical conditions and must now be retrofitted—or replaced—to achieve resilience in the face of declining freshwater supplies. But such efforts raise complex challenges. First, adjustments may not only be costly but may engender significant social and political conflict.[11] Second, some adaptation measures will inevitably compete with concurrent mitigation efforts, necessitating trade-offs. Finally, intersectoral cooperation regarding the water-energy nexus (which has historically not been the norm) will be critical.

The strategies required to sustain a robust hydrologic cycle fall into three principal categories: restoring water sources; finding alternative water sources; and creating integrated systems for water capture, use, and reuse. The first major section of this chapter considers both restoration and diversification, and the second considers integrated systems.

In some parts of the world, excessive withdrawal fostered by modern extraction, pumping, and piping regimes has undermined formerly sustainable water supplies. Projects undertaken in India have demonstrated, however, that reverting to nonindustrial technologies holds promise as means of maintaining better water balance. Forward-looking adaptive strategies may also augment water resources through relatively simple approaches to collection and storage. In some of the most arid parts of the world, new sourcing methods include advanced desalination technologies that hold promise, but they must reduce their carbon footprints in order to become truly sustainable.

Sourced from the Land: Revitalizing India's Tank Systems

Although blessed by an abundance of rivers, India suffers from wide regional variations in the distribution of water resources. Dependence on the monsoon season (typically from June to September) for nearly three-quarters of the nation's annual precipitation[12] adds to the variability of access to the resource—hence the ubiquitous reliance on rainwater capture and storage.[13]

India's water infrastructure reveals the country's ancient lifeline. Historically, rainwater for domestic use and crop irrigation was harvested and impounded in lakes or "tanks" (artificial reservoirs constructed across a slope). Built by villages for more than 2,000 years, with sizes averaging 10 hectares (about 25 acres) in size, these tanks rely on downhill check dams—temporary or permanent small dams built across a catchment area to confine upland water flow. As constructed natural systems the tanks provide vital ecosystem services, including nutrient recycling, groundwater recharge, support for habitat diversity, and, in times of heavy rains, flood mitigation.[14] Historically, responsibility for tank maintenance fell to the community, and members of lower castes were charged with weeding and removing built-up silt from the tanks.[15]

In the Godavari River basin, which spans almost the entirety of India's midsection, water-tank-based irrigation has historically been central to agriculture.[16] In the semi-arid Maner sub-basin, all 24 of the micro-basins relied on tank systems to support water-intensive crops such as maize, rice, and cotton. In the late 1980s, however, when the Land Reforms Act put state governmental authorities in charge of tank management and put an end to local decision making, maintenance effectively ceased. Subsequent government efforts to restore the tanks' functionality were unsystematic and failed to account for the basic ecology and hydrology of the tank system.[17] Inflows decreased, and silt eroding from the surrounding deforested catchment areas accumulated rapidly, dramatically reducing the tanks' storage capacity.[18]

Meanwhile, there was an increase in the use of structural approaches to obtaining water, including groundwater extraction, bore-well drilling, and the construction of hydroelectric dams. Canals and open irrigation ditches were also built to divert water. Water shortages in the Godavari basin have been further compounded by climate disturbances. As of 2009 the area's population was expected to nearly double by 2050—with water needs following suit.[19]

From 2004 to 2006 the World Wildlife Federation, working with Modern Architects for Rural India (MARI), a nongovernmental organization, supported a pilot project to revive tanks in the Maner sub-basin. As the first stage in the initiative, 12 tanks were desilted in order to demonstrate the economic viability of micro-restoration (as opposed to state-sponsored macro-infrastructural projects). Meanwhile, community participation strategies were used to identify the social and policy tools needed to scale up such an effort.[20]

After the excavation of 73,000 tons of sediment, the performance of the 12 tanks in an 11-hectare (about 27-acre) area serving 42,000 people improved: irrigation capacity increased by 900 hectares,[21] and because the tanks could store more runoff from the monsoons, water pumping ceased, along with the large associated electrical costs. The restoration of the tanks also increased the opportunity to recharge groundwater during high-rainfall years, which could then be drawn on during prolonged drought. Because tank water is fed by gravity, the additional pressure of increased water volumes allowed it to flow greater distances, reaching more farmers.[22] Clay silt, rich in nutrients and carbon, provides sufficient fertilizer for 600 hectares (about 1,480 acres) of farmland. The excavation also reduced the need for inorganic fertilizers and improved soil quality, strengthening plants against crop pests and thereby lowering pesticide use.[23] According to the farmers, the augmented topsoil increased moisture retention from four days to seven, further benefiting crops.[24] Other environmental benefits—principally the restoration of the density and diversity of avian and fish stocks in the water tanks—were attributable to the formation of 16 human-made silt and soil islands mounded in the wetlands, a redeployment that averted the cost of removing them. Finally, by intensifying cropping, this low-energy, soft-path solution increased carbon fixation (photosynthesis) throughout the area.[25]

Local farmers paid almost three-quarters of the $100,000 cost, largely through in-kind labor, but the direct and indirect agricultural benefits of the restoration helped recover the project costs quickly, and even provided a profit.[26] The project's annual economic returns were valued in 2008 at Rs 5,850,500 ($98,609)—a figure that excludes increases in milk production owing to the increased availability of fodder, as well as the augmented fish production attributable to the tanks' ability to accommodate larger water volumes.[27] The largest returns came from the increased yields on the affected 50 hectares (124 acres), where the production of groundnuts and maize realized the biggest gains.[28]

Yet another economic dividend of the restoration of the tanks was increased local employment (including the reemployment of washermen), which reduced overall outmigration of farm laborers to urbanizing areas in search of jobs.[29] Village committees for tank maintenance were reconvened, and wages were offered for silt excavation. For the landless poor, the benefit of wages was compounded by earnings from the enlarged farms' higher yields and the increase in fish stocks. Working through a complex system of interrelated factors, the revitalized tanks improved climate resilience, rejuvenated agriculture, restored social structures, and increased local employment.

There are 208,000 village water tanks across India, many similarly degraded, whose potential restoration represents a low-cost, low-tech, locally meaningful approach to providing a sustainable water supply.[30] Improving India's traditional water systems could not only avert or reduce the need for large-scale projects and increase climate-change resilience, but could move local communities in the direction of *gram swaraj*—village self-determination—which Mahatma Gandhi viewed as instrumental to a democratic India.[31] Projections have shown that in the Maner sub-basin alone, desilting the remaining tanks by approximately 15 feet would make it possible to store as much as 2.94 billion cubic meters (777 billion gallons) of water for this parched region, which would go a long way toward achieving water self-sufficiency.[32] Such an initiative stands in contrast to the massive water infrastructure interventions currently under consideration, including the $4-billion Polavaram Dam, on the lower Godavari River—which would displace a quarter of a million people and inundate 60,000 forested hectares (about 148,000 acres).[33]

Sourced from the Air: Urban Rainwater Harvesting Options and Policies in Seoul, South Korea

As traditional patterns and methods of water sourcing become unreliable due in part to climate instability, vulnerabilities will increase in areas that are already experiencing shortages. Monsoonal areas, including South Korea, are subject to the world's most unpredictable precipitation patterns. Thus, most South Korean cities rely heavily on centralized water supplies drawn from dammed reservoirs and often piped great distances at high cost. Uneven rainfall (more in summer, less in spring) creates significant challenges for Seoul, a city of 10 million. A very dry spring may bring damage from mountain fires, only to be followed by monsoon flooding, with casualties and property losses.[34]

A successful pilot program for harvesting urban rainwater—operating since 2007 and supported by the Seoul National University's Rainwater Research Center—has had a positive effect on city policy and is likely to influence other municipalities. Star City, a dense development occupying a tight, 6.25-hectare (15.4-acre) site with large commercial properties and a residential population of nearly 5,000, captures about 67 percent of the site's annual rainfall in its rainwater harvesting system, a climate-change adaptation strategy designed to supplement the centralized municipal water source (fig. 7-1). The multipurpose system controls stormwater, reduces energy consumption, supports firefighting, and offsets the use of potable water, thereby conserving freshwater supplies.

Roof water from the four main residential towers and terraces (approximately 50,000 square meters, or about 12 acres) is piped into three 1,000-cubic-meter-capacity storage tanks located three stories below the largest tower.[35] The first tank, whose water level is monitored by a remote-controlled system, is usually kept low or empty in order to accommodate storm runoff from the site. In advance of a storm, the tank's remaining contents are emptied into the drainage system; after the storm has passed, the contents are discharged slowly. The second tank accepts roof water that is then filtered through a self-cleaning, soil- and sand-based filtering system. This water is used to flush public toilets, to wash the site, and to meet the substantial irrigation needs of the complex's gardens. The third tank holds surplus water from the second tank, reserved for firefighting and other emergency uses.

Figure 7-1. Star City, Seoul, Korea. (Courtesy of The Jerde Partnership Inc.—Design Architect.)

With this system in place, residents were credited approximately $80,000 annually in their water rates, largely because of reduced water use at the site as well as reduced energy consumption at the wastewater treatment plant. In return for developer financing of the approximately $450,000 upfront additional cost, which will be paid back in eight years, the city allowed a 3 percent increase in the allowable floor area.[36] In 2005, on the basis of the success of Star City and other local rainwater-harvesting systems, the government of Seoul enacted ordinances stipulating the installation of such systems in new public buildings and providing subsidies for private systems.[37] Although the regulations have not been strenuously enforced, they were revisited and upgraded in 2008.[38]

The simple technology of rainwater harvesting alters the entire paradigm of water management, transforming it from an essentially linear flow that begins at a remote dam and courses through pumping stations and water distribution lines to sewers—to a decentralized, location-specific arrangement that banks water for local use related to need. In addition to addressing water shortages, rainwater harvesting offers a number of co-benefits: controlling floods and their attendant pollution; offsetting potable demand by putting rainwater to use; creating a dedicated water supply for firefighting and other emergency uses; and, finally, providing locally managed, on-site treatment—which is less expensive than centrally managed, end-of-pipe water treatment.[39]

Sourced from the Sea: The Promise of Desalination

Today nearly 3,000 desalination plants worldwide produce 27 million cubic meters (7,133 million gallons) of freshwater from seawater daily.[40] But the two most widely used technologies—multistage flash, which relies on repeated evaporation and condensation, and reverse osmosis, a process in which saltwater is driven, under pressure, through a semipermeable nano-membrane—require the expenditure of thermal and mechanical energy.[41] Current desalination methods, on a global average, use approximately 84.5 barrels of oil annually to produce 1 cubic meter (264 gallons) of potable water daily.[42]

Solarized desalination plants capture energy for direct use (photovoltaic [PV] panels generate electricity for the reverse osmosis process), thereby maximizing renewable resources. Alternatively, desalination plants can employ solar thermal energy: a solar still, a low-tech, greenhouse-type construction, uses solar heat to replicate the way in which seawater evaporates and then condenses in high, cool clouds, producing rainwater. Plants based on this model, however, have several disadvantages and are therefore rarely commercially scaled: first, the plants are space-intensive; second, they have high initial costs; third, unrecovered heat loss during condensation lowers efficiency. Most renewable-energy-based desalination plants in operation rely on PV-driven reverse-osmosis systems. Wind turbines—especially offshore, or in coastal areas where high winds prevail—can be readily coupled with reverse-osmosis units, keeping the energy consumption used in desalination relatively close to the place of generation.[43]

A promising technology for commercialized, renewable-energy-powered desalination plants is concentrated solar power (CSP). Concentrated solar power uses mirrors or lenses to concentrate a large area of sunlight onto a small area. Electrical power is produced when the concentrated light, converted to heat, drives a steam turbine. Efficient desalination relies heavily on closely matching the input power to the desalination load, and the fluctuating energy generated by wind or PV alone cannot efficiently support an operation with a constant power demand.[44] Power matching requires energy storage, which CSP obtains from the use of molten salt batteries that are coupled with the generation complex.

Renewable-energy-powered desalination is moving closer to technical maturity, but globally, the number of installations remains quite low. So far, cost has been the principal barrier. Another concern that applies to all desalination plants is the potential ecological harm from the discharge of hypersaline brine, the main by-product of desalination. Because dewatering and concentrating brine is by itself a highly energy-intensive process, the preferred disposal method is the discharge of brine into local waters. If the salts extracted in the course of desalination are not recovered for use as common salt, they can be converted into higher-value products used in the chemical or mining industries, which could potentially be colocated near desalination plants. Such an arrangement would prevent any brine from being released to the sea, but the technology involved in upgrading the sea salts for chemical or mining uses comes at a high cost, too.

The Solar-Powered Al Khafji Water Desalination Plant— Ash Sharqiyah, Saudi Arabia

The Al Khafji Water Desalination Plant, completed in 2013 and powered by alternative energy, bolsters water resources in Ash Sharqiyah, Saudi Arabia's largest province. The delivery of almost 8 million gallons a day of desalinized water, drawn from the Arabian Gulf, meets the needs of 100,000 people, helping to offset the province's current high rate of water withdrawal. As a reflection of commitment to reducing environmental impact, this showcase project is coupled with a 10-megawatt (MW) solar plant using a new CSP technology that concentrates the sun 1,500 times on a solar cell to boost efficiency.[45]

The plant relies on reverse osmosis, and new, nano-sized membranes—developed by the King Abdulaziz City for Science and Technology and the IBM Joint Center for Nanotechnology Research—increase efficiency. Grid power extends the plant's operation during nighttime hours.

Although the new CSP technology has a high initial cost, the plant's developers chose to use it to demonstrate the efficacy of the technology. With the nation's other combined power and desalination plants consuming more than 1.5 million barrels of oil per day, the Al Khafji Water Desalination Plant—the first large-scale, solar-powered operation of its kind—is just the beginning of a series, according to the King Abdulaziz City for Science and Technology.[46]

Low-Carbon Water for High-Value Crops: The Seawater Greenhouse

For the estimated 1.75 billion occupants of water-stressed regions,[47] agricultural uses must compete with domestic and industrial water consumption; accessing sufficient freshwater for growing food is thus an impending challenge.[48] Because conventional desalination is costly, in both economic and energy terms, water-stressed regions have come to rely on food imported from water-rich regions, rendering them economically and even politically dependent.[49] By colocating food and freshwater production, the Seawater Greenhouse offers a promising agricultural solution for arid regions.

The Seawater Greenhouse, which was developed by Charlie Paton, founder and managing director of Seawater Greenhouse Ltd., was first employed in Tenerife, one of the Canary Islands, in 1994. His elegantly simple, low-carbon process, which runs almost entirely on solar energy, recapitulates the hydrologic humidification/dehumidification cycle in which seawater is first evaporated by the sun, then cools down to form clouds and returns to the earth as fog, rain, or dew.

Seawater is trickled down a porous front-wall evaporator—a spongy honeycomb filter through which air is drawn into the greenhouse; as the air passes over the filter, its humidity increases and air temperature drops. As the air continues to move through the greenhouse, heated by the sun, it absorbs still more water vapor, which has been transpired by the plants. The hot, fully saturated air is then forced across metal pipes containing cold seawater. The condensate (distilled water) that collects around the pipes is stored for irrigation use. Watering needs in the greenhouse are reduced though the greenhouse's naturally high humidity and the practice of intercropping plants, which produces shade.[50]

A number of beneficial features have been integrated into the process. The initial evaporator filters out pests, while the further application of highly saline water to plants' leaves and produce acts as a biocide, eliminating the need for pesticides. Nutrients captured from the processed brine are used for fertilizer, and the extracted salt is transformed into gourmet crystals sold by the greenhouse owners. Nearby, surplus water produced by the greenhouse is used to support citrus crops. The greenhouse has also shown unexpected benefits to local ecology: the cool, moist air that flows out of the structure supports a much enhanced local plant life.

In 2010, the process was further commercialized with high-tech features at Sundrop Farms, a 2,000-square-meter (about one-half-acre) structure in Port Augusta, near Australia's Spencer Gulf. In 2014, Sundrop Farms will expand current operations by 20 hectares (49.4 acres). When fully ramped up, annual food production is expected to yield approximately 100,000 kilograms (about 110 tons) of hydroponically grown tomatoes—an amount 15 to 30 times higher than conventional field production for the same area, which will quickly recoup the $2-million upfront costs and significantly boost local employment.[51]

If implemented on underutilized coastal land near consumer markets, this integrated approach to year-round production of freshwater and crops could be widely applied in other arid regions. In many other parts of the globe—including the entire Mediterranean basin, as well as parts of Africa, the Middle East, Mexico, coastal Southern California, Australia, and East Asia—the substitution of seawater for scarce inland waters would be a great boon, providing the benefits of interconnected food and water security coupled with energy savings.[52]

The Sahara Forest Project: Pilot Facilities in Qatar and Jordan

According to the World Bank, between 2010 and 2050 water scarcity in large parts of the globe—North Africa, most of the Middle East, and parts of East Asia—will increase by nearly

40 percent.[53] In these regions, transitioning the water sector toward sustainability calls for three imperatives: increasing conservation and efficiency, making greater use of treated wastewater, and desalinating seawater. To avert the massive CO_2 emissions associated with fossil-fuel-powered desalination, however, it is essential to transition to renewable energy sources.[54]

A seawater greenhouse and concentrated solar-power plant facility in Doha, Qatar (fig. 7-2), among the first pilot initiatives of the Sahara Forest Project (SFP), opened in December 2012 and had harvested its first barley crop by 2013. The Sahara Forest Project is planning a larger pilot, close to Aqaba, Jordan, that will similarly combine water, energy, and food production—but will also produce algae in some of the waste brine, thereby sequestering carbon. Once the cultivation of this renewable fuel source is commercialized, the plant will be carbon-negative. As yet another secondary benefit, the plant's soils will sequester carbon by taking up biomass residues.

As of this writing, no date had been set for the start of construction. Once the Qatar and Jordan facilities have been subject to a full environmental impact assessment, they will be followed by a huge, 20-hectare (about 50-acre) demonstration center planned by SFP near Aqaba, Jordan, on government-

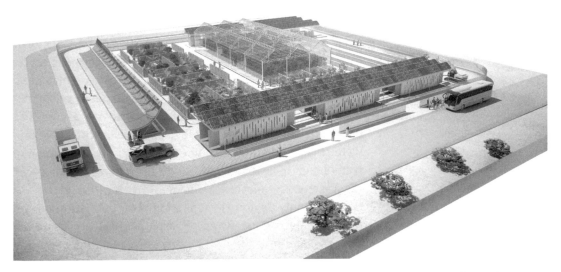

Figure 7-2. Desert re-vegetation around a saltwater infrastructure, Sahara Forest Project Pilot Facility, Mesaieed, Qatar Sahara Forest Project, Seawater Greenhouse, Doha, Qatar (© Sahara Forest Project).

donated land that includes an easement for a pipeline carrying Red Sea water 15 kilometers (9.3 miles) inland for desalination, cultivation, and energy production.[55] The center will be a hybrid system that will take advantage of process synergies among power generation, desalination, and evapotranspiration (the evaporation of water from soil and the transpiration of water by plants). Efficiency will be optimized through the use of CSP: mirrors will concentrate solar energy to drive a steam turbine generating electricity. The waste heat will also be used in the greenhouses, for water evaporation in the seawater desalination process. The seawater will be further utilized in the colocated cultivation of sea-loving plant species such as algae, which can be used for large-scale bio-energy production. The key to the success of the system is to maximize the use of resources, including waste products. In this case, saltwater will be used in several forms, and at various stages, to produce freshwater, grow crops, and even produce bio-fuel.

Wastewater Reuse—Orange County, California

By their nature, both surface and underground water resources cut across jurisdictional boundaries. Improving sustainable management of water resources in the face of climate-induced water insecurity calls for transformative approaches: the water sector must recognize that all water resources (fresh, storm-, and wastewater) are interconnected and must be collaboratively managed. Integrated Water Resources Management (IWRM), which may be defined as a partnership among stakeholders at various levels of government, focuses on managing water resources holistically to ensure water quality and quantity.[56] When California passed its IWRM Act of 2002, for example, over the next four years it began to support integrated watershed and aquifer planning through the authorization of water bonds in 46 regions covering 82 percent of the state.[57]

Wastewater reuse—exemplified in the discussion of Orange County, California—is an example of a holistic management approach. Wastewater recycling deserves a place in the array of water-management strategies: in addition to reducing the need to import water from new sources, it reduces or eliminates the need to discharge treated wastewater into surface waters (see box 7-1).[58]

Box 7-1. Recycling Wastewater: Examples from Belgium and Namibia

Over the past several decades, improved treatment methods have rendered the reuse of wastewater more common. On Belgium's western Flemish coast, freshwater for six coastal communities had historically been drawn from a small local aquifer beneath a sand dune, triggering saltwater infiltration. Since 2002, effluent from the nearby Wulpen wastewater treatment plant has undergone membrane-filtration treatment before being used for aquifer recharge, an approach that has regenerated the barrier against saltwater intrusion and improved drinking water quality.[1]

In Namibia, one of the most arid nations in sub-Saharan Africa, almost twice as much water is typically lost to evaporation as is consumed.[2] When demand-management measures—including strict regulation of water use for equipment, irrigation, and swimming pools—proved insufficient, wastewater reclamation proved a viable solution for Windhoek, the capital city of 2 million. The city's approach to reuse, which is more direct than aquifer replenishment, moves water recycling to the next level.

At the first phase of treatment, domestic and industrial effluent are separated; the purification processes of the domestic water that follow include ozonation (treatment with ozone) and membrane ultrafiltration. Reprocessed water accounts for only 25 percent of the city's daily potable requirements, but the amount can be increased to 50 percent if necessary to meet demand.[3] Monitoring of microorganism indicators, taste-testing campaigns, education, marketing, and media outreach have enabled the system to gain the confidence of the public.

1. Emmanuel Van Houtte and Johan Verbauwhede, "Operational Experience with Indirect Potable Reuse at the Flemish Coast," *Desalination* 218, no. 1 (2008): 207.

2. Petrus L. Du Pisani, "Direct Reclamation of Potable Water at Windhoek's Goreangab Reclamation Plant," *Desalination* 188, no. 1 (2006): 79–80.

3. J. Lahnsteiner and G. Lempert, "Water Management in Windhoek, Namibia," *Water Science & Technology* 55, no. 1 (2007): 446.

In the United States, the earliest examples of wastewater reuse were in industry and for the irrigation of crops and golf courses. Although the use of recycled wastewater increased by as much as 15 percent a year between 1976 and 2007,[59] as of 2005, most of the 3,300 water-reuse projects registered in the United States yielded non-potable water.[60] As far back as 1976, however, the Orange County, California, Water District (OCWD) had embraced a strategy that diversified its portfolio of water resources while addressing some of the early effects of climate change on water supply and sea level. Since then the agency has had worldwide influence, leading the effort to reclaim water for aquifer recharge through the advanced treatment of sewage effluent.

OCWD's achievement of indirect potable reuse—the recycling of highly treated wastewater effluent for aquifer recharge—represents a leap forward in integrated water-resources planning. This achievement demanded an unusual level of cooperation across government jurisdictions and regulatory bodies involved in sanitation, water quality, and public health. Significantly, the innovation also addressed the most significant barrier to wastewater reuse: public resistance.

Orange County sits in a desert climate and has largely depended on the combined strategies of aquifer management and water importation. By the 1950s, a surging population and intense agricultural demand led to excessive withdrawal of aquifer water, and the county's water table dropped below sea level, inducing a flow of seawater into the aquifer that extended inland as far as five miles.[61] To control this intrusion, the OCWD began to import freshwater at high cost, which was introduced into the aquifer groundwater to create a pressurized barrier against encroaching contamination. In 1976, the OCWD established Water Factory 21, obviating this practice. Instead of piping wastewater out to sea after it had been subjected to primary treatment, the facility used what were then state-of-the-art cleansing techniques to subject it to further processing. Some of the water was then used as a hydraulic barrier against seawater intrusion; the rest was used for groundwater reinjection, to replenish OCWD's aquifer directly.[62]

By the 1990s, faced with the rising volume of the county's effluent, the sanitation department began to consider building a new, $200-million ocean outfall—a discharge pipe into the sea. Instead, through a 2007 joint venture with OCWD they expanded the water-recycling facility, which now produces over 96 million cubic meters (3,390 cubic feet) of treated wastewater annually.[63] Through microfiltration, reverse osmosis, and ultraviolet disinfection, effluent from what is now known as the Groundwater Replenishment System (GWRS) achieves near-distilled quality, exceeding all state and federal drinking-water standards. About 50 percent of the water goes to expanding the seawater barrier; the rest is pumped to one of two places: the OCWD recharge facility, which is 13 miles away, or to a "percolation lake" with permeable soil, where the water is filtered over a six-month period before blending into the water table, for return as drinking-water supply.[64]

This holistic integration required significant cooperation between the water and sanitation departments—a challenge to the more typically "siloed" agencies. The departments also undertook an aggressive program, including both consultation and educational outreach, to engender public acceptance of the treatment process. Thanks to endorsements from environmental and public-health experts and organizations, as well as extensive, ongoing communication with the community—including businesses, other government agencies, and the health and medical sectors—the GWRS ultimately earned not only public trust but overwhelming public support.[65]

Water for All in Singapore

Home to one of the busiest ports in the world, the geographically blessed island of Singapore sits at the crossroads of global trade, boasting a successful free-market economy and an affluent and highly educated population. A nation that has thrived despite limited natural resources, Singapore is beginning to see the costs of aggressive development: the rain forest that once covered the island is now limited to the Bukit Timah Nature Reserve, and the small watersheds that made up a part of the nation's freshwater resources have been further reduced in size.

Historically, Singapore has developed its water infrastructure with the same utilitarian efficiency that created its thriving economy. The many waterways crisscrossing the country have been armored to prevent erosion—a gray-infrastructure approach that has been convenient for shipping and business, but has proven aesthetically and environmentally disastrous. Among other environmental harms, the structures inhibit natural infiltration and storage.

Under a treaty set to expire in 2061, Singapore imports freshwater from Malaysia—an option that is fraught with political uncertainty. To manage demand, develop and expand local water sources, and wean the country from foreign water supplies, Singapore's statutory Public Utilities Board (PUB), the nation's publicly operated water utility with purview over gas and electric, has implemented a sophisticated set of policy measures. Through progressive programs and integrated infrastructural solutions, the nation is optimizing its limited water resources while restoring its native waterways and recovering the natural beauty of the island.

The PUB's mission statement—"Water for All: Conserve, Value, Enjoy"—is guiding the transition from hard- to soft-path management—a top-down process that is being implemented gradually, through efficient administration and a well-designed regulatory framework.[66] Guided by both comprehensive and strategic plans, the overall vision involves more than 100 projects, at various scales, to be implemented over 10 to 15 years.[67] To build community support and foster stewardship, in addition to instituting comprehensive policies to reduce water demand, the PUB has developed a number of programs—the Four Taps, the 3P Partnership, and ABC Waters—each of which has several subprograms and associated education efforts.

Implemented in 2006, Four Taps is a strategic plan designed to achieve water autonomy within 50 years. To minimize the amount of water imported from Malaysia (the first "tap"), the plan focuses on the other three: creating local catchments, using NEWater (reclaimed water), and developing desalinated supplies.

Local catchment involves an integrated system of 15 reservoirs fed by an extensive storm-drainage system. The catchment area for the recently established Marina Reservoir (in the heart of the city), the island's largest, is one-sixth the size of Singapore and currently supplies 10 percent of the country's water demand.[68]

NEWater, a separate tap developed under the 3P Partnership, is projected to supply 50 percent of the nation's water by 2060.[69] NEWater effectively multiplies available water sources;[70] the success of the public-relations campaign in overcoming aversion to the use of reclaimed water (known as "toilet to tap") testifies to the value of engaging residents as partners.

Industry partners, who receive incentives for research and development, have been essential to the creation of new technologies, including energy-efficient desalination plants. A reverse-osmosis plant currently provides sufficient high-quality potable water to meet 30 percent of Singapore's water needs.[71] One promising technology uses waste heat from industry to offset the energy intensity of desalination, thereby increasing the amount of water that can be sourced from this tap at the same cost.[72]

The 3P Partnership (people, public, private) draws together the general public, government, and the corporate sector to manage the demand side through mandatory water conservation, water tariffs, and education. ABC Waters, the most visible component of the PUB strategy, uses the tagline "Active, Beautiful, Clean Water for All." An environmentally progressive initiative to restore ecological function and improve urban living, ABC Waters has two principal components: a green infrastructure plan and a public-relations campaign designed to support the restoration and augmentation of water bodies by reframing the value of water to society. Soft-path water infrastructure, such as rain gardens, green roofs, bioswales, and dry ponds, has been judiciously sited to complement existing hard path systems. To mitigate peaks and regulate flow, rainwater is treated on-site, then slowly released into streams. Singapore's pervasive use of relatively simple technology also serves cultural and recreational purposes: infrastructural improvements are enhanced by aesthetic modifications and integrated with art, leisure activities, and educational experiences.

The multifunctional Marina Barrage, which crosses downtown's large Marina Bay, is perhaps Singapore's most ambitious infrastructural asset: in addition to serving as a tidal barrier and flood-control mechanism, the barrage is transforming the enclosed marina into a major freshwater reservoir and recreational area (fig. 7-3). Visitors pass through new, tropical botanic parklands en route to a two-story, green-roofed visitors center

Figure 7-3. Aerial view of Marina Barrage and Visitor Centre, Singapore. (Courtesy of CDM Smith.)

(which is wrapped around the pump house for the hydraulic gates) that showcases Singapore's environmental accomplishments. The intersection of innovative design, environmental features, and community amenities is representative of the PUB's approach to the holistic management of water resources.

Conclusion

Particularly when combined with other anthropogenic pressures, climate-related effects are putting increasing strain on freshwater resources. No part of the world will be entirely immune to shifts in water availability due to changes in the large-scale hydrological cycle. In many locales these shifts will lead to a reduction in easily accessible freshwater supplies. In consequence, water provision, along with other key sectors—including agriculture, industry, and energy production—must begin to transition away from mining "fossil water," the deep-water aquifers that are no longer being replenished by infiltration. Along with groundwater recharge, the sectors must seek out alternative sources of supply and increase options for reuse.

In many agricultural areas, water infrastructure should augment storage capacity by building reservoirs and by restoring groundwater recharge to its natural functioning. In water-short or water-stressed urban areas, where stormwater is typically jettisoned, its capture, treatment, and storage for non-potable use should be considered. Rainwater harvesting, one of the most modest technologies for combating water shortages, is paradoxically not very advanced, particularly at the urban scale. In the United States, for example, only a handful of cities and states have overturned regulations prohibiting the indoor use of rainwater on the basis of health and safety concerns. A study undertaken by the Natural Resources Defense Council in 2011 found that if 50 percent of roof areas captured the first inch of rainfall for non-potable use, annual savings in Atlanta, Georgia, and Chicago, Illinois, would be $25.9 million and $20.6 million, respectively.[73] And according to an analysis undertaken at the University of Arizona, similar rooftop rainwater capture in Tucson—one of the most arid cities in the country—could reduce residential water use by 30–40 percent.[74]

Another line of defense against water shortfalls for coastal communities will be hybrid renewable-energy generation and desalination. Fortunately, many of the coastal regions with the greatest water shortages are at latitudes with plentiful solar access.[75] Arid coastal areas in the United States, for example, could begin to take advantage of process synergies among power generation, desalination, and agriculture. Finally, waste-water recovery for treatment and non-potable reuse (as in Orange County and Windhoek) can help stabilize and enlarge available resources.

New and recycled sources for water consumption may yet prove insufficient, however, in the context of the energy-water nexus. For instance, water resources long dedicated to agriculture may need to be diverted, out of necessity, to critical refor-estation efforts (intended to store carbon), or for the cultivation of bioenergy resources intended to displace carbon-based fuels. Initiatives in arid and semi-arid areas, including desalina-tion and the reuse of wastewater, will be energy-intensive; and then there's the problem of waste brine.

Because of resource limitations and dense populations, small island nations like Singapore may be leading the way in water sourcing via integrated-systems management. IWRM, a vital element in sustainable water management, addresses all water sources and transactions in the hydrologic cycle and is crucial to negotiating complex jurisdictional boundaries and engaging all affected sectors.

Ultimately, cooperation between water and energy infra-structure is particularly imperative to decrease the carbon intensity associated with the procurement and delivery of freshwater. Applied thoughtfully, the integration of resources—whether low-tech, as in the case of the Godavari Tank restora-tions, or high-tech, as in the Qatar and Jordan Sahara Forest Projects—can not only reduce the waste of a precious resource at lower energy costs but can become a catalyst for improved agricultural production.

8. Ways Forward: Think Systematically, Experiment Locally

This book's introduction recounted the tragic failure, in 2007, of the I-35W Bridge in Minneapolis. In its place today, the St. Anthony Falls Bridge is a forward-looking piece of infrastructure that bolsters safety, anticipates alternative transit modes, trims operating energy costs, and incorporates community amenities. Like the other projects worldwide highlighted throughout this book, the new bridge embodies many of the priorities of post-industrial infrastructure. Attending to the challenges we face in the United States—the emphasis of this closing chapter—the bridge rebuilding reminds us that we have the technical knowledge and tools to move forward; what we need now is both vision and leadership to create the policy and financing vehicles to make future-proofing possible.

The extraordinary scale of needed infrastructural building and maintenance in the United States raises a number of questions. In the absence of a national infrastructural agenda, who will assume leadership? Can funding be leveraged through existing or retooled financial institutions—and if not, what policy instruments might be used to address funding gaps? How can decision makers be guided to transcend compartmentalized thinking and create the partnerships, cross-sector strategies, and designs that are needed to deliver multifunctional public works?

Given the drawn-out economic recovery and the prevailing congressional gridlock, genuine progress toward infrastructural revitalization seems unlikely, at least in the short term, despite ever-more-urgent calls from industry, civil society, and professional organizations. Ideally, a reinvigorated national vision would align federal, state, and local policy in support of next-generation investments—first, by eliminating injurious subsidies and discouraging environmental externalities (the social costs of environmental damages); and second, by augmenting market incentives and establishing financing mechanisms that favor next-generation investments. A proactive federal government would promote and fund projects of multijurisdictional, regional, or national significance, such as interstate transit improvements, and integrated water-resource management, and help accelerate rollouts of the smart grid. A central lending authority (along the lines of the proposed National Infrastructure Bank) could streamline access to funding and increase public-private investment. Finally, a proactive federal government would support research, piloting, and development of next-generation infrastructural technology in much the same way that the EU or European national governments have underwritten pilot projects in Lille, France; the Netherlands; and Lolland, Denmark.

While the heroic era of federally led projects—from canals to railroads to rural electrification and interstate highways—may perhaps be behind us, with federal-level funding and support, other levels of government may be better poised to move them forward. Since making its investment in major programs such as interstate highways, water distribution, and treatment systems before the 1980s, the federal government has devolved much of the work involved in infrastructure planning, expansion, and maintenance to state and local governments—which now own approximately 97 percent of American bridges, roads, and highways. Half of all water filtration systems and about 80 percent of wastewater systems are owned and operated by municipalities and local governments.[1]

The infrastructural landscape of the twenty-first century will be complex, and the creation of integrated, cross-sector projects at the most local level possible will require transformative leadership and organizational capacity. When it comes to siting issues, the fact that land-use decision making is largely under local control means that local governments are likely to be more nimble than their state—let alone federal—counterparts. In practical terms, most public services are local issues; cities and towns deal in the particulars. Given the extent of state and local government involvement in infrastructure investment and authority over project planning and implementation, these levels of government are potential hubs of leadership and innovation.

With or without federal guidance, state and local governments can assert control over their own destinies. States can even cooperate to address problems at the regional scale, to help leverage existing financing or assemble new financing. Local governments can engage in fiscally creative arrangements—through tax-increment financing, special-assessment districts, user fees, targeted tax increases, bond issues, and ballot initiatives. Armed with the right policy tools and, in particular, supported by public-private partnerships, state and local governments can proactively advance the next generation of coordinated public works. Thus, the strategies described in this chapter are directed to the state and local officials who are poised to offer more agile leadership in the realm of transformational infrastructure planning, including partnering with progressive utilities, regulatory agencies, and new investment entities. Precedents exist for "think[ing] systematically and experiment[ing] locally,"[2] and they can be built on in the coming years.

This final chapter outlines specific steps for moving the nation toward the development of multifunctional, cross-sector infrastructural systems—specifically, by mobilizing funding, developing innovative policies, and creating new delivery models for blended assets. In accordance with the five principles that form the framework for this book, the projects that state and local governments need to foster will have these priorities in common: optimization through combination; low- or zero-carbon heat and power; productive amalgamation of constructed and natural systems; inclusion of community assets; and smart adaptation to climate uncertainty.

State and Local Governments: Agents of Experimental Change

Exemplary US infrastructure projects make apparent that local entities can spearhead ambitious, multipronged infrastructural initiatives (see, for example, Mt. Poso Biomass Cogeneration Plant, or the University of New Hampshire's EcoLine partnership, in chapter 3: California's Arcata Wastewater Treatment Plant, in chapter 4; and Orange County's Water Factory 21, in chapter 7). Making such accomplishments more commonplace, however, will require new policy mechanisms and access to funding at the state or local government level.

Frustrated by general political paralysis in Washington, D.C., today, state and local leaders are beginning to undertake their own actions, some in collaborations that cross state lines. In response to climate change, for instance, already more than 1,054 US mayors[3] and 36 states[4] (plus the District of Columbia) had developed greenhouse-gas-reduction plans as of 2012.[5] Nine northeastern US states had signed a regional agreement in 2005 to reduce CO_2 emissions by some 24 million tons per year to 165 million tons per year. In February 2013, they agreed to a lower cap of 91 tons per year in 2014, with further reductions at a rate of 2.5 percent a year until 2020.[6]

Absent federal initiative, many city and state leaders are similarly initiating alternative infrastructure-development mechanisms. Voters in Oklahoma City, for instance, agreed in 2009 to a 1 percent local sales tax that will generate more than three-quarters of a billion dollars over seven years for a series of metropolitan area projects (MAPs) backed by the local chamber of commerce and private sector contributions.[7] Through MAPs, the city is improving parks and bike trails, and creating a streetcar system and transit hub.[8] Moreover, by bundling and integrating projects, the city will achieve construction economies. The Chicago Infrastructure Trust (detailed below) will leverage private investment in support of otherwise budget-breaking, cross-sector urban projects. A significant 2012 initiative called the West Coast Infrastructure Exchange (WCX) is indicative of bold new moves being made by neighboring state officials to address emergent energy, water, and transportation concerns. Governors, treasurers, and infrastructure development agencies of California, Washington, and Oregon have joined forces with officials from British Columbia in a collaborative venture that will facilitate alternative infrastructure investments, bundling public and private funds, and developing new delivery models to create crucial merit- or "performance-based" energy, water, and transportation projects serving their regions.

Financing Mechanisms for Next-Generation Projects

Beginning in the late 1980s, infrastructure investment began to shift from the federal to the state level. To fill the gap created by diminishing federal grants and to capitalize on the remaining federal allocations, states developed alternative investment vehicles. In 1987, the Federal Water Quality Act established state revolving funds (SRF) for water- and wastewater-treatment infrastructure in every state; these have funded more than $100 billion in infrastructure improvements since 1992. State infrastructure banks (SIBs) that support transportation initiatives were initially established as subsets of SRFs through individual, state-specific enabling legislation in the mid 1990s and extended in 2005; many were capitalized through federal highway-authorization bills. Today 33 states have a SIB, although as many as 10 are underactive or inactive because, in several cases, states have not replenished the expended funds.[9]

SRFs, SIBs, and "green banks," such as the Connecticut Clean Energy Finance and Investment Authority, are typically not-for-profit institutions, operating under state regulation, that combine private banking functions with public oversight. All three offer opportunities to capitalize projects through revolving funds, financial structures in which the repayment of principal, bonds, interest, and fees replenishes the available capital. SRFs have been used primarily to finance surface-transportation projects and water-related improvements, as well as some renewable-energy projects. SIBs and green banks were initially capitalized from various grant sources with significant state matches.

Because of their low lending rates, SIBs could become the most valuable and versatile means of increasing state and locally led infrastructure spending. Because they are accountable only to state entities within which they are housed (many are under state departments of transportation), SIBs have, in past, avoided federal procurement delays, and can thus be more flexible and more responsive to local needs. Because of their formal selection processes, SIBs may also better insulate project selection decisions from political influence. Significantly, SIBs can be used to leverage private funding and project expertise that can sustain local economic development.[10]

SIBs have varying degrees of decision-making authority. Some states appoint external oversight bodies, but most SIBs have a board or advisory committee charged with guiding project selection and providing general oversight; such boards or committees may be comprised of representatives from other agencies, along with gubernatorial or legislative appointees. In some cases, the boards include a citizen's oversight committee with appointed members; there may also be requirements that all meetings be public.[11]

The California Infrastructure and Economic Development Bank (known as the California I-Bank) is widely regarded as one of the most successful SIBs, and it has been put forward by the Urban Land Institute and others as a model for a national infrastructure bank.[12] It is located within the California Business, Transportation, and Housing Agency, but acts as an independent entity. Since its one-time appropriation of $181 million in 1999, the I-Bank's operations have been funded solely from borrower closing fees, loan repayments, and the bank's interest earnings. The bank's broad powers enable it to provide low-cost, long-term infrastructure financing. Significantly, the I-Bank underwrites a full range of public works, including water-supply and sewage-treatment facilities, educational and recreational facilities, and public transit, streets, highways, and storm drainage.[13] Projects are assigned priority according to criteria that take into account project impact (overall job creation and retention), local community employment, quality of life and community amenities, economic need, land-use strategies, environmental protection, and leverage capacity.

One of the I-Bank's bond programs, the Infrastructure State Revolving Fund (ISRF), gives municipalities, counties, districts, and redevelopment agencies access to funding that can be leveraged through other local, state, and federal grants and loans.[14] Between mid-2000 and mid-2010, the ISRF approved 95 loans totaling over $400 million.[15] The I-Bank, like the Chicago Infrastructure Trust (CIT; see below), is a model of interagency creativity, using a crosscutting approach to project development and financing that specifically encourages "transformative infrastructure projects."[16] Embraced by unions, nongovernmental organizations, and private-sector leaders, the I-Bank leverages state funds to upgrade public infrastructural assets, engaging in customized project financing that includes private investors.

A similar innovative mechanism for infrastructure development is the Chicago Infrastructure Trust (CIT)—a bold, $7-billion investment endeavor conceived by Chicago mayor Rahm Emanuel and established by city ordinance in 2012. Designed to create jobs and leverage private investment, the CIT will be used to construct or retrofit essential services from airports to commuter-rail to parks, schools, and utilities. In a coordinated effort designed to reduce future street cuts, for instance, broadband cables will be laid at the same time that an estimated 900 miles of water pipes and 750 miles of sewer lines are replaced.[17] Applauded in 2012 by the US Conference of Mayors as an outside-the-box initiative and a blueprint for cities that want to control their own infrastructural destiny, the CIT is a viable model with wide potential application in other large cities.[18]

Public-Private Partnerships and the Rise of Private Infrastructure Investment

Not only can public-private partnerships (PPPs) help fill gaps in the financing and delivery of public infrastructure, but they also offer opportunities for greater private-sector participation in the financing, design, construction, and, in many cases, the operation and maintenance of public works. PPPs can be used for one-off projects or applied to ongoing capital programs. Among their potential benefits are cost savings; completion of projects on time and within budget; and, of course, lower government outlays. When concession contracts (agreements between government and a private company) are structured properly, deferred maintenance (attributable to government budget shortfalls) can be reduced or eliminated.[19]

In the United Kingdom, PPPs represent between 10 and 13 percent of national investment in public infrastructure, and the use of the model is increasing rapidly in India and Japan.

Canada and Australia have used PPPs for water and wastewater projects, as have Ireland, the Netherlands, and other European nations.[20] With the exception of various toll roads and other highway infrastructure in Illinois, Indiana, and Texas, PPPs are still novel in the United States. Creating a supportive climate for state and local PPPs depends on the passage of state-level enabling legislation, the development of sound legal frameworks for contracts, the fair allocation of risk, and careful structuring of operations and maintenance concessions.[21]

Since 2005 significant monies from around the globe have been pooled in private funds dedicated to infrastructure investment driven by the private sector's awareness of a cash-strapped public sector and the revenue potential of such investment. Billions of dollars of such capital are vested with firms such as Morgan Stanley, GE-Credit Suisse First Boston, and J. P. Morgan.[22] Meanwhile, large investors such as insurance companies and pension funds are diversifying their holdings through infrastructure investment, anticipating predictable and reasonable returns with relatively modest risk.[23] A Dutch pension fund, for example, has invested €2 billion in infrastructure with hopes to increase to €5 billion by 2015; and in 2010 the Ontario Teachers' Pension Plan invested C$7.1 billion in infrastructure—more than 6 percent of its total assets.[24]

As of 2012, $810 million from US pension funds had been invested in Australian assets such as ports, power stations, and freeways,[25] a circumstance that raises a question: Why export investment, rather than using it to meet burgeoning needs at home? Change may be at hand, however. Public employees' and teachers' retirement systems in California, Kansas, and Washington State have stated their intention to allocate a small percentage of their assets to infrastructure.[26] In what is perhaps the most significant indicator of a potential trend in private investment—and one in response to climate change, at that—is the decision, on the part of the Teachers' Retirement System of the City of New York, to invest $1 billion in critical, post–Hurricane Sandy infrastructure improvements.[27]

The importance of PPPs for the future-proofing of public works cannot be underestimated. First, PPPs like the CIT allow several projects to be bundled, which can work in favor of conjoined, cross-sector projects. Second, PPPs have the flexibility to use alternative procurement methods such as design/build contracts and performance-based contracting (commitments that projects achieve specific, measurable performance standards)—

which, when compared with the rigidity and specificity of typical government procurement processes, can promote greater design innovation. Third, under PPPs, contracts for next-generation assets can be awarded according to best value—factoring in additional benefits—rather than being awarded on the basis of the lowest price. Finally, as funding becomes more difficult to obtain, the combination of innovative procurement methods and design/build/operate efficiencies can encourage alternative delivery models that favor complex, integrated projects.

Nevertheless, PPPs face challenges. The public is wary of privatization—and some of this wariness comes from the concern, not entirely unfounded, that private capital comes at a higher cost. Other drawbacks can include the lack of public institutional capacity to deal with the complexity of contract models. On the other hand, these concerns can be surmounted by the use of "public-private partnership units" (successfully used in other countries)—entities established explicitly to undertake quality control and standardization, render technical advice, and develop appropriate policy.[28]

Embedding the Five Principles in Funding Decisions

According to a 2002 federal review of transportation financing, SRF project-selection methods vary widely, ranging from "first-come, first-served" to a combination of objective and subjective criteria, including project objectives and financial assessments. With respect to selection criteria, the report singled out the Florida Department of Transportation for best practices: after financial considerations, the department's criteria include "economic benefits, new technologies (intelligent transportation), environmental benefits, and intermodal enhancements."[29] Both the CIT and the I-Bank also rely on triple-bottom-line criteria.[30]

What mechanisms might both SRFs and SIBs use to promote next-generation projects? One option is to proactively encourage particular types and combinations of development by establishing outcome-oriented threshold or supplementary criteria, as well as award and allocation formulas that are aligned with the five axioms of next-generation public works: multipurpose, low-carbon infrastructure that is tightly coordinated with natural systems, well integrated into social contexts, and capable of adapting to a changing climate. Selection criteria along the lines of those outlined in box 8-1 would encourage integrated, multidimensional planning.

Box 8-1. Sample Supplemental Evaluation Criteria for SIBs or SRFs Financing
Next-Generation Infrastructure[1]

Eligible project sponsors

Departments; agencies; commissions; towns; cities; counties; nonprofit corporations formed on behalf of an applicant; special districts; assessment districts; joint powers authorities within the state; and any combination of these categories.

Project types

Streets; state and county highways; drainage, water-supply, and flood-control facilities; ports; parks and recreational facilities; power and communications facilities; public transit; sewage-collection and treatment facilities; solid-waste collection and disposal facilities; and other publicly occupied facilities affiliated with these systems.

Supplementary scoring criteria for prioritizing projects

Beyond threshold eligibility, including economic need and financial economic feasibility, projects shall provide a full life-cycle cost analysis (LCCA), including project agency and user costs. Assessments are also to include, to the extent possible, identification and valuation of major negative externalities as well as the environmental and social co-benefits attributable to the project. Infrastructure projects shall be evaluated and accorded funding priority over single-purposed or conventionally designed infrastructure facilities and according to their fulfill-ment of the following supplementary criteria. Specifically, they shall:

Support mixed land use

- Mixed use of property by two or more project types (as listed above).
- Shared use of roads, operation, and maintenance facilities and utilities.
- Use of (1) previously urbanized property, preferably brownfields; (2) vacant or underutilized urban or suburban land; (3) land immediately adjacent to developed property.

Reduce energy and greenhouse-gas emissions

- Designs that promote operational energy efficiency and/or conservation.
- Reduced energy demand through partial, on-site production of green power; purchase of green power to offset use of electrical grid; connection to other sources of distributed power; and/or utilization of exergy; or,
- Energy produced by local waste-to-energy process or procured from anaerobic digestion of organic waste or wastewater (biogas).
- Priority given to grouped and/or conjoined projects that reduce energy use and environmental impacts through the recovery and exchange of waste, wastewater, or waste heat.

Inclusion of green infrastructure

- Systems planned in accordance with integrated water-resource management programs.
- On-site water harvesting, retention, and/or treatment for reuse or for direct infiltration.
- Reduction of potable water use and substitution of stormwater or gray water for cooling and other non-potable uses.
- Reliance on green infrastructure measures to eliminate stormwater runoff.
- Measures reducing energy demand and/or chemical use for water treatment and distribution.

Social and/or economic benefits

- Improved quality of life, attractiveness, and long-term economic competitiveness for the community.
- Full environmental remediation and mitigation of site and environs.
- Job creation and/or community employment per dollar of financing.
- Inclusion of community facilities or other new educational, cultural, or recreational uses that provide local jobs.
- Provision of quality-of-life measures and/or community amenities.

Climate adaptation measures

- Incorporation of place-based measures to achieve resilience for facilities exposed to extreme weather events, or sited in climate-sensitive areas (e.g., coastlines, rivers, storm tracks), with priority given to soft infrastructure.
- Inclusion of safeguards (e.g., redundancy) to reduce cross-sectoral cascading failures.
- Provisions for water harvesting, storage, cleaning, and beneficial reuse.
- Integrated water capture, storage, use, and reuse.

---

1. Some language is in part adapted from "Criteria, Priorities, and Guidelines for the Infrastructure State Revolving Fund (ISRF) Program," report of the California Infrastructure and Economic Development Bank (Board-Approved Criteria dated January 29, 2008).

Another means to the same end would put forward-looking evaluation criteria in the hands of an independent body, such as a state-level infrastructure commission tasked with reviewing— or encouraging—multipronged capital endeavors. A number of commissions or committees— some, for instance, legislatively mandated, others executive-appointed, and still others in the form of blue-ribbon panels—have already been charged with state or local strategic decision making with regard to infrastructure investment. Examples include the Special Public-Private Infrastructure Commission established by the Commonwealth of Massachusetts; New York State's 2100 Commission, which targets statewide resilience measures; the Infrastructure Committee created by Marathon County, Wisconsin; and San Francisco's Commission on Community Investment and Infrastructure (one of two committees that replaced the city's redevelopment agency).

Ideally, an infrastructure commission would be made up of nonpartisan, appointed or elected experts authorized to foster and coordinate cross-sector projects and link them to a state or local financing system. The commission would include representatives from state agencies or local government departments (e.g., energy, water services, environmental protection, transportation, parks) as well as regulatory, private-sector, and nongovernmental members. Their role would be broad: overall policy making, the establishment of performance metrics for desired outcomes, review of capital-improvements programs, approval of the design of large projects, and possibly also troubleshooting and general oversight (see box 8-2).

Box 8-2. Proposed State (or Large City) Infrastructure Commission: Roles and Responsibilities

- Advocate for and work to develop cross-sector infrastructural improvements that (1) link energy, water, wastewater, waste, and transportation; (2) offer co-benefits; and (3) include complementary utilities, industries, or businesses.
- Help accelerate planning and financing for interlinked, multi-sector projects by highlighting potential revenue from the combination of functions (e.g., recovered energy, water, or nutrients).
- Promote best practices in integrated infrastructure development through advocacy and outreach, providing advisory technical expertise as necessary.
- Work with zoning or other regulatory authorities to facilitate amendments or variances that will support the development of multifunctional infrastructural facilities.
- Serve as broker and facilitator, helping to connect state and local authorities, service providers, regulators, consumers, and other stakeholders to the state bank's private investors and equity owners.
- Encourage the sharing of capital costs by arranging blended state (or city) funds from capital programs for transportation, roads, streets and highways, wastewater, energy, water, and parks departments.
- Ensure long-term engagement with stakeholders in affected communities and regions.
- Develop performance metrics that incorporate internal efficiencies, energy cascades, resource recycling, land-use intensity, and other value-added environmental and social benefits of colocation.
- Coordinate interstate initiatives with peer infrastructure commissions.
- Partner with public or private academic institutions undertaking research in new technologies.
- Help leverage private investment.

Policies and Tools for Next-Generation Infrastructure

States and local governments can muster the political will and funding to circumvent federal paralysis by implementing creative enabling programs such as those in Chicago, California, and Oklahoma. Working with existing infrastructure banks, revolving funds, or nonprofit trusts (or creating new ones), governors and state legislators, local executives and governing boards, agency or department heads, development authorities, nongovernmental organizations, developers, and public or private utility providers can begin to broker ambitious projects, encouraging the various infrastructure sectors to think more horizontally and collaboratively toward making future-proofing a "value-added" new norm. The following five sections examine each of the principles in turn, highlighting some current approaches, along with programs and tools that are helping to advance next-generation infrastructure.

Foster Inter-departmental Planning for Combined Projects

State and local governments, working with utility partners, can use their land-use authority to support infrastructural clustering. In practical terms, this may mean, at the state level, the designation of economic-development districts, or at the local level, undertaking zoning changes so that both industrial and commercial zones can accommodate infrastructural mixed use, or amalgamated utilities. As a hypothetical example, such an assemblage would include: (1) distributed energy cogeneration, conjoined with (2) decentralized storm and/or wastewater treatment, and (3) organic- and solid-waste-handling facilities, allowing for heat recovery, biogas production, and water reuse along with other by-product capture for revenue production. The same locale might even support a bus or truck depot, incorporating biogas refueling in the same location (per the example from Lille, France). If such a development were sited on a brownfield, it might be able to capitalize on funding from city or state supplemental brownfields RLFs or the federal Environmental Protection Agency's Brownfields Area-Wide Planning Pilot Programs or Multi-Purpose Pilot Grants). Local governments partnered with innovative utilities can foster the redevelopment of brownfields or dead malls (dated, deserted, or largely vacant shopping centers) as eco-infrastructural parks—sites that can host distributed infrastructure facilities, along with tenants that could contribute to or make use of resources generated on-site.

State- and local-government sustainability plans are ideal frameworks for considering the capital programs of various infrastructure sectors in tandem, in order to identify opportunities to cluster or coordinate construction, upgrades, or expansions. Sustainability and climate-action plans—such as New York City's PlaNYC 2030, Santa Monica's 15x15 Climate Action Plan, and the 2015 Sustainable Chicago Action Agenda—provide both the necessary vision and the integrated environmental, economic, and social frameworks with which to realize infrastructural clustering.

The EcoDistrict model, which was developed by the Portland State Institute for Sustainable Solutions, suggests governance and financing frameworks under which local government, utilities, developers, and others can jointly undertake complex, district-scale infrastructure improvements.[31] Successful pilots have been conducted in Denver, Portland (Oregon), and Seattle. Denver's Living City Block, for example, is a consortium of otherwise unrelated residential and commercial building owners that undertakes infrastructure upgrades, including renewable and energy-efficiency improvements, in lower downtown.[32]

Scale Up Green Power at the State and Local Levels

The move toward lower-carbon power generation, green power purchasing, and distributed energy production will demand levels of political, socioeconomic, and technological transformation that are certain to prove challenging for many individuals, corporations, and even elected officials in the United States. Nonetheless, many Fortune 500 entities, state and local government administrations, and American voters see such a shift as inevitable if the nation's long-term energy security and green job prospects are to improve, and as private entrepreneurship and technology gains help proliferate investments in green power.[33] As early adopters of policies and technical strategies designed to support decarbonization, state and local governments may continue to be the principal actors in a major societal shift.

States already offer fiscal incentives to support the low-carbon energy market, primarily through the adoption of Renewable Portfolio Standards. As of 2012 these obligatory targets ranged from roughly 10 percent by 2015 in North Dakota and South Dakota, to 30 percent by 2030 in California.[34] In addition, states have worked to lower barriers to implementing carbon reductions; net metering, which allows electricity customers to generate renewable energy and offset their consumption, is controlled by state public utility commissions, as are interconnection policies, which specify the technical safety requirements for grid-connected, distributed generation systems. Net metering has been adopted by 45 states and interconnection policies have been adopted in 44 states and Washington, D.C.[35]

States can help level the playing field for renewable-energy generation through carbon-reduction targets and green-power policies—initiatives that are not being undertaken at the federal level. Between 2002 and 2008 the US government awarded the fossil-fuel industry more than $72 billion in subsidies, whereas federal investments in the renewable-energy industry totaled a mere $12.2 billion.[36] While federal subsidies to the fossil-fuel industry are unlikely to be phased out, states can exert leverage through policies that factor in the full social and environmental benefits of clean power. One such lever is carbon credits (also known as carbon offsets). In October 2012, California legislators established the first cap-and-trade program in the United States—which may be the world's second largest after the EU. Under the program, the state grants and then auctions off carbon allowances or carbon credits to emitters. Proceeds from these sales, projected to be $10 billion by 2016, will be invested in infrastructure that further reduces greenhouse-gas emissions.[37]

Additional policy initiatives are needed to provide higher rewards to distributed providers of clean power. In Europe, one of the reigning policy mechanisms is the feed-in tariff (FIT), a premium that utilities pay for renewable power production that (1) reflects the value of the avoided environmental costs otherwise incurred by the use of fossil fuel, (2) eliminates the uncertainties of power-purchase agreements (fluctuations in prices in a deregulated market), and (3) renders renewable-energy projects much more financially feasible.[38] FITs have so far been deployed in a handful of US jurisdictions. Among the dozen-plus states that use them are California, which led the way in 2006; Hawaii and Vermont, both of which implemented FITs in 2009; and Oregon, which implemented FITs in

2010. Among the municipalities that have established FITs are Gainesville, Florida, and Sacramento, California.

States can also use their authority to designate zones or districts as sites for advanced energy projects.[39] Significant examples include energy improvement districts (EIDs), which are based on the model of business improvement districts (BIDs). Like BIDs, EIDS (which are also known as "neighborhood energy partnerships") consist of a number of participants forming a legal entity. But whereas BIDs engage in aesthetic and infrastructural improvements, EIDs finance and administer their own local energy-generation resources—issuing bonds and installing privately owned distribution lines to serve their members. In 2007, Connecticut passed enabling legislation for EIDs that use distributed systems and combined heat and power.[40]

Another applicable policy mechanism, legislated in four states so far, is Community Choice Aggregation (CCA), which permits the creation of limited service areas—classes of customers that might even include groups of municipalities and counties—that generate their own renewable power but distribute it through conventional means.[41]

The Connecticut Clean Energy Financing and Investment Authority (CEFIA), the country's first clean-energy funding authority, is an important PPP model with the potential to support cross-sector infrastructural initiatives. A quasi-public funding entity created to scale up renewable and clean energy across the state by leveraging public and private funds, CEFIA was established in July 2011 through a $1.25-million award from the American Recovery and Reinvestment Act of 2009.[42] Through innovative financing tools, surcharges on electric bills, and private investments, CEFIA underwrites the development of new technologies and assists with project financing. As a program, it reduces reliance on grants, rebates, etc. Such a model could be used to support the types of infrastructural ecologies examined in this book, such as anaerobic digesters for energy production and combined heat and power systems.

Most important, other states could utilize the CEFIA model in combination with their infrastructure banks, SRFs, or other existing grant programs to leverage greater capital investment.[43] Given that federal clean energy policies and programs are currently in a holding pattern or are actively retrenching, the CEFIA model is a useful means of addressing funding gaps, particularly in light of state and local budgetary constraints.

Local governments can also make headway by implementing low-carbon district energy reliance on grid-connected renewable systems. In Minnesota, the nonprofit District Energy St. Paul, launched as a demonstration project in 1983 to meet the needs of the downtown business community, today operates a 1.2 MW (thermal equivalent) system that heats 185 buildings and cools 100. It operates a locally resourced, biomass-fueled cogeneration plant and in 2011 added one of the nation's largest solar hot-water systems.[44]

Despite progress, low- or no-carbon energy sources still face an uneven playing field. One way to address this inequity is to require that pro forma cost analyses reflect the many benefits of low- or no-carbon generation. Generally speaking, distributed generation reduces externalities by, for example, reducing transmission losses and decreasing the need for expensive and "dirtier" peak-load generation (older plants usually brought on line last to cover peaks). More-innovative and comprehensive policies for the evaluation of infrastructure proposals would monetize such benefits, revealing the lower costs associated with low- and no-carbon energy sources and thereby helping to break through market barriers.

Promote Soft-Path Synergies for Water Infrastructure

Soft-path approaches to water collection, storage, treatment, and use are typified by distributed, nonstructural, integrated mechanisms that augment centralized storm- and wastewater-treatment facilities and may even reduce the need for their expansion. Such projects continue to demonstrate lower first costs and maintenance costs, while increasing resilience, providing ecological restoration, and offering numerous civic benefits. Finally, soft-path infrastructure can be coterminous with forests, wetlands, parks, recreation areas, and scenic territories.

Given their abundant advantages, soft-path projects may well become the linchpin of local infrastructural investment. In light of entrenched preferences for hard-path, industrial-era approaches, however, the transition demands overcoming numerous barriers: the various agencies involved in water are often separated by bureaucratic silos; the applicable codes and ordinances tend to be fragmented;[45] funding and regulation of water-related projects is segmented; there is a bias, within the engineering field, against decentralization; and finally, the public is generally unaware of the characteristics and positive potential of soft-path solutions.

With the assistance of federal grants distributed by EPA, local governments construct, operate, and maintain approximately 95 percent of the country's water-infrastructure networks.[46] In fiscal year 2012, EPA awarded $1.5 billion to the Clean Water State Revolving Fund (CWSRF) program and $918 million to the Drinking Water State Revolving Fund.[47] Much of that funding, however, has been dedicated to hard-path public works. A national commitment to soft-path approaches—through subsidies, loan guarantees, and other mechanisms, such as mandatory life-cycle and external cost-benefit analyses—could help reverse this bias. If, for example, soft-path approaches like those used in New York City's upstate watershed-protection programs were more the rule than the exception, localities could avert further investments in hard-path water-filtration treatment.

Most of the soft-path innovations described in chapter 4 overcame regulatory obstacles and cobbled together funding from various sources through a combination of citizen advocacy and local leadership. But ultimately, barriers to soft-path, municipal-scale innovations cannot be overcome without federal guidance and assistance—including both funding and the development of model codes that will permit cross-sector integration and foster the use of alternative and distributed technologies.[48] The federal government could strengthen support for local, soft-path approaches using financial incentives within its subsidy programs such as EPA's CWSRF, as well as through other water-related subsidy programs administered by the US Departments of Agriculture and Housing and Urban Development.[49] In 2009, for example, under EPA's CWSRF, $800 million in the American Recovery and Reinvestment Act funds was set aside for the Green Project Reserve to support more than 50 projects incorporating decentralized wastewater systems.[50]

In May 2012, the US Senate approved the Water Protection and Reinvestment Act of 2012 (HR6249). Modeled closely on the Transportation Infrastructure Financing Innovations Authority (TIFIA), HR6249 is a deficit-neutral program that would rely on the assessment of small water fees to reduce interest rates and thereby supplement SRF loans. Eligible soft-path projects would include community water systems; protection of groundwater and surface sources; implementation of water-efficient, energy-efficient, and renewable generation technologies; and wastewater and stormwater reuse and control. At the time of writing, the bill was referred to subcommittee for the House of Representatives' consideration.[51]

Building institutional capacity for soft-path approaches will require changes in state and local regulations. For example, changes to planning, zoning, and building codes can be devised to support the incorporation of natural hydrologic functions into land uses. Such instruments can also foster projects that combine water infrastructure with energy, transportation, or waste infrastructure, or that promote resource sharing (cascading) between energy and water infrastructure (e.g., the recovery of heat and energy from the organic wastes in wastewater). A more unified permitting system would overcome the bureaucratic silos that inhibit integration.[52] Aided by federal research and through the funding of programs such as the National Community Decentralized Wastewater Demonstration Project,[53] states and localities could eventually develop more performance- and context-based codes, as opposed to prescriptive requirements for filtration, stormwater, and sanitary wastewater treatment.[54]

Local elected and appointed officials can sponsor inter-agency and multi-stakeholder coordination of capital improvements, so that investments in water infrastructure can be combined with those from other sectors in order to maximize public benefits and improve land values. To support the inclusion of ecosystem enhancements as part of infrastructure projects at the capital-programming level, planning and budgeting policies can be designed to monetize the benefits associated with ecological systems such as environmental restoration and improvements in public health, job creation, and scenic value. Many federally sponsored grants, loans, and other payment programs already allow such quantification of benefits.[55]

There are signs that some of these advances could soon be under way. In the Water Environment Federation's 2013 publication *The Water Resources Utility of the Future: A Blueprint for Action*, water-industry leaders foresee the water utility becoming "manager of valuable resources, a partner in local economic development, and a member of the watershed community seeking to deliver maximum environmental benefits at the least cost to society … by reclaiming and reusing water, extracting and finding commercial uses for nutrients and other constituents, capturing waste heat and latent energy in biosolids and liquid streams, generating renewable energy using its land and other horizontal assets, and using green infrastructure to manage stormwater . . . to improve urban quality of life more broadly."[56]

Site Community-Friendly Facilities Sensitively

Sensitized by a legacy of LULUs (locally unwanted land uses) in minority and low-income areas, an increasingly savvy public is attuned to the environmental, health, and property risks associated with the siting of infrastructure assets. Developers of next-generation facilities will need to empower local stakeholders, build public trust, address fair-share issues, and acknowledge special responsibilities to their host communities. In addition, developers must eliminate adverse effects and engage the community in ongoing monitoring. Finally, developers can facilitate shared use and foster the inclusion of collateral benefits. Taken together, such measures will help ensure that infrastructure assets are beneficially embedded in, and connected to, the communities and regions they serve.

The paramount challenge in facility siting is addressing the disparity between locally concentrated risk or harm, whether real or perceived, and the widely distributed advantages. A fair siting process achieves *distributive justice*—a balance between burdens and benefits.[57] In practical terms, distributive justice means that risks, responsibilities, and rewards are balanced in such a way that benefits to the host community outweigh adverse impacts.

In Canada, an innovative "open siting" policy approach for siting LULUs relies on a voluntary system: the government or utility proponent engages in broad outreach to potential host communities, detailing economic opportunities and outlining the environmental and public safety standards. Communities are then invited to offer their sites for evaluation, retaining the choice to opt out if selected. Once a site has been chosen, the proponent holds public referenda to obtain community input on design and to ensure community buy-in. Community representatives are included among the project managers and also participate in environmental monitoring. Among the benefits that host communities typically gain are a commitment to hire local workers and to engage in workforce-diversity practices.[58]

Community Benefits Agreements (CBAs) are another useful policy option. Developed in the late 1990s, CBAs are legally binding agreements negotiated by civil-society groups and public representatives or private interests in return for local acceptance of major public or private development projects. Prior to agreement negotiation, the public participates in a siting review, prioritizing local concerns. In addition to agreeing to engage in mitigation measures based on the best available technology, the developer then offers compensation packages that include benefits designed to offset any minor residual impacts.[59] Compensation may include property-value guarantees, local employment options, improved housing, and recreational or cultural facilities. Monitoring provisions are also included. The downside of CBAs is that they depend on community-wide organizing and strong leadership, neither of which may always be present. Moreover, legal services may be costly for a community to obtain. Finally, the validity of CBAs has not yet been fully tested in court.[60]

Chapter 5, "Destigmatizing Infrastructure," describes a number of infrastructure projects that incorporate innovative features such as recreational, educational, and community facilities. Such ancillary uses can in some cases catalyze community acceptance, and in other cases represent the outcome of negotiations. As a policy instrument, a mix of uses and good design can help dilute the stigma that might otherwise be associated with a complex.

The megacommunity, another emerging practice, is a self-governance model in which representatives from multiple stakeholder groups voluntarily come together to solve complex problems.[61] Because the control of a megacommunity is distributed, no one group or sector dominates; instead, the functioning of the group is grounded in a set of organizing principles that include diversity, adaptability, and an aspiration toward "convergence" of goals and objectives through proactive alignment of interests. The entire process is characterized by open communication and negotiated decision making—both of which work to optimize the whole, rather than just some of the parts. The megacommunity is thus an apt model for the development of complex, post-industrial infrastructure projects. The Bolivia-to-Brazil pipeline (chapter 5) is a good example of a megacommunity; however, the same term could also just as easily be applied to a number of other collaborative initiatives considered in the book: Hammarby Sjöstad (chapter 2), the Lolland Community Facility Testing Partnership, and the Minewater project (both chapter 3).

Overall, policy instruments such as CBAs, or megacommunities that foster trust, embody openness and transparency, limit risks to stakeholders, ensure informed consent, and provide negotiated compensation must be the new norm for infrastructure investments. Other instruments, yet to be invented, will need to foster greater proactive community participation, mobilize capacity for cross-sector coordination, and ensure the incorporation of value-added civic functions into infrastructural complexes.

Adapt to an Uncertain Future

Each hazard of climate instability—flooding, drought, temperature extremes, and increasingly frequent and intense storms and coastal surges—inevitably transcends jurisdictional, agency, and departmental boundaries. Moreover, the interdependence of infrastructural systems compounds risk: a single vulnerability can trigger cascading failures. Adaptation measures addressing climate change demand holistic approaches.

While planning and implementation must remain local, such efforts must occur within the framework of higher-order policy: a coherent set of federal planning objectives designed to work across all levels of government. Under mandates from the Interagency Climate Change Adaptation Task Force and the President's Council on Environmental Quality, federal agencies, for example, are already required to prepare adaption plans that could serve as templates for state and local government. Cross-jurisdictional consistency can generate a stable and predictable fiscal climate for investment in mitigation and adaptation measures.

While there may be voluntary design programs that begin to address resiliency,[62] other federal leadership is needed as well, in terms of national standards and codes, for the construction and operation of critical infrastructure. Since these have been developed on the basis of historical climate data, they are slow to change, and must be brought up to date using more-recent climate models.[63] A national climate service should be established to address the impacts of climate change; among other activities, such a service would supply geographically specific information for high-risk regions.[64] Canada, for instance, is using an asset management framework to update standards related to snow loads, permafrost, and drainage systems.[65]

Even in the absence of federal guidance, however, some significant planning work has already been undertaken. Since the mid-2000s, over 100 state, county, and municipal governments have drawn up climate-adaptation plans—either comprehensive or focused on single sectors. The plans feature short- and long-term resiliency strategies to address drought, urban water management, natural hazards, public health, rising shorelines, and other areas subject to climate change.[66] In keeping with the five axioms that form the framework of this book, however, state and local policies should capitalize on crosscutting issues by promoting integrated adaptation planning.

States can use financing policies to guide public and private utility owners to incorporate climate adaptation into their capital-asset planning frameworks. In addition to addressing costs, such frameworks should contain detailed asset inventories, including component life spans and maintenance and replacement cycles. Integrating climate adaptation into capital planning would allow facility upgrades to be integrated into an ongoing, carefully thought-out process. Priority should be assigned to cost-effective nonstructural solutions such as improved maintenance and new operating protocols.

State or local government policy makers must make holistic approaches to investment obligatory—through agency directives, in the course of negotiating PPPs, and through the criteria for access to revolving funds, grants, and loans. Programs should encourage adaptation initiatives that integrate "no-regrets" measures, as well as strategies with low or even no costs to taxpayers. As noted in chapters 6 and 7, no-regrets measures create short-term additional benefits even if long-term climate protection is never put to the test. Examples abound: reservoir expansion increases water supply while enabling the reservoir to serve as a retention system during flooding from major storms; green infrastructure provides urban cooling and beautification while mitigating carbon emissions; the structures of seawalls or dikes can accommodate railways, bikeways, or roads; and the infiltration of recycled water forms a barrier against saltwater intrusion while also amplifying domestic water resources.

Far-sighted state and local officials can advocate for cross-sector solutions by posing the right questions, approaching the right entrepreneurial partners, brokering co-development agreements, assembling financing, facilitating community input, and obtaining regulatory approvals. Without project champions, projects like wetlands wastewater treatment in Arcata, California; minewater district heating in Heerlen, Holland; biogas fuel in Lille, France; and the waste-transfer station / recycling center in Phoenix, Arizona, could not have been realized.

To develop integrated solutions, however, decision makers must increasingly rely on the skills of the design sector. The teams that are best equipped to offer bold, innovative responses will include architects, planners, and landscape architects; public health experts; civil, structural, mechanical, and electrical engineers; and ecologists and hydrologists, as well as members of a number of other subspecialties. Procurement criteria for design services (including long-term design-build-operate contracts) should (1) require broad-based professional collaborations and design joint ventures, and (2) be developed to require holistic solutions that achieve beneficial social, economic, and environmental outcomes.

Energy, water, waste-handling and transportation assets have long been the purview of engineering specialists. However, by incorporating the wide-ranging, integrative thinking idiomatic to architects, landscape architects, and planners, infrastructure developers can produce value-added outcomes. These design professionals may be more likely to perceive potential economies of scale, appreciate site context, and be sensitive to pattern and spatial relationships, all of which can yield opportunities for resource exchange. Designers are also trained to engage in integrative, complex problem solving that uses conceptual frameworks to produce formal and functional synthesis. They are especially adept at combining amenity with utility by envisioning opportunities for public, educational, or recreational space in unusual places. Finally, they are emboldened by opportunities for incongruous juxtaposition: Naka's "museum of garbage," the Amager Baake's snow-covered waste-to-energy plant, and Arcata's wildlife marshes and wastewater treatment are representative examples.

The practice of integrative, cross-disciplinary design transcends the siloed habits of the modernist paradigm. It favors collaborative, systems-based approaches that can leverage resources across jurisdictional boundaries. Two unusual proposals underscore this point. To create the Teatro del Agua (Water Theater), an outdoor performing-arts venue and desalination plant located in the abandoned industrial port area of Las Palmas, in Spain's Canary Islands, engineer Charlie Paton (inventor of the Seawater Greenhouse) and Grimshaw Architects (designers of the IJburg Bridge and the Croton Filtration Treatment Plant) teamed up. Their scaled-up and reshaped version of the Seawater Greenhouse desalination process is positioned to intercept the prevailing seawater-laden breezes. The captured air is conducted through solar-heated evaporators, then across deep, seawater-cooled pipes, allowing freshwater to condense. This huge network of evaporator and condenser cells is arranged like fish scales on a tall, arched armature. This arresting structure becomes the backdrop for a handsome outdoor civic space intended as a new performing arts venue (fig. 8-1).

A second example—which has not been implemented but which has inspired invaluable debate on adaptation measures—builds on insights gained from the Netherlands. Anticipating the storm surges of Hurricanes Irene and Sandy by half a decade, architects, landscape architects, and engineers under the Fellows of the American Institute of Architect's 2007 Latrobe Prize Fellowship envisioned alternative coastal protection measures that might be deployed throughout New York Harbor—specifically, a variety of soft-path, multifunctional

Figure 8-1. Rendering of proposed Teatro del Agua (Solar Desalination Plant and Amphitheater), Tenerife, Canary Islands, Spain (© Grimshaw Architects).

adaptations—including wetland parks, oyster beds, and other interventions designed to buttress the shoreline and absorb storm-surge energy (fig. 8-2). These concepts were further developed for "Rising Currents," a 2010 show at the Museum of Modern Art. In the curator's words, the exhibit succeeded in "catalyzing debate, raising the awareness of the issues of cli-

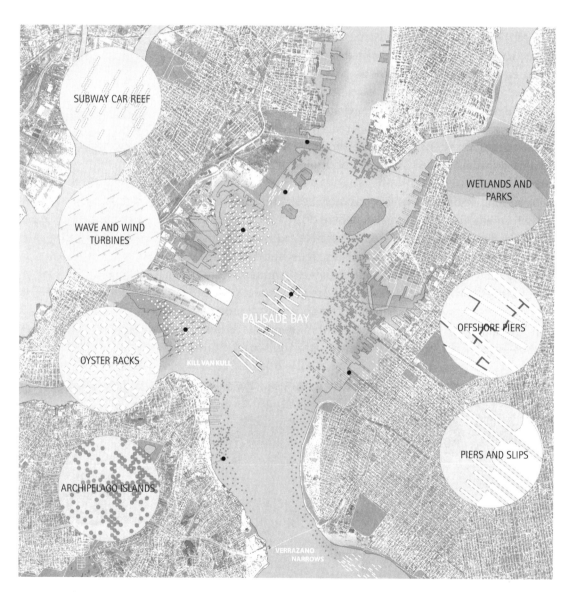

Figure 8-2. Proposed "Soft Infrastructure" for Palisade Bay in the New York Upper Harbor, from On the Water | Palisade Bay, Hatje Cantz Verlag, 2010 (© Guy Nordenson and Associates, Catherine Seavitt Studio, and Architecture Research Office).

mate change and rising sea levels, and, perhaps most importantly, elevating the role of design in tackling issues of climate change."[67]

The legacy of industrial-era infrastructure—one of independent, single-purpose assets, and "non-reimbursed," or one-way flows—must increasingly yield to post-industrial solutions modeled on the multidimensional, closed-loop exchanges characteristic of ecosystems. Over recent decades, urban planning has moved away from the modernist model in which activities were isolated by zone and facilities by use. In keeping with this effort, shouldn't public works begin to reconnect, network, and capitalize on the benefits of integrated energy, water, waste, and other services? Innovative hybrids, multifunctional complexes that are attuned to local contexts that renounce carbon, that regenerate natural systems, that are open to public occupation, and that anticipate future climates are prospective ways forward. America's infrastructure needs are dauntingly large, complex, and urgent. Ultimately, if we are to regain not only economic stability but also prosperity, if we are to remain a creative and competitive nation, we will need to demonstrate the capacity for holistic thinking and integrative action.

Notes

Chapter 1

1. National Transportation Safety Board, "Collapse of I-35W Highway Bridge / Minneapolis, Minnesota / August 1, 2007" (accident report, National Transportation Safety Board NTSB/HAR-08/03, Washington, DC, 2008), xiii, www.dot.state.mn.us/i35wbridge/ntsb/finalreport.pdf (accessed May 12, 2013).

2. Ibid., 22.

3. Ibid., 157.

4. Paul Hawken, Amory Lovins, and L. Hunter Lovins, *Natural Capitalism: Creating the Next Industrial Revolution* (Boston: Little, Brown and Company, 1999).

5. Felix Rohatyn, *Bold Endeavors: How Our Government Built America, and Why It Must Rebuild Now* (New York: Simon & Schuster, 2009).

6. The $3.6-trillion figure largely reflects a replacement-in-kind approach, a concept critiqued herein. See: American Society of Civil Engineers, "Report Card for America's Infrastructure," 2009 and 2013 (Reston, VA: ACSE, 2009), www.infrastructurereportcard.org/a/#p/overview/executive-summary (accessed May 11, 2013).

7. Keith Miller, Kristina Costa, and Donna Cooper, "Infographic: Drinking Water and Wastewater by the Numbers," Center for American Progress, October 11, 2012, www.americanprogress.org/issues/economy/news/2012/10/11/41256/infographic-drinking-water-and-u.swastewater-by-the-numbers/ (accessed June 13, 2012).

8. ASCE, "2013 Report Card for America's Infrastructure," 2, www.infrastructurereportcard.org/a/#p/drinking-water/investment-and-funding (accessed May 4, 2013).

9. ASCE, "2009 Report Card for America's Infrastructure," https://apps.asce.org/reportcard/2009/grades.cfm 58.

10. ASCE, "2013 Report Card for America's Infrastructure," www.infrastructurereportcard.org/a/#p/wastewater/conditions-and-capacity.

11. ASCE, "2013 Report Card for America's Infrastructure," www.infrastructurereportcard.org/a/#p/energy/conditions-and-capacity.

12. The Brattle Group, "Transforming America's Power Industry: The Investment Challenge 2010–2030" (2008), www.brattle.com/_documents/uploadlibrary/upload725.pdf (accessed February 12, 2013).

13. Center for American Progress analysis of FHWA data reported in: Federal Highway Administration, *2008 Status of the Nation's Highways, Bridges, and Transit*. Estimates are in 2006 dollars.

14. ASCE, "2013 Infrastructure Report Card," www.infrastructurereportcard.org/a/#p/bridges/conditions-and-capacity.

15. Last updated in 2001. See: US General Accounting Office (now Government Accountability Office), "U.S. Infrastructure: Funding Trends and Federal Agencies' Investment Estimates," GAO-01-986T (testimony before the Subcommittee on Transportation and Infrastructure, Committee on Environment and Public Works, US Senate, Washington, DC, July 2001).

16. Benjamin Tal, "Capitalizing on the Upcoming Infrastructure Stimulus," CIBC World Markets Inc., Occasional Report #66, January 26, 2009, http://research.cibcwm.com/economic_public/download/occrept66.pdf (accessed July 12, 2012).

17. Urban Land Institute and Ernst & Young, "Infrastructure 2009: A Global Perspective" (Washington, DC: Urban Land Institute, 2009), 15. The discrepancy between US and EU infrastructure spending can be partly explained by the EU's tradition of tax-based public spending, which leverages private-sector capacity to build highways, schools, waterworks, and other civil structures.

18. Peter Baker and John Schwartz, "Obama Pushes Plan to Build Roads and Bridges," *New York Times*, March 29, 2013.

19. Ecosystem services have been divided into: provisioning services such as food, fuel, and fiberwood products; regulating services such as climate regulation, disease regulation, and pollination; and cultural services such as education, recreation, and tourism.

20. Steven M. Rinaldi, James P. Peerenboom, and Terrence K. Kelly, "Critical Infrastructure Interdependencies," *IEEE Control Systems*, December 2010, 13.

21. Ibid., 14.

22. Paul N. Edwards, "Infrastructure and Modernity: Force, Time, and Social Organization in the History of Sociotechnical Systems," in *Modernity and Technology*, ed. Thomas J. Misa, Philip Brey, and Andrew Feenberg (Cambridge: MIT Press, 2003), 193.

23. David Holmgren, *Permaculture Principles and Pathways Beyond Sustainability* (Holmgren Design Services, 2002), 165.

24. Teresa Domenech and Michael Davies, "Structure and Morphology of Industrial Symbiosis Networks: The Case of Kalundborg," *Procedia Social and Behavioral Sciences* 10 (2011): 79–89.

25. Rinaldi et al., 11.

26. T. D. O'Rourke, "Critical Infrastructure, Interdependencies, and Resilience," *The Bridge—National Academy of Engineering*, no. 1 (Spring, 2007): 23.

27. "Drought Blamed for Blackout in Ecuador," *Latin American Herald Tribune*, November 19, 2009, www.laht.com/article.asp?ArticleId=347191&CategoryId=14089 (accessed February 13, 2011).

28. Melissa Bailey and Paul Bass, "You Can Drink the Water," *New Haven Independent*, July 7, 2010, www.newhavenindependent.org/index.php/archives/entry/dirty_water_alert/ (accessed February 14, 2011).

29. US Energy Information Administration, "Energy in Brief, 2011," www.eia.gov/energy_in_brief/article/major_energy_sources_and_users.cfm (accessed February 13, 2011).

30. US Energy Information Administration, "U.S. Energy-Related Carbon Dioxide Emissions, 2011," www.eia.gov/environment/emissions/carbon/ (accessed February 13, 2011).

31. World Wide Fund for Nature (WWF) and Booz & Company, "Reinventing the City: Three Prerequisites for Greening Urban Infrastructures," 2010, 1, http://awsassets.panda.org/downloads/wwf_low_carbon_cities_final_2012.pdf (accessed March, 10, 2011).

32. Ibid.

33. Holmgren, 156.

Chapter 2

1. "SMART (Stormwater Management and Road Tunnel), Kuala Lumpur, Malaysia," *Road Traffic-Technology*, www.road traffic-technology.com/projects/smart/ (accessed January 12, 2013).

2. United Nations Development Pro-gramme, "Kuala Lumpur, Malaysia, Case Study (Mixed Use Tunnel)," November 2012, www.esc-pau.fr/ppp/documents/featured_projects/malaysia_kuala_lumpur.pdf (accessed January 11, 2013).

3. Ibid., 28.

4. Gusztav Kados and Yeoh Hin Kok, "Stormwater Management and Road Tunnel (SMART)," in *Underground Space—The 4th Dimension of Metropo-lises*, ed. Jiri Barkak, Ivan Hrdina, Georgij Romancov, and Jaromir Zlamal (London: Taylor & Francis Group, 2007), 1183.

5. Since 1989 the United Nations Human Settlements Programme has been acknowledging "initiatives which have made outstanding contributions in various fields such as shelter provision, highlighting the plight of the homeless, leadership in post-conflict reconstruc-tion, and developing and improving the human settlements and the quality of urban life." See: UN-Habitat, "UN-Hab-itat Announces Scroll of Honour Call for Applications," July 17, 2012, www.unhabitat.org.

6. The plant is described in greater detail in chapter 5.

7. In New York City, street cuts, or trench-ing to access utilities in a typical right-of-way, average 12 times annually. By increasing the number of players, utility deregulation has only exacerbated the problem. See: American Public Works Association, "Locations of Utilities in Public Rights-of-Way: Examples from Various Cities" (paper presented at Utilities & Public Right-of-Way Commit-tee Summit, Atlanta, GA, February 29, 2000).

8. Arthur R. McDonald, "Success in the Trenches," *Transmission and Distribution World*, December 2001, http://tdworld.com/mag/power_success_trenches/ (accessed September 20, 2010).

9. Sandy Mitchell, "Prince Charles Is Not Your Typical Radical," *National Geo-graphic*, May 2006, http://ngm.national geographic.com/features/world/europe/england/cornwall-text/1 (accessed September 20, 2010).

10. "State-of-the-Art Infrastructure in Place at Marina Bay" (press release, Urban Redevelopment Authority of Singapore June 16, 2006), www.ura.gov.sg/pr/text/pro6-40.html (accessed February 2, 2011).

11. Solarius.com, "Disney's Magic Kingdom Utilidors Map," November 2007, www. solarius.com/dvp/wdw/mk-tunnels-large.htm.

12. Taipei Municipal Rapid Transit Newsletter No. 247 (interim report, January 2008; Web version 105, March 2012).

13. Thomas Nordmann and Luzi Clavadetscher, "PV on Noise Barriers," *Progress in Photovoltaics: Research and Applications* 12, no. 6 (September 2004): 494–95.

14. FAR Systems, "Noise Barriers with Photovoltaic Panels: Energy That Makes No Noise," Barriera A22 (installation description), www.barrierafotovoltaica. it/index.php/en/-barriera-a22 (accessed February 11, 2011).

15. Ibid., 128.

16. H. K. V. Lotsch, Adolf Goetzberger, and Volker U. Hoffman, *Photovoltaic Solar Energy Generation* (Springer Series in Optical Sciences, vol. 112, 2005), 127.

17. The World Bank, "Jamuna Bridge—A Boost for Bangladesh's Economy," World Bank—Transport in South Asia, http://go.worldbank.org/I4JRJD65V0 (accessed September 24, 2010).

18. Construction of the 4.8 km-long bridge was supported by the World Bank together with the Asian Development Bank, Japan's OECF, and the government of Bangladesh and, according to the World Bank, includes measures to mitigate the project's environmental impacts, including resettlement, compensation of project-affected persons, fisheries, and wildlife, and environmental monitoring. See: www.worldbank. org/projects/P009509/jamuna-bridge?lang=en.

19. "Forecasting Wind Data from Cell Phone Towers," *Alternative Energy News*, November 30, 2010, www. alternative-energy-news.info/forecast-wind-data-cell-phone-towers (accessed April 21, 2011). See also: www.onsemble. ws/.

20. H. Koch, G. Ottenhenning, and E. Zochling, "Improving the Physical Security and Availability of Substations by Using New Switchgear Concepts" (paper presented at Power Engineering Society General Meeting, IEEE, vol. 2, June 12–16, 2005), 1145, 1148, doi: 10.1109/ PES.2005.1489265.

21. Jafar Taghavi and Keith Tieszen. "Anaheim Park's Substation Hidden Within." *Transmission and Distribution World* (Penton Business Media, April 2007), www.anaheim.net/utilities/IMAGES/ ParkSubinTDWorld.pdf (accessed July 12, 2012).

22. Ward Pincus, "GIS Substations That Embellish, Not Blemish the Urban Streetscape," *Living Energy* (Siemens publication, no. 1, November 2009), 55, www.energy.siemens.com/us/pool/hq/ energy-topics/livingenergy/downloads/ Social_acceptance_substations_that_ embelish.pdf (accessed January 2011).

23. Ibid., 56.

24. Hope Cohen, "The Neighborly Substation: Electricity, Zoning, and Urban Design" (white paper, Manhattan Institute, Center for Rethinking Development, December 2008), 12, www. policyarchive.org/handle/10207/ bitstreams/14677.pdf (accessed February 6, 2011).

25. Cohen, 17.

26. Taghavi and Tieszen.

27. Sustainable Energy Australia (SEA), "Wind Farm Basics," May 2004, www.synergy-wind.com/BP1_Basics.pdf.

28. Matthew Brower, "Agricultural Impacts Resulting from Wind Farm Construction," New York State Department of Agriculture and Markets for NYSERDA, 2005.

29. Windustry, "Minwind III–IX, Luverne, MN: Community Wind Project," www.windustry.org/minwind-iii-ix-luverne-mn-community-wind-project (accessed February 20, 2011).

30. Alinta Energy, "Alinta Wind Farm Fact Sheet," www.docstoc.com/docs/5317344/Alinta-Wind-Farm-fact-sheet-The-Alinta-Wind-Farm (accessed February 2, 2011).

31. Sustainable Energy Australia (SEA), "The Compatability of Wind Farming with Traditional Farming in Australia," May 2004, 6–8, http://www.w-wind.com.au/downloads/CBP9_Traditional.pdf (accessed March 1, 2012).

32. Alexandre Filgueiras and Thelma Maria V. e Silva, "Wind Energy in Brazil—Present and Future," Renewable & Sustainable Energy Reviews 7, no. 5 (October 2003): 439–51.

33. Offshore-Wind Energie, "Wind Farms," Germany's Federal Ministry for the Environment, Nature Conservation, and Nuclear Safety, www.offshore-windenergie.net/en/wind-farms (accessed November 24, 2013).

34. Alfred Wegener Institute for Polar and Marine Research, "Marine Aquaculture, Maritime Technologies and ICZM," www.awi.de/en/go/aquaculture (accessed March 3, 2012).

35. T. Michler-Cieluch, G. Krause, and B. H. Buck, "Reflections on Integrating Operation and Maintenance Activities of Offshore Wind Farms and Mariculture," Ocean & Coastal Management 52, no. 1 (January 2009).

36. Shari Blalock, "Purafil ESD Eliminates Wastewater Odors in Barcelona, Spain," Journal AWWA 99, no. 9 (September 2007): 108–10.

37. Dennis Rondinelli and Michael Berry, "Multimodal Transportation, Logistics, and the Environment," European Management Journal 18, no. 4 (2000): 398–410.

38. Ibid.

39. US Department of Transportation, National Commission on Intermodal Transportation, Toward a National Intermodal Transportation System—Final Report (Washington, DC: USDOT, September 1994), http://ntl.bts.gov/DOCS/325TAN.html.

40. City of Raleigh, NC, "Union Station: Raleigh's Multimodal Transit Center," www.raleighnc.gov/projects/content/PlanUrbanDesign/Articles/Union Station.html (accessed November 20, 2013). See also: North Carolina Department of Transportation website, www.ncdot.gov/projects/raleighunion station/.

41. Congresswoman Nancy Pelosi at the August 10, 2010, ground-breaking ceremony for San Francisco Intermodal Transportation Facility, http://abclocal.go.com/kgo/story?section=news/local/san_francisco&id=7604826 (accessed August 14, 2010).

42. Ibid.

43. Transbay Transit Center, "Economic Benefits," http://transbaycenter.org/project/transit-center/economic-benefits (accessed December 31, 2010). See also: San Francisco Redevelopment Agency, "Redevelopment Plan for the Transbay Project Redevelopment Area," Ordinance No. 124-05, June 21, 2005, and Ordinance No. 99-06, May 9, 2006.

44. *Intermodal Surface Transportation Efficiency Act of 1991*, HR 2950, 102nd Congress, 1st session (Washington DC: January 3, 1991).

45. San Francisco Redevelopment Agency, "Redevelopment Plan for the Transbay Redevelopment Project Area," adopted June 21, 2005. See: www.sfredevelopment.org/index.aspx?page=54.

46. See: Transbay Transit Center website, http://transbaycenter.org/.

47. The TJPA was created in 2001 by the City and County of San Fancisco, the Alameda–Contra Costa County Transit District and the Peninsula Corridor Joint Powers Board.

48. Data centers are estimated to represent 1 percent or more of world energy use. See: Tarmo Virki, "Cloud Computing Goes Green Underground in Finland," Reuters, November 29, 2009, www.reuters.com/article/2009/11/30/idUSGEE5AS01D20091130.

49. Bobbie Johnson, "Web Providers Must Limit Internet's Carbon Footprint, Say Experts," *Guardian*, May 3, 2009, www.guardian.co.uk/technology/2009/may/03/internet-carbon-footprint.

50. US Environmental Protection Agency, ENERGY STAR Program, *Report to Congress on Server and Data Center Energy Efficiency*, EPA response to Public Law 109-431, August 2007.

51. Cavern Technologies, "Green Solutions," www.caverntechnologies.com/why-cavern/green-solutions.

52. Jeffrey Burt, "HP Touts 4 Green Data Centers," *eWeek*, October 14, 2009. www.eweek.com/c/a/Green-IT/HP-Touts-Four-Green-Data-Centers-426947/1/ (accessed October 2, 2010).

53. Juha Sipilä, Helsingin Energia, "The World's Most Eco-Efficient Data Center" (presentation for Uptime Institute Symposium, New York, May 2010), www.helen.fi/pdf/Uptime_Institute_presentation.pdf, accessed October 2, 2010.

54. Ratnesh Sharma et al., "Design of Farm Waste-Driven Supply Side Infrastructure," Hewlett-Packard Laboratories (presented at ASME 2010 4th International Conference on Energy Sustainability ES2010, Phoenix, May 17–22, 2010).

55. Robert McMillan, "Microsoft to Power Data Center with Sewage-Sourced Methane," *Wired*, November 20, 2012, www.wired.co.uk/news/archive/2012-11/20/microsoft-powers-data-centre-with-sewage.

56. Wolfgang Unterberger, Hans Hofinger, and Thomas Grünstäudl, "Utilization of Tunnels as Sources of Ground Heat and Cooling—Practical Applications in Austria," iC Group of Companies website, www.ic-group.org/uploads/media/TunnelsGroundHeat_en.pdf (accessed February 11, 2011).

57. A heat pump is a device that warms or cools a building by transferring heat from a relatively low-temperature reservoir to one having a higher temperature.

58. Gaby Ochsenbein, "Alpine Caviar and Papayas Come to Switzerland," *Swissinfo*, January 1, 2009, www. swissinfo.ch/eng/Home/Archive/ Alpine_caviar_and_papayas_come_ to_Switzerland.html?cid= 7127408 (accessed October 31, 2010).

59. Jonas R. Bylund, "Planning, Projects, Practice: A Human Geography of the Stockholm Local Investment Programme in Hammarby Sjöstad" (doctoral thesis, Stockholm University, 2006), 66.

60. Ibid., 77.

61. Hiroaki Suzuki et al., *Eco2 Cities: Ecological Cities as Economic Cities* (Washington, DC: World Bank Publications, 2010), 185–93.

62. CABE (Commissioner for Architecture and the Built Environment), "Hammarby Sjöstad, Stockholm, Sweden," case study, 2009, http:// webarchive.nationalarchives.gov. uk/20110118095356/http:/www.cabe. org.uk/case-studies/hammarby-sjostad (accessed August 22, 2013).

63. The main source of heating in Hammarby Sjöstad is district heating. Thirty-four percent of this heat comes from purified waste water, 47 percent from combustible household waste, and 16 percent from bio fuel (figures refer to 2002).

64. Suzuki et al., 187.

65. Successful measures achieved include annual reductions of: nonrenewable energy use (11,000 MW); CO_2 800 tonnes; NO 1,000 kg (2,204 lbs.); SO_2 2,400 kg (5,291 lbs.); phosphorus discharge to water, 1,500 kg (3.307 lbs.) and to air, 260 kg (573 lbs.).

66. Karolina Brick, "Follow-up of Environmental Impact in Hammarby Sjöstad— Sickla Udde, Sickla Kaj, Lugnet, and Proppen" (report summary, Grontmij AB, March 2008), www.hammarby sjostad.se/inenglish/pdf/Grontmij%20 Report%20eng.pdf (accessed January 4, 2011).

67. Suzuki et al., 21.

Chapter 3

1. Fred Pearce, "From Ocean to Ozone: Earth's Nine Life-Support Systems— Climate Change," *NewScientist*, February 24, 2010, www.newscientist.com/ article/dn18577-earths-nine-lifesupport-systems-climate-change.html.

2. US Department of Energy and US Environmental Protection Agency, *Guide to Purchasing Green Power* (Washington, DC, March 2010), 4, www.epa.gov/ greenpower/documents/purchasing _guide_for_web.pdf (accessed April 1, 2012).

3. Ibid., 2.

4. Shaoni Bhattacharya, "European Heat Wave Caused 35,000 Deaths," *NewScientist*, October 10, 2003, www. newscientist.com/article/dn4259- european-heatwave-caused- 35000-deaths.html (accessed April 22, 2012).

5. Lisa Song, "Heat Waves Putting Pressure of Nuclear Power's Outmoded Cooling Technologies," *InsideClimate News*, May 4, 2011, http://insideclimatenews.org/news/20110504/nuclear-power-water-climate-change-heat-cooling (accessed February 22, 2012).

6. "Officials Say Sandy Transport Damage in Billions," *WABC Eyewitness News*, December 6, 2012, http://abclocal.go.com/wabc/story?section=news/local/new_york&id=8911130.

7. US Environmental Protection Agency, "Sources of Greenhouse-Gas Emissions," EPA Climate Change, www.epa.gov/climatechange/ghgemissions/sources/electricity.html (accessed September 20, 2012).

8. US Energy Information Administration, "Most States Have Renewable Portfolio Standards," *Today in Energy*, February 3, 2012, www.eia.gov/todayinenergy/detail.cfm?id=4850.

9. Union of Concerned Scientists, "The Promise of Biomass: Clean Power and Fuel—If Handled Right," September 2012, www.ucsusa.org/assets/documents/clean_vehicles/Biomass-Resource-Assessment.pdf (accessed June 2, 2012).

10. Robert D. Perlack, Lynn L. Wright, Anthony F. Turhollow, and Robin L. Graham, "Biomass as Feedstock for a Bioenergy and Bioproducts Industry: The Technical Feasibility of a Billion-Ton Annual Supply" (research project of the US Department of Energy and the US Department of Agriculture, April, 2005), www.eere.energy.gov/biomass/publications.html (accessed April 24, 2011).

11. Union of Concerned Scientists, "How Biomass Energy Works," 2010, www.ucsusa.org/clean_energy/our-energy-choices/renewable-energy/how-biomass-energy-works.html (accessed July 24, 2012).

12. Sibel Korhaliller, "The UK's Biomass Energy Development Path," International Institute for Environment and Development, November 2010, 1.

13. The Mt. Poso Cogeneration Plant is owned and operated by Mt. Poso Cogeneration Company LLC, a 50-50 partnership of DTE energy Services, based in Michigan, and Macpherson Energy Corporation, based in California.

14. Mt. Poso Cogeneration Company website: www.mtposo.com (accessed April 12, 2012).

15. "Macpherson Energy Converts Mt. Poso Cogeneration Plant to Renewable Center," *Oil and Gas Observer*, November 17, 2010, www.oilandgasobserver.com/news/macpherson-energy-converts-mt-poso-cogeneration-plant-to-renewable-center-/000532 (accessed April 12, 2012).

16. Dave Hyams, Senior Vice President, Solem & Associates, Public Relations Manager for Mt. Poso, in conversation with author, April 16, 2012.

17. "Mt. Poso Cogeneration Company Completes Conversion of Power Plant from Coal to 100% Renewable Biofuel Energy," *Business Wire* (press release, February 22, 2012), www.businesswire.com/news/home/20120222006396/en/Mt.-Poso-Cogeneration-Company-Completes-Conversion-Power (accessed July 2, 2012).

18. Ibid.

19. Desmond Smith, "Strategy and Imple-mentation of Biomass Conversion at Mt. Poso," *Biomass Magazine*, January 2010, http://biomassmagazine.com/ articles/3380/strategy-and-implementation-of-biomass-conversion-at-mt.-poso (accessed July 2, 2012).

20. Ibid.

21. Nickolas J. Themelis, "An Overview of the Global Waste-to-Energy Industry," *Waste Management World*, review issue, July–August 2003.

22. Amy Quinton, "School to Tap Trash Dump's Methane for Energy," *All Things Considered*, National Public Radio, December 13, 2006.

23. Jody Record, "EcoLine Behind the Scenes," *University of New Hampshire Campus Journal*, October 28, 2009, http://unh.edu/news/campusjournal/ 2009/Oct/28ecoline.cfm (accessed March 12, 2011).

24. In 2010, Waste Management Inc. cur-rently has more than 110 landfill gas-to-energy facilities nationwide powering 400,000 homes every day and offset-ting almost two million tons of coal per year. See: "Landfill Gas to Energy," Waste Management, www.thinkgreen. com/landfill-gas-to-energy (accessed May 28, 2011).

25. With 20 times the global-warming potential of carbon dioxide, methane is considered a pollutant. According first to the Clean Air Act and then the EPA's Resource Conservation and Recovery Act, large landfills must control emis-sions in at least this minimal manner rather than release them to the atmosphere.

26. US Environmental Protection Agency, "Project Profile—University of New Hampshire EcoLine™ Cogeneration System," US EPA Landfill Methane Out-reach Program, 2010, http://epa.gov/ lmop/projects-candidates/profiles/ universityofnewhampshire.html (accessed July 12, 2012).

27. Ibid.

28. Ibid.

29. Sarah Lozanova and John Laumer, "UNH Taps Local Landfill for Energy," Waste Management: Think Green program, July 1, 2008, http://thinkgreen.com/ pointofview/?p=6 (accessed June 26, 2011).

30. Record, "EcoLine."

31. Deborah McDermott, "Landfill Gas Now Powering UNH," May 31, 2009, *Seacoast Online* http://info.nhpr.org/node/24918 (accessed June 16, 2011).

32. Gregory Meighan, "Eco-ceptional: EcoLine Wins EPA Project of the Year," *The New Hampshire*, February 4, 2010, www.tnhonline.com/eco-ceptional-1.1115428#.UaIbI5WTNmA.

33. Lozanova and Laumer, "UNH Taps Local Landfill."

34. US Environmental Protection Agency, "An Overview of Landfill Gas Energy in the United States," Landfill Methane Outreach Program, June 2012, www.epa. gov/lmop/documents/pdfs/overview. pdf (accessed June 21, 2012).

35. Recycling Works!, Sierra Club, and Inter-national Brotherhood of Teamsters, "The Danger of Corporate Landfill Gas-to-Energy Schemes and How to Fix It," 2010, www.teamster.org/sites/ teamster.org/files/6310GreenhouseGas

Reportrevisedlowres.pdf (accessed May 4, 2012).

36. Toby Sterling, "The Hague Announces Project to Warm 4,000 Houses Using Geothermal Heating," *Environmental News Network*, July 4, 2007.

37. Nuon and Capital Cooling, "Showcase of District Cooling Systems in Europe—Amsterdam," http://old.iea-dhc.org/download/Showcases_District_Cooling_Amsterdam.pdf (accessed March 6, 2013). See also the project write-up as a best-practice reported by the C40 Cities Climate Leadership Group, part of the Clinton Climate Initiative: www.c40cities.org/best practices/energy/amsterdam_cooling.jsp (accessed March 6, 2013).

38. "Seawater to Heat Houses in Duindorp," TheHague.com, August 24, 2009, www.denhaag.nl/en/residents/to/Seawater-to-heat-houses-in-Duindorp.htm.

39. Sterling, "The Hague."

40. Peter Op't Vel and Erwin Roijen, "The Minewater Project Heerlen: Low Exergy Heating and Cooling in Practice," from Maryke Van Staden and Francesco Musco, eds., "Local Governments and Climate Change: Sustainable Energy Planning and Implementation in Small and Medium-Sized Communities," *Advances in Global Change Research* 39, Springer Science+Business Media (2010): 317.

41. Jean Weijers and Erwin Roijen, "The Minewater Project," *Renewable Energy Netherlands 2011*, www.cyclifier.org/project/minewater-project/ (accessed May 1, 2011).

42. "Minewater as a Renewable Energy Resource," Interreg IIIB NWE ENO (2010), 7, http://skrconline.net/content/images/stories/documents/mine_water_renewable_energy_guide.pdf (accessed May 1, 2011).

43. "Minewater as a Renewable Energy Resource," 7.

44. Ibid., 21.

45. Ibid., 18.

46. Andrew Hall, John Ashley Scott, and Helen Shang, "Geothermal Energy Recovery from Underground Mines," *Renewable and Sustainable Energy Reviews* 15 (2011): 917.

47. Peter Op't Veld and Elianne Demollin-Schneiders, "The Mine Water Project Heerlen, the Netherlands: Low Exergy in Practice" (proceedings of Clima 2007 WellBeing Indoors, Helsinki, 2007), 5, www.chri.nl/upload/art.%20mine waterproject.pdf (accessed May 1, 2011).

48. Ibid., 27.

49. "Minewater as a Renewable Energy Resource," 7.

50. Ibid., 18.

51. Hall et al., 923.

52. Georg Wieber and Stefan Pohl, "Mine Water: A Source of Geothermal Energy—Examples from the Rhenish Massif" (proceedings of the International Mine Water Association Symposium, Karlsbad, 2008), 1.

53. George R. Watzlaf and Terry E. Ackman, "Underground Mine Water for Heating and Cooling Using Geothermal Heat Pump Systems," *Mine Water and the Environment* 25 (2006): 10.

54. Trieu Mai et al., "Renewable Electricity Futures Study," National Renewable Energy Laboratory, Golden, CO, 2012, www.nrel.gov/docs/fy13osti/52409-ES.pdf.

55. The firm is perhaps best known for having designed the Olympic Velodrome for London's 2012 summer events.

56. Jörg Schlaich, Rudolf Bergermann, Wolfgang Schiel, and Gerhard Weinrebe, "Design of Commercial Solar Updraft Tower Systems—Utilization of Solar Induced Convective Flows for Power Generation," Structural Engineering International 14, no. 3, 1 (August 2004): 23.

57. Ibid.

58. Ibid., 5.

59. Ibid., 6.

60. Ibid.

61. Wolf-Walter Stinnes, "Greentower: Performance Guarantees through Insurance Policies" (proceedings of the Industrial and Commercial Use of Energy Conference, 2004), http://ebookbrowse.com/2004-stinnes-greentower-performance-guarantees-through-insurance-policies-pdf-d193600969.

62. Darius Snieckus, "EnviroMission in Texas Deal," Recharge News, May 24, 2013, www.rechargenews.com/solar/americas/article1327682.ece (accessed May 25, 2013).

63. EnviroMission website updated 2013, www.enviromission.com.au/EVM/content/home.html.

64. "1 km Australian Solar Tower Seeking Approval," Solar Australia, February 6, 2012, http://solarmagazine.com.au/news/1km_australian_solar_tower_seeking_approval/065934/.

65. Fritz Crotogino, Klause-Uwe Mohmeyer, and Roland Scharf, "Huntorf CAES: More Than 20 Years of Successful Operation" (paper from Compressed Air Energy Storage Meeting, Orlando, March, 2001).

66. Kelsey Higginbotham, "A Natural Way to Store Energy—The Dakota Salts Way," Today's Energy Solutions, April/May 2009, 28.

67. "Salt Miner Is Working Up the Numbers for Energy Storage in North Dakota," Renewable Energy News, no. 19, February 19, 2009, http://renews.biz/tag/americas/ (accessed March 2, 2011).

68. Eric Wesoff, "Compressed Air Storage Beats Batteries at Grid Scale," GreentechMedia, March 3, 2011, www.greentechmedia.com/articles/read/compressed-air-energy-storage-beats-batteries/ (accessed April 11, 2011).

69. "Gartner Estimates ICT Industry Accounts for 2 Percent of Global CO_2 Emissions," Gartner Inc., Gartner Newsroom press release, April 26, 2007, www.gartner.com/it/page.jsp?id=503867 (accessed July 4, 2012).

70. Carbon dioxide equivalent is a measure used to compare the emissions from various greenhouse gases based upon their global-warming potential. See: Climate Group and the Global e-Sustainability Initiative, "SMART 2020: Enabling the Low-Carbon Economy in the Information Age," 2008, 6, www.smart2020.org/_assets/files/02_Smart2020Report.pdf (accessed March 22, 2011).

71. Google, "Our Carbon Footprint: 2011," Google Green, www.google.com/green/bigpicture/#/intro/infographics-1.

72. Rich Miller, "Google Buys Wind Power to Green Oklahoma Grid," *Data Center Knowledge,* April 21, 2011, www.datacenterknowledge.com/archives/2011/04/21/google-buys-wind-power-to-green-oklahoma-grid/ (accessed April 30, 2011).

73. Preetika Rana, "India Carbon Emissions at 'Disturbing' Levels," *Wall Street Journal: India,* December 4, 2012, http://blogs.wsj.com/india realtime/2012/12/04/india-carbon-emissions-at-disturbing-levels/ (accessed October 22, 2011).

74. Mridul Chadha, "Solar Powered Cell-phone Towers in India to Reduce 5 Million Tons CO_2, Save $1.4 Billion Every Year," *Cleantechnica,* March 24, 2010, http://cleantechnica.com/2010/03/24/solar-powered-cellphone-towers-in-india-to-reduce-5-million-tons-co2-emissions-save-1-4-billion-every-year/ (accessed April 22, 2011).

75. Ibid.

76. Katherine Tweed, "Why Cellular Towers in Developing Nations Are Making the Move to Solar Power," *Scientific American,* January 15, 2013, www.scientificamerican.com/article.cfm?id=cellular-towers-moving-to-solar-power.

77. "Indus Towers Launches Pilot Program to Power 2,500 Cell Phone Towers with 'Outsourced' Solar Power Model," *Panchabuta,* February 1, 2011, http://panchabuta.com/2011/02/01/indus-towers-launches-initial-program-to-power-2500-cell-phone-towers-with-outsourced-solar-power-model/ (accessed April 22, 2011).

78. "Solar Power to Be a Must for Mobile Towers," *Times of India,* October 22, 2010, http://articles.timesofindia.indiatimes.com/2010-10-22/computing/28249057_1_solar-power-mobile-towers-cell-towers (accessed April 21, 2011).

79. The exception is in desert wastelands, where immense photovoltaic systems have become more common.

80. "What Floats?" Far Niente Winery Weblog, www.farniente.com (accessed April 12, 2012).

81. "Floating Solar Power Energizes New Jersey American Water Treatment Plant" (press release, American Water Works, October 19, 2011), www.amwater.com (accessed August 3, 2012).

82. Manas Dasgupta, "India's Gujarat State: Tapping Solar Power, Avoid Water Wastage," *Hindu,* March 6, 2003, www.indiaafricaconnect.in/index.php?param=news/4227.

83. Mark Horn, "Plant Profile: Neely Waste-water Reclamation Facility," *Water Environment & Technology* 24, no. 4 (2012): 54–55. (A publication of Water Environment Federation, Alexandria, VA.)

84. Ibid., 3.

85. ICLEI-Europe / Northumbria University, "Lille Metropole, France: Urban-Rural Linkages Fostering Sustainable Development in Europe" (case study, submitted 2008), http://ec.europa.eu/regional_policy/archive/conferences/urban_rural/doc/caselille.pdf (accessed June 24, 2011).

86. Biogasmax, "A European Project for Sustainable Development," www.biogasmax.eu/biogasmax-project-

biogas-and-biofuel/biogas-and-biofuel-for-sustainable-developpement.html (accessed June 03, 2011).

87. Darryl D'Monte, "Lille: City of the Future," *InfoChange India*, August 23, 2010, www.energy-cities.eu/db/lille_113_en.pdf (accessed June 3, 2011).

88. Energie-Cités and Municipality of Lille, France, "Biogas/Biofuel: Lille, France," 1999, www.energy-cities.eu/db/lille_113_en.pdf (accessed June 2, 2011).

89. D'Monte.

90. "Transfer Centre and Organic Recovery Centre" (General Presentation Lille Metropole Communauté Urbaine, 2009), www.biogasmax.eu/media/organic_recovery_centre_lille__085752800_1634_26112009.pdf (accessed June 2, 2011).

91. Ibid.

92. D'Monte.

93. Ibid.

94. Silvia Magnoni and Andrea M. Bassi, "Creating Synergies for Renewable Energy Investments, a Community Success Story from Lolland Denmark," *Energies* (2009): 1155.

95. Ibid., 1153.

96. Ibid., 1154.

97. In the years 2001–2005, annual subsidies have ranged between $340 million and $519 million. See: Magnoni, 1159.

98. Ibid., 1162.

99. Ibid., 1155.

100. Ibid.

101. Ibid.

102. Ibid, 1163.

103. A similarly sophisticated cross-sector networking scheme will be seen in the Svartsengi Resource Park, discussed in chapter 5.

104. Jeffrey Ball, "Tough Love for Renewable Energy: Making Wind and Solar Power Affordable," *Foreign Affairs* 91, no. 3 (May/June 2012): 125–6.

105. M. Maureen Hand, "Renewable Electricity Futures," Utility Variable-Generation Integration Group, Fall Technical Workshop, Omaha, Nebraska, October 24, 2012, NREL/PR-6A20-56834, www.nrel.gov/docs/fy13osti/56834.pdf (accessed June 22, 2010).

Chapter 4

1. Dana F. Gumb Jr., "Staten Island History and Bluebelt Land Acquisitions," *Clear Waters*, vol. 39, New York Water Environment Association Inc., 2009, 22–25, http://urbanomnibus.net/redux/wp-content/uploads/2010/12/Staten-Island-History-and-Bluebelt-Land-Acquisitions.pdf (accessed April 12, 2013).

2. The author prefers the term "soft-path water paradigm" over "green infrastructure"—a much too generalized term. From the term applied by Amory Lovins to energy systems, "soft-path" infrastructure is well defined in: Valerie I. Nelson, "A Soft-Path Paradigm Shift: Federal Policies to Advance Decentralized and Integrated Water Resource Management," Coalition for Alternative Wastewater Treatment of Gloucester, Massachusetts, 2007, http://sustainablewaterforum.org/fed/report.pdf (accessed December 13, 2012).

3. Nelson, Ibid., 20.

4. US Environmental Protection Agency, *Water on Tap: What You Need to Know* (Washington, DC, December 2009), http://water.epa.gov/drink/guide/upload/book_waterontap_full.pdf.

5. Center for Sustainable Systems, University of Michigan, "U.S. Wastewater Treatment Factsheet," Pub No. CSS04-14, 2011, http://css.snre.umich.edu/css_doc/CSS04-14.pdf.

6. US Environmental Protection Agency, *Inventory of U.S. Greenhouse Gas Emissions and Sinks 1990–2009* (Washington, DC, April 15, 2011), www.epa.gov/climatechange/Downloads/ghgemissions/US-GHG-Inventory-2011-Complete_Report.pdf (accessed December 2, 2012).

7. Organization for Economic Cooperation and Development, "Infrastructure to 2030: Telecom, Land Transport, Water and Electricity" (Paris, France, 2006), www.oecd.org/futures/infrastructureto2030/ (accessed December 14, 2012).

8. Valerie I. Nelson, "Soft-Path Integrated Water Resource Management: Training, Research, and Development Needs," National Decentralized Water Resources Capacity Development Project, Washington University, St. Louis, MO, and the Coalition for Alternative Wastewater Treatment, Gloucester, MA, vii, http://ndwrcdp.werf.org/documents/SOFT_PATH_TRDneeds_WEB.pdf (accessed December 14, 2012).

9. US Central Intelligence Agency, "Country Comparison: Roadways," *CIA World Fact Book*, 2008, www.cia.gov/library/publications /the-world-factbook/rankorder/2085rank.html.

10. Lance Frazer, "Paving Paradise: The Peril of Impervious Surfaces," *Environmental Health Perspectives* 113, no. 5 (July 2005): A456–62.

11. *Working landscape* may be defined as a landscape where the production of market goods and the functioning of ecosystem services are mutually reinforcing.

12. Evapotranspiration is the use and evaporation of water by vegetation.

13. Seattle Public Utilities, City of Seattle, "Street Edge Alternatives," www.seattle.gov/util/environmentconservation/projects/drainagesystem/greenstormwaterinfrastructure/completedgsiprojects/streetedgealternatives/ (accessed June 11, 2012).

14. Ibid.

15. Charles McKinney, Chelsea Mauldin, and Deborah Marton, eds., "High Performance Landscape Guidelines: 21st Century Parks for New York City," The Design Trust, City of New York Parks and Recreation, 2010, 210, www.nycgovparks.org/sub_about/go_greener/design_guidelines.pdf (accessed March 21, 2012).

16. This reuse of concrete from the site conserves, according to the landscape architect, almost 2 billion BTU of embodied energy, while avoiding 60 tons of carbon emissions for a new concrete median. See: Yuka Yoneda, "Jagged Chunks of Sidewalk Reused to Create Unique Median for Queens Plaza," Inhabitat NYC, March 9, 2011, http://inhabitat.com/nyc/jagged-chunks-of-sidewalk-reused-to-create-unique-median-for-queens-plaza/.

17. Penny Lee, Senior Planner, Long Island City at New York City Department of City Planning, interview with the author, March 3, 2012.

18. US Environmental Protection Agency, "Combined Sewer Overflow Demographics," National Pollutant Discharge Elimination Systems (NPDES), http://cfpub.epa.gov/npdes/cso/demo.cfm?program_id=5 (accessed February 4, 2012).

19. The team consists of: Waterfront Toronto; Phillips Farevaag Smallenberg Landscape Architects; Jill Anholt, sculptor; Teeple Architects; and TMIG, infrastructure consultant.

20. Waterfront Toronto, "Sherbourne Common Fact Sheet," last updated July 28, 2011, www.waterfrontoronto.ca (accessed February 1, 2012).

21. The ultraviolet equipment shares its foundation with a park pavilion situated above it, which features a café, mechanical equipment storage, and restrooms (whose toilets use gray water).

22. James Roche, Director, Parks Design and Construction, Waterfront Toronto, interview with author, April 12, 2012.

23. Paul McRandle, "Philadelphia Cleans Up Storm Water with Innovative Management," National Geographic, Daily News, July 6, 2012, http://news.nationalgeographic.com/news/2012/06/120606/philadelphia-storm-water-runoff/ (accessed November 20, 2012).

24. US Environmental Protection Agency, Green Infrastructure Case Studies: Municipal Policies for Managing Stormwater with Green Infrastructure (Washington, DC: Office of Wetlands, Oceans, and Watersheds, August, 2010), 50, www.epa.gov/owow/NPS/lid/gi_case_studies_2010.pdf (accessed June 1, 2012).

25. Alisa Valderrama and Larry Levine, "Financing Stormwater Retrofits in Philadelphia and Beyond," Natural Resources Defense Council, February 2012, www.nrdc.org/water/files/StormwaterFinancing-report.pdf (accessed November 12, 2012).

26. Water treatment processes are physically and chemically separated into primary, secondary, and tertiary stages.

27. As a secondary treatment method, the algae growth found in oxidation ponds or lagoons further decomposes material in the bacterial production of oxygen.

28. US Environmental Protection Agency, Arcata, California—A Natural System for Wastewater Reclamation and Resource Enhancement (Washington, DC: US EPA Office of Water, September 1993), 4, www.epa.gov/owow/wetlands/pdf/Arcata.pdf (accessed October 20, 2011).

29. David J. Tenenbaum, "Constructed Wetlands: Borrowing a Concept from Nature," Environmental Health Perspectives 112, no. 1 (January 2004): 4.

30. Amanda Suutari, "USA—California (Arcata)—Constructed Wetland: A Cost-Effective Alternative for Wastewater Treatment," EcoTipping Points Project, June 2006, www.ecotippingpoints.org/our-stories/indepth/usa-california-arcata-constructed-wetland-wastewater.html (accessed January 2013).

31. BOD (biological oxygen demand) is a widely used indirect measurement of organic matter present in water.

32. Humboldt State University, CH2M-Hill, and PBS&J, "Free Water Surface Wetlands for Wastewater Treatment: A Technology Assessment," US Environmental Protection Agency, Office of Water, June 1999, 6–15, http://water.epa.gov/type/wetlands/restore/upload/2004_12_20_wetlands_pdf_FW_Surface_Wetlands.pdf (accessed November 17, 2012).

33. City of Arcata, "Wildlife Sanctuary," www.cityofarcata.com/departments/environmental-services/water-wastewater/wildlife-sanctuary (accessed January 11, 2012).

34. Amanda Suutari and Gerald Marten, "Eco Tipping Points: How a Vicious Cycle Can Become Virtuous," *Earth Island Journal* (Summer 2007): 30.

35. US Environmental Protection Agency, *Constructed Wetlands Treatment of Municipal Wastewaters* (Cincinnati, OH: Office of Research and Development, September 1999), http://water.epa.gov/type/wetlands/restore/upload/constructed-wetlands-design-manual.pdf.

36. Humboldt State University et al., 1–9.

37. *Wadi* is the Arabic term for a seasonal stream.

38. Mohammad al-Asad and Yildirim Yavuz, "Wadi Hanifa Development Plan" (on-site review report, Arriyadh Development Authority, 2258 SAU, 2007), 4, www.archnet.org/library/downloader/file/1405/file_body/FLS1237.pdf (accessed December 5, 2011); see also: Wael al-Samhour and Mashary

al-Naim, "Wadi Hanifa Wetlands" (on-site review report, Arriyadh Development Authority, 2258 SAU, 2007), 4, www.archnet.org/library/downloader/file/2223/file_body/FLS1808.pdf (accessed December 5, 2011).

39. George Stockton (landscape architect and planner), President, Moriyama & Teshima Planners, Limited, conversation with author, March 5, 2012.

40. Abdulaziz A. Alhamid, Saleh A. Alfayzi, and Mohamed Alfatih Hamad, "A Sustainable Water Resources Management Plant for Wadi Hanifa in Saudi Arabia," *Journal of King Saud University*, Engineering Sciences, vol. 19, no. 2 (2007): 217.

41. Moriyama & Teshima Architects, with Buro Happold, "Wadi Hanifah Restoration Project," Arriyadh Development Authority, March 2010, www.mtplanners.com/M&T%20Wadi%20Hanifah%20Restoration%20Project%20Booklet%20-%202010-03-S.pdf (accessed March 8, 2012).

42. Stockton.

43. Moriyama et al., 9.

44. Ibid., 11.

45. Ibid., 25.

46. Ibid., 11.

47. Ibid., 9.

48. Ibid., 11.

49. al-Asad and Yavuz, 15.

50. Ibid., 35.

51. High Commission for the Development of ArRiyadh, "Wadi Hanifah Rehabilitation Program," ArRiyadh City website, http://www.ada.gov.sa (accessed December 11, 2011).

52. Stockton.

53. Ibid.

54. Moriyama et al., 33–35.

55. National Research Council, *Valuing Eco-system Services: Toward Better Environmental Decision-Making* (Washington, DC: National Academies Press, 2005), 156.

56. The agreement was renewed in 2011 with a further $100 million in City funding commitments.

57. National Research Council, *Valuing Ecosystem Services*, 159.

58. "New York City Watershed: Memorandum of Agreement between the City of New York, the State of New York, and the U.S. Environmental Protection Agency et al.," January 21, 1997, www. nysefc.org/Default. aspx?TabID=76&fid=389#dltop (accessed January 3, 2012).

59. Aesthetic standards that are not health-based are considered secondary by EPA, but *not* by New York City Department of Health.

60. Salome Freud, "Why New York City Needs a Filtered Croton Supply," New York City Department of Environmental Protection, May 2003, 9, www.nyc.gov/ html/dep/pdf/croton/whitepaper.pdf (accessed January 29, 2012).

61. In 2007 EPA granted the City a 10-year Filtration Avoidance Determination Renewal based on the City's strong record of watershed protection.

62. New York City Water Board, "Public Information Regarding Water and Wastewater Rates," April 2010, http:// ditmasparkblog.com/wp-content/ uploads/DEP-Blue-Book-Arial-15-one-page-per-22.pdf (accessed January 29, 2012).

63. David Burke, Associate Principal, Grimshaw Architects, conversation with author, May 26, 2010.

64. David Burke, "Water Systems for Urban Improvements," Grimshaw Architects, *Blue: Water, Energy and Waste*, vol. 1 (2009): 62.

65. Great Ecology Firm, "Croton Water Treatment Plant," http://greatecology. com/projects/croton-water-treatment-plant/ (accessed January 29, 2012).

66. Burke, "Water Systems," 63.

67. Ibid.

68. Chapter 6 will describe some of the responses to water scarcity in a warming world.

Chapter 5

1. Mirele Goldsmith, "Citizen Opposition to the Croton Water Treatment Plant" (paper presented at Sixth Biennial Conference on Communication and Environment, Cincinnati, OH, July 2001), 4.

2. The design team includes: Grimshaw Architects, Ken Smith Landscape Architect, Great Ecology, Rana Creek Ecological Design, and Hazen and Sawyer/ AECOM Joint Venture.

3. Matt Chaban, "Fore! Nation's Largest Green Roof atop Bronx Water Plant Doubles as Driving Range," *The Architect's Newspaper*, February 26, 2009, http://archpaper.com/news/articles. asp?id=3231.

4. National Commission on Energy Policy, *Siting Critical Energy Infrastructure: An Overview of Needs and Challenges*

(white paper, Washington, DC, June 2006), www.energycommission.org (accessed February 16, 2012).

5. In 2002 the larger Greenpoint/Williamsburg area was also host to some 30 solid-waste transfer stations, a medical-waste incinerator, a radioactive-waste storage facility, 1,000 industrial firms, and 30 high-hazardous-waste storage facilities. See: Jason Corburn, "Combining Community-Based Research and Local Knowledge to Confront Asthma and Subsistence-Fishing Hazards in Greenpoint/Williamsburg, Brooklyn, New York," *Environmental Health Perspectives* 110, Supplement 2 (April 2002): 245.

6. The first plume, which is almost double the size of the *Exxon Valdez* oil spill in Alaska, remained undiscovered until 1978. See: "The Big Spill," *New York Times*, New York Region Opinion, September 30, 2007, www.nytimes.com/2007/09/30/opinion/nyregion opinions/CInewtown.html (accessed February 17, 2010).

7. Newtown Creek Alliance, "About the Creek: Newtown Creek Information," www.newtowncreekalliance.org/history/ (accessed February 17, 2010). Newtown Creek was not declared a Superfund Site until 2010.

8. The Clean Water Act requires wastewater to be treated to remove at least 85 percent of certain pollutants before post-treatment water, known as effluent, is discharged into surrounding waterways.

9. Water-Technology.net, "Newtown Creek Water Pollution Control Plant, USA," Net Resources International, www.water technology.net/projects/newtown/ (accessed February 18, 2010).

10. Catherine Zidar, Executive Director, Newtown Creek Alliance, interview with author, March 25, 2010.

11. Still in existence, the group continues to negotiate mitigation measures, secure remediation of environmental damage, and help local residents and businesses address concerns about health and quality.

12. Carol Steinsapir, "Moving Forward: A Progress Report on the Environmental Benefits Program" (draft report, New York City, January 1993), 1.

13. "DEP Opens Visitor Center at Newtown Creek," (press release, NYC Department of Environmental Protection, April 24, 2010), www.nyc.gov/html/dep/html/press_releases/10-40pr.shtml (accessed March 12, 2012). See also: "New York City's Wastewater," City of New York, Department of Environmental Protection, www.nyc.gov/html/dep/html/wastewater/index.shtml (accessed March 12, 2012).

14. City of New York, Department of Environmental Protection, "2011–2114: 2011 Progress Report," www.nyc.gov/html/dep/pdf/strategic_plan/dep_strategy_2011_update.pdf (accessed April 21, 2012).

15. Elisabeth Rosenthal, "Europe Finds Clean Energy in Trash, but U.S. Lags," *New York Times*, April 12, 2010.

16. European Commission, "Environment in the EU27," Eurostat News Release 43/2010, March 19, 2010, http://epp.eurostat.ec.europa.eu/cache/ITY_PUBLIC/8-19032010-AP/EN/8-

19032010-AP-EN.PDF (accessed April 22, 2012).

17. Ibid.

18. US Environmental Protection Agency, *Municipal Solid Waste Generation, Recycling, and Disposal in the United States: Facts and Figures for 2009* (Washington, DC, December, 2010), www.epa.gov/epawaste/nonhaz/municipal/pubs/msw2009-fs.pdf (accessed June 2012).

19. Furans are volatile organic compounds obtained from wood oils.

20. Nickolas J. Themelis, "An Overview of the Global Waste-to-Energy Industry," *Waste Management World* (July–August 2003): 40–47.

21. Erica Gies, "Waste-to-Energy Plants a Waste of Energy, Recycling Advocates Say," *New York Times*, July 4, 2008, Business section.

22. Letter to M. Zannes of the Integrated Waste Services Association from EPA Assistant Administrators Marianne Horinko and Jeffrey Holmstead, February 14, 2003.

23. P. Ozge Kaplan, Joseph DeCarolis, and Susan Thorneloe, "Is It Better to Burn or Bury Waste for Clean Electricity Generation?" *Environmental Science & Technology* 43, no. 6 (2009): 1711.

24. Syndicat Intercommunal de Traitement des Ordures Ménagères, "ISSEANE: The Future Issy-les-Moulineaux Household Waste Sorting and Energy Production Centre," SYCTOM de L'agglomeration Parisienne, 2007, 4, www.syctom-paris.frww.syctom (accessed September 12, 2011).

25. Ibid., 9.

26. Ibid.

27. Ibid., 6.

28. Tom Freyberg, "Can an Energy from Waste Plant be a Work of Art?" *Sustainable Solutions*, February/March 2009, 33.

29. Masanori Tsukahara and Hitachi Zosen Corporation, "Presentation of Japanese Technology of Waste to Energy," *JASE-World, Waste to Energy Sub WG*, November 14, 2012, www.mofa.go.jp/region/latin/fealac/pdfs/4-9_jase.pdf (accessed September 30, 2011).

30. B. Harden, "Japan Stanches Stench of Mass Trash Incinerators," *Washington Post*, November 18, 2008.

31. City of Hiroshima, Urban Design Section, City Planning Division Urban Development Bureau, www.city.hiroshima.lg.jp/ (accessed July 3, 2011).

32. City of Hiroshima, "Introduction to the Facilities of Hiroshima," International Relations Division, Department Citizens' Affairs Bureau of Hiroshima, www.city.hiroshima.jp/ (accessed July 30, 2011).

33. Harden.

34. Another lively invention by this celebrated ecological artist is the whimsically biomorphic Spittelau Thermal Waste Treatment Plant upgrade in Vienna, completed in 1992. What is less well known is that at Spittelau Hundertwasser went beyond mere cosmetic gestures and insisted in his contract that the facility incorporate more-advanced pollution controls. His revisions are now part of the global standard for flue-gas-treatment processes.

35. Jim Witkin, "Skiing Your Way to 'Hedonistic Sustainability,'" *New York Times*, February 16, 2011.

36. Babcock & Wilcox Vølund, "Waste-to-Energy Plant Amager Bakke, Copenhagen, Denmark," fact sheet 2013, www.volund.dk/en/Waste_to_Energy/References/~/media/Downloads/Brochures%20-%20WTE/Amager%20Bakke%20-%20Copenhagen%20-%20Denmark.ashx.

37. Vanessa Quirk, "BIG's Waste-to-Energy Plant Breaks Ground, Breaks Schemas," *ArchDaily*, March 5, 2013, www.archdaily.com/339893 (accessed March 16, 2013).

38. Christopher Sensenig, "Willamette River Water Treatment Plant—Wilsonville, OR," *Places* 13, no. 3 (2004): 6–9.

39. Edward Walsh, Rex Warland, and D. Clayton Smith, *Don't Burn It Here: Grassroots Challenges to Trash Incineration* (University Park, PA: Penn State University Press, 1997), 157. See also: US Environmental Protection Agency, "Wastes, Non-hazardous Waste, Municipal Waste," www.epa.gov/osw/nonhaz/municipal/wte/basic.htm.

40. Karen Stein, "Making Art of Trash," *Architectural Record* (June 1994).

41. William Morrish, "Raising Expectations [Place Debate: Revisiting the Phoenix Public Art Plan]," *Places* 10, no. 3 (July 1996): 63.

42. Christine Temin, "Rising in Phoenix: A Model for Public Art," *Boston Globe Magazine*, July 24, 1994.

43. The concept of "Solving for Pattern," according to Wendell Berry's essay of the same title, is the process of discovering solutions that solve multiple problems while avoiding creation of new ones. While originally used in reference to agriculture, the term has been picked up by the green-design community.

44. Michael Singer, Ramon Cruz, and Jason Bregman, "Infrastructure and Community: How Can We Live with What Sustains Us?" Environmental Defense and Michael Singer Studio, 2007, 14, http://ne.edgecastcdn.net/000210/ebs/100107_sustainable/pdfs/singer.pdf (accessed August 21, 2011).

45. Herbert Muschamp, "When Art Is a Public Spectacle," *New York Times*, August 20, 1993, Arts section.

46. City of Phoenix Public Works Department, "Solid Waste Strategic Plan 2010," City of Phoenix, http://phoenix.gov/webcms/groups/internet/@inter/@dept/@pubworks/@news/documents/web_content/056272.pdf (accessed August 21, 2011).

47. Sarah E. Graddy, "Creative and Green: Art, Ecology, and Community" (masters thesis, University of Southern California, 2005).

48. Ibid., 15.

49. Singer et al.

50. Imported fossil fuel supports fishing and land transportation. See: Arni Ragnarsson, "Geothermal Development in Iceland 2005–2009" (proceedings of the World Geothermal Congress 2010, Bali, Indonesia, April 25–29, 2010), 1.

51. The term *primary energy* refers to energy forms required by the energy sector to generate the supply of energy carriers used by society.

52. These figures date from 2009. See: Ragnarsson, 3–4.

53. Einar Gunnlaugsson and Gestur Gislason, "District Heating in Reykjavik and Electrical Production Using Geothermal Energy," Orkuveita Rekjavikur, www.or.is/media/files/District%20heating-092s3PaperIGC20032003.pdf (accessed August 26, 2012).

54. Geothermal plants are recognized in the United States by statute as a renewable resource, with their heat energy considered indefinitely available.

55. A case study of a coal plant updated with scrubbers and other emissions control technologies emits 24 times more carbon dioxide, 10,837 times more sulfur dioxide, and 3,865 times more nitrous oxides per megawatt-hour than a geothermal steam plant. See: Alyssa Kagel, Diana Bates, and Karl Gawell, "A Guide to Geothermal Energy and the Environment," *Geothermal Energy Association* (2005): 2, www.geo-energy.org (accessed December 21, 2011).

56. Kagel et al., 41.

57. Magnea Gudmundsdottir, Asa Brynjolfsdottir, and Albert Albertsson, "The History of the Blue Lagoon in Svartsengi" (proceedings of the World Geothermal Congress 2010, Bali, Indonesia, April 25–29, 2010).

58. Daniel Gross, "Iceland Has Power to Burn," *Newsweek*, April 5, 2008.

59. Albert Albertsson and Julius Jonsson, "The Svartsengi Resource Park" (proceedings of the World Geothermal Congress, Bali, Indonesia, April 25–29, 2010), 2.

60. Iceland has one of the highest numbers of cars per capita in the world. See: K.-C. Tran and Albert Albertsson, "Utilization of Geothermal Energy and Emissions for Production of Renewable Methanol" (proceedings of the World Geothermal Congress, 2010, Bali, Indonesia, April 25–29, 2010), 1.

61. This synthesis gas is a fuel gas mixture consisting primarily of hydrogen, carbon monoxide, and very often some carbon dioxide.

62. Tran and Albertsson, 2.

63. Ibid., 1.

64. "Iceland as a Green Saudi Arabia" (press release, Carbon Recycling International [CRI]), www.carbonrecycling.is/index.php?option=com_content&view=article&id=52%3Aiceland-as-a-green-saudi-arabia&catid=2&Itemid=6&lang=en (accessed March 16, 2013).

65. Albertsson and Jónsson, 2.

66. Washington, Oregon, Idaho, Wyoming, Utah, California, Nevada, Arizona, and New Mexico.

67. Kagel et al., i.

68. Massachusetts Institute of Technology, "The Future of Geothermal Energy: Impact of Enhanced Geothermal Systems (EGS) on the United States in the 21st Century," US Department of Energy, 2006, www1.eere.energy.gov/geothermal/egs_technology.html (accessed March 15, 2013).

69. Ibid., 1–5.

70. The World Bank, "Brazil—Gas Sector Development Project, Sao Paulo Natural Gas Distribution Project," World Bank

Project Performance Assessment Report (December 1, 2003), 90, www-wds.worldbank.org/ (accessed October 12, 2011).

71. Mark Gerenscer et al., *Megacommunities: How Leaders of Government, Business and Non-Profits Can Tackle Today's Global Challenges Together* (New York: Palgrave/Macmillan, 2008).

72. Petrobras also developed an effective procedure for handling claims from affected populations. See: Kay Patten Beasley, "Bolivia-Brazil Gas Pipeline Project—Environmental Assessment, Executive Summary," November 1996, 27, www-wds.worldbank.org/servlet/WDSContentServer/WDSP/IB/2000/02/24/000009265_3980313101727/Rendered/INDEX/multi_page.txt (accessed March 17, 2013).

73. Juan D. Quintero, "Best Practices in Mainstreaming Environmental & Social Safeguards into Gas Pipeline Projects: Learning from the Bolivia-Brazil Gas Pipeline Project (GASBOL)," The World Bank Energy Sector Management Assistance Program, July 2006, 22, www-wds.worldbank.org/ (accessed October 1, 2011).

74. World Bank Report No. 22201, "Implementation Report (SCL-42650) on a Loan in the Amount of US$130 Million to the Transportadora Brasileira Gasoduto Bolivia-Brasil S.A., for a Gas Sectored Development Project—Bolivia Gas Pipeline," June 27, 2001, 13.

75. World Bank, "Implementation Report," 11.

76. Quintero, 26.

77. Ibid, 27.

78. World Bank, "Implementation Report," 39.

79. Quintero, 42.

80. World Bank Project Assessment Report.

81. George Ledec and Juan D. Quintero, "Bolivia-Brazil Gas pipeline Project (GASBOL): Minimizing Project Footprint," in *Mainstreaming Conservation in Infrastructure Projects: Case Studies from Latin America*, World Bank, June 2007, 8, http://siteresources.worldbank.org/INTBIODIVERSITY/Resources/Mainstream-Infrastructure-web.pdf (accessed October 9, 2011).

82. Gerenscer et al., 75.

Chapter 6

1. Royal Haskoning, "Integrated Coastal Zone Development: A Process Approach Based on ComCoast Experiences" (technical report, WP1 ComCoast project, 2007), 6–7. See also the Natura 2000 Networking Programme website: www.natura.org/sites_uk_abbotts.html (accessed November 4, 2012).

2. A May 15, 2013, study showed that among 11,944 papers expressing a position on anthropogenic global warming, 97.2 percent endorsed the consensus position on anthropogenic causation. See: John Cook et al., "Quantifying the Consensus on Anthropogenic Global Warming in the Scientific Literature," *Environmental Research Letters* 8, no. 2 (2013): 024024, doi:10.1088/1748-9326/8/2/024024.

3. Union of Concerned Scientists, "Findings of the IPCC Fourth Assessment Report: Climate Change Science," www.

ucsusa.org (accessed November 4, 2012). See also: Miguel Llanos, "Sea Level Rose 60 Percent Faster than UN Projections, Study Finds," *NBC News*, November 28, 2012, http://worldnews.nbcnews. com/_news/2012/11/28/15512957-sea-level-rose-60-percent-faster-than-un-projections-study-finds.

4. Discussions of mitigation measures center on three questions: (1) Who will reduce emissions (i.e., both developed and developing nations)? (2) How much will emissions be reduced (i.e., what baseline will be used, and what will be the extent of the reductions measured against that baseline)? (3) How quickly will reductions occur? Mitigation proposals include various strategies to reduce, sequester, or offset GHG emissions—through cap-and-trade, carbon taxes, or other mechanisms.

5. UK Cabinet Office, "Introduction, Definitions, and Principles of Infrastructure Resilience," in *Keeping the Country Running: Natural Hazards and Infrastructure* (London: Civil Contingencies Secretariat, Cabinet Office, 2011), www.gov.uk/ government/uploads/system/uploads/ attachment_data/file/78902/section-a-natural-hazards-infrastructure.pdf.

6. C. S. Hollings, "Resilience and Stability of Ecological Systems," *Annual Review of Ecology and Systematics* 4 (1973): 9.

7. Ibid.

8. Union of Concerned Scientists—USA, "Infographic: Sea Level Rise and Global Warming," www.ucsusa.org/ global_warming/science_and_impacts/ impacts/infographic-sea-level-rise-global-warming.html (last revised April 16, 2013).

9. Gordon McGranahan, Deborah Balk, and Bridget Anderson, "The Rising Tide: Assessing the Risks of Climate Change and Human Settlement in Low-Elevation Coastal Zones," *Environment and Urbanization* 19, no. 1 (2007): 22, doi: 10.1177 /0956247807076960.

10. Matt Rosenberg, "Polders and Dikes of the Netherlands," About.com, http://geography. about.com/od/ specificplacesofinterest/a/dykes.htm (accessed November 27, 2012). See also: Pavel Kabat et al., "Climate-Proofing the Netherlands," *Nature* 438 (2005): 283.

11. Aleksandra Kazmierczak and Jeremy Carter, "Adaptation to Climate Change Using Green and Blue Infrastructure: A Database of Case Studies" (Manchester, UK: University of Manchester, 2010), 19.

12. Pavel Kabat, et al., "Dutch Coasts in Transition," *Nature Geoscience* vol. 2 (July 2009): 4.

13. I. Watson and C. W. Finkl, "State of the Art in Storm-Surge Protection: The Netherlands Delta Project," *Journal of Coastal Research* 6 (1990): 741, www. jstor.org/stable/4297737.

14. Johan van der Tol, "Barriers and Dams: Exporting Holland's Sea Defenses," Radio Netherlands Worldwide, October 4, 2011, www.rnw.nl/english/article/ barriers-and-dams-exporting-hollands-sea-defences (accessed November 27, 2012).

15. Dacher L. Frohmader, "The Eastern Scheldt Storm Surge Barrier," *Concrete Construction* (May 1991): 385.

16. "Deltawerken-Nature," www.delta werken.com/Nature/14.html (last modified 2004, accessed November 27, 2012).

17. Bianca Stalenberg, Han Vrijling, and Yoshito Kikumori, "Japanese Lessons for Dutch Urban Flood Management" (proceedings of "Water Down Under," Adelaide, Australia, 2008). See also: Jun Inomata, "Multiple Use of Flood Prevention Facilities in Japan," National Institute for Land and Infrastructure Management, Ministry of Land, Infrastructure, and Transport, www.mlit.go.jp/river/trash_box/paper/pdf_english/19.pdf (accessed April 29, 2013).

18. Netherlands Ministry of Transport, Public Works, and Water Management, "A Different Approach to Water: Water Management Policy in the 21st Century," Ministry of Transport, Public Works and Water Management, Amsterdam, Netherlands, 2000, 12.

19. H. van Schaik, F. Ludwig, M. R. van der Valk, and B. Dijkshoorn, "Climate Changes Dutch Water Management," Co-operative Programme on Water and Climate and Netherlands Water Partnership, Delft, Netherlands, 2007, 15.

20. "Deltawerken—The Delta Works Website," www.deltawerken.com/The-Delta-Works/1524.html (accessed November 27, 2012).

21. "Room for the River: First Dairy Farmer Moves to New Farm on 6m-High Mound in Overdiepse Polder," Dutch Water Sector, August 11, 2012, www.dutchwatersector.com/news-events/news/3384-room-for-the-river-first-dairy-farmer-moves-to-new-farm-on-6-m-high-mound-in-overdiepse-polder.html (accessed January 11, 2013).

22. "Overdiepse Polder—Overdiepse Polder River Widening," Waterschap Branbantse Delta, www.brabantsedelta.nl/overdiep/english/overdiepse_polder (accessed November 29, 2012).

23. Climatewire, "How the Dutch Make 'Room for the River' by Redesigning Cities," Scientific American, January 20, 2012, www.scientificamerican.com/article.cfm?id=how-the-dutch-make-room-for-the-river (accessed November 29, 2012).

24. H. van Schaik, F. Ludwig, and M. R. van der Valk, eds., Climate Changes Dutch Water Management (Delft, The Netherlands: Netherlands Water Partnership, August 2007).

25. "Guiding Models for Water Storage: Possibilities for Water Storage and Multiple Space Use in the Dutch River Area" (ESPACE project report, Nijmegen/Oosterbeek, Netherlands, September 2004), 41.

26. Studio Marco Vermeulen, "Selected Projects," www.marcovermeulen.nl/ (accessed November 11, 2012).

27. Armando Carbonell and Douglas J. Meffert, "Climate Change and the Resilience of New Orleans: The Adaptation of Deltaic Urban Form," Lincoln Land Institute, 2009, 5–10, http://siteresources.worldbank.org (accessed February 2011.)

28. David Waggonner, Han Meyer, et al., "New Orleans after Katrina: Building America's Water City" (unpublished paper).

29. Interview with David Waggonner, July 25, 2013.

30. Ibid.

31. Gordon Russell, "Planners, Inspired by Dutch, Now Hope to Build," *The Advocate*, Baton Rouge, LA, July 22, 2013.

32. Joseph Mathew, "Strategic Alternatives for Coastal Protection: Multipurpose Submerged Reefs" (presentation in the 11th Meeting of the Coastal Protection and Development Advisory Committee [CPDAC], Chennai, January 4, 2010), 3–8.

33. Kerry P. Black, "Artificial Surfing Reefs for Erosion Control and Amenity: Theory and Application," *Journal of Coastal Research*, special issue no. 34 (2001): 2.

34. Kerala Department of Tourism, "Kovalam Reef: An Initiative of Government of Kerala for Coastal Protection, Ecology Enhancement and Eco-recreation," Government of Kerala, India, 2010.

35. Mike Christie and Oliver Colman, "An Economic Assessment of the Amenity Benefits Associated with Alternative Coastal Protection Options" (paper presented by International Association of Agricultural Economists, 2006 Annual Meeting, Queensland, Australia, August 12–18, 2006), 5.

36. Kerry P. Black and Shaw Mead, "Design of Surfing Reefs," *Reef Journal* 1 (2009): 177.

37. S. T. Mead, "Multiple-Use Options for Coastal Structures: Unifying Amenity, Coastal Protection, and Marine Ecology," *Reef Journal* 1, no. 1 (2009): 297.

38. Rhys A. Edwards and Stephen D. A. Smith, "Subtidal Assemblages Associated with a Geotextile Reef in South-East Queensland, Australia," *Marine and Freshwater Research* 56, no. 2 (2005): 133.

39. K. Saito, "Japan's Sea Urchin Enhancement Experience," in *Sea Urchins, Abalone, and Kelp: Their Biology, Enhancement, and Management*, ed. Christopher M. Dewes, University of California, California Sea Grant College Conference, Bodega Bay, CA, March 18–21, 1992.

40. Lina Kliucininkaite and Kai Ahrendt, "Modelling Different Artificial Reefs in the Coastline of Probstei," *RADOST Journal Series* 5 (2011): 40.

41. M. Raybould and T. Mules, "Northern Gold Coast Beach Protection Strategy: A Benefit-Cost Analysis" (technical report, Gold Coast City Council, 1998).

42. Jinu Abraham, "Campaign against Artificial Reef Kovalam," India Tourism Watch, December 11, 2010, http://indiatourismwatch.org/node/6 (accessed November 29, 2012).

43. Xavier Leflaive et al., "Water," in *OECD Environmental Outlook to 2050: The Consequences of Inaction* (OECD Publishing, 2012).

44. Young Ho Bae, Kyeong Ok Kim, and Byung Ho Choi, "Lake Sihwa Tidal Power Plant Project," *Ocean Engineering* 37, no. 5 (2010): 454, doi:10.1016/j.oceaneng.2010.01.015.

45. Larry Parker and John Blodgett, "Greenhouse Gas Emissions: Perspectives on the Top 20 Emitters and Developed Versus Developing Nations" (CRS report for Congress, 2008), 16.

46. Neil Ford, "Seoul Leads Tidal Breakthrough: Development of the 254MW Sihwa Tidal Power Plant in South Korea Could Lead to Further Advances in Tidal

Power Technology," *International Water Power & Dam Construction* 58, no. 10 (October 1, 2006): 10–12.

47. Bae et al., 454.

48. Man-ki Kim, "Korea Building World's Largest Tidal Power Plant," *The Korea Herald*, March 30, 2010, www.koreaherald.com/view. php?ud=20090727000009.

49. Korea Electric Company (KEPCO), "Korea Tidal Power Study—Phase I, KORDI, DIST." (technical report, Shawinigan Engineering Company, 1978), 180.

50. Robert Williams, "How France Eclipsed the UK with Brittany Tidal Success Story," *Ecologist*, November 10, 2011, www.theecologist.org/News/ news_analysis/678082/how_france_ eclipsed_the_uk_with_brittany_tidal_ success_story.html.

51. Corlan Hafren Limited, "The Severn Barrage Regional Vision," *Engineer*, October 2010, 1, www.theengineer.co.uk/ Journals/1/Files/2010/10/18/ Halcrow%20Severn_Barrage_ Vision_oct_2010.pdf (accessed April 22, 2013).

52. Bi-direction turbines operate under water flow in either direction. Low-head turbines are those set within a fall of water less than 5 meters.

53. Where tidal power is derived from Earth's oceanic tides, wave energy is produced when electricity generators are placed on the surface of the ocean. See: Oregon State University, "About Marine Energy—Making Waves," Northwest National Marine Renewable Energy Center, http://nnmrec.oregon state.edu/ocean-wave-energy (accessed January 15, 2013).

Chapter 7

1. Charles Vörösmarty quoted in: Fiona Harvey, "Global Majority Faces Water Shortages 'Within Two Generations,'" *Guardian*, May 24, 2013, www. guardian.co.uk/environment/2013/ may/24/global-majority-water- shortages-two-generations (accessed June 2, 2013).

2. Food and Agriculture Organization (FAO), "World Agriculture: Towards 2015/2030," ed. Jelle Bruinsma (London: Earthscan, 2003), 27, www.fao.org/ fileadmin/user_upload/esag/docs/ y4252e.pdf (accessed July 19, 2012).

3. B. C. Bates, Z. W. Kundzewicz, S. Wu, and J. P. Palutikof, eds., "Climate Change and Water," IPCC Technical Paper VI (Geneva: IPCC Secretariat, 2008), 4.

4. "A Shortage of Capital Flows," *The Economist*, October 9, 2008, www. economist.com/node/12376698 (accessed November 21, 2012).

5. Nick Cashmore, "Remaining Drops— Freshwater Resources: A Global Issue," CLSA U Blue Books, 2006, 20, www. pacinst.org/reports/remaining_drops/ CLSA_U_remaining_drops.pdf (accessed November 21, 2012).

6. Philip Mote, Alan Hamlet, Martyn P. Clark, and Dennis P. Lettenmaier, "Declining Mountain Snowpack in Western North America," *Bulletin of the American Meteorological Society* 86 (2005): 44, doi: 10.1175/BAMS-86-1-39.

7. Jonathan Overpeck, *Assessment of Climate Change in the Southwest United States*, ed. Greg Garfin (Washington, DC: Island Press, 2012), 1–20.

8. "Pajaro River Watershed: History and Background," Action Pajaro Valley, www.pajarowatershed.org/Content/10109/HistoryandBackground.html (accessed June 21, 2012).

9. US Environmental Protection Agency, *National Water Program 2012 Strategy: Response to Climate Change*" (public comment draft 2012), 2, http://water.epa.gov/scitech/climatechange/2012-National-Water-Program-Strategy.cfm (accessed July 7, 2012).

10. Where renewable water in a country is below 1,700 m³ per person per year, that country is said to be experiencing water stress; below 1,000 m³ it is said to be experiencing water scarcity; and below 500 m³, absolute water scarcity.

11. Kathleen A. Miller, Steven L. Rhodes, and Lawrence J. MacDonnell, "Water Allocation in a Changing Climate: Institutions and Adaptation," *Climatic Change* 35, no. 2 (1997): 157.

12. Rakesh Kumar, R. D. Singh, and K. D. Sharma, "Water Resources of India," *Current Science* 89, no. 5 (2005): 794.

13. World Wildlife Fund (WWF), "Water for Life: Lessons for Climate Change Adaptation from Better Management of Rivers for People and Nature," ed. Jamie Pittock (Switzerland: WWF, 2008), 18, http://assets.panda.org/downloads.50_12_wwf_climate_change_v2_full_report.pdf.

14. K. Lenin Babu and S. Manasi, "Estimation of Ecosystem Services of Rejuvenated Irrigation Tanks: A Case Study in Mid-Godavari Basin" (proceedings of the IWMI-TATA Water Policy Research Program "Managing Water in the Face of Growing Scarcity, Inequity, and Declining Returns: Exploring Fresh Approaches," Hyderabad, April 2–4, 2008), 283.

15. Biksham Gujja, Sraban Dalai, Hajara Shaik, and Vinod Goud, "Adapting to Climate Change in the Godavari River Basin of India by Restoring Traditional Water Storage Systems," *Climate and Development* 1 (2009): 232.

16. Ibid., 230. (N.b. India's peninsular rivers, such as the Godavari, do not receive Himalayan snowmelt.)

17. Gujja et al., "Adapting to Climate Change," 232.

18. Babu and Manasi, "Estimation of Ecosystem Services," 284.

19. Gujja et al., "Adapting to Climate Change," 237.

20. Ibid., 233.

21. Ibid., 233–5.

22. Babu and Manasi, "Estimation of Ecosystem Services," 290.

23. Gujja et al., "Adapting to Climate Change," 235.

24. Babu and Manasi, "Estimation of Ecosystem Services," 286.

25. Ibid.

26. WWF, "Water for Life," 18.

27. Gujja et al., "Adapting to Climate Change," 235.

28. Ibid., 287.

29. Babu and Manasi, "Estimation of Ecosystem Services," 292.

30. Ibid., 238.

31. Nilesh Heda, "Conservation of Riverine Resources through People's Participation: North-Eastern Godavari Basin,

Maharashtra, India" (final report), Rufford Small Grant for Nature Conservation (UK: Samvardhan, 2011), 14.

32. Gujja et al., "Adapting to Climate Change," 233.

33. WWF, "Water for Life," 18.

34. Mooyoung Han, "Innovative Rainwater Harvesting and Management Practice in Korea" (Korea: Seoul National University, 2007), 1.

35. Mooyoung Han, J. S. Mun, and H. J. Kim, "An Example of Climate Change Adaptation of Rainwater Management at the Star City Rainwater Project" (Seoul, Korea: Seoul National University, 2008), 2.

36. Mooyoung Han and Klaus W. König, "Rainwater Harvest System—Star City, Seoul," *fbr-Wasserspiegel* 4, 2008, 3, www.fbr.de/fileadmin/user_upload/files/Englische_Seite/Han_WS_1_2009_engl_webseite.pdf (accessed July 24, 2012).

37. Mooyoung Han and S. R. Kim, "Improving a City's LWIR with Rainwater Harvesting," *Water & Wastewater Asia* (2007): 32.

38. Bill McCann, "Seoul's Star City: A Rainwater Harvesting Benchmark in Korea," *Water21* (2008): 18.

39. Jungsoo Mun and Mooyoung Han, "Rainwater Harvesting and Management Spotlighted as a Key Solution for Water Problems in Monsoon Region" (Seoul, Korea: Seoul National University), 3, www.researchgate.net/publication/228790709_Rainwater_Harvesting_and_Management_spotlighted_as_a_key_solution_for_water_problems_in_monsoon_region (accessed July 21, 2012).

40. Fulya Verdier, "MENA (Middle East/North Africa) Regional Water Outlook, Part II: Desalination Using Renewable Energy," report prepared for the World Bank (Stuttgart, Germany: Fichtner, March 2011).

41. Ibid., 4–15, 20.

42. Mohamed A. Eltawil, Zhao Zhengming, and Liqiang Yuan, "A Review of Renewable Energy Technologies Integrated with Desalination Systems," *Renewable and Sustainable Energy Reviews* 13, no. 9 (2009): 2246.

43. Anibal T. De Almeida and Pedro S. Moura, "Desalination with Wind and Wave Power," *Solar Desalination for the 21st Century*, ed. L. Rizzuti et al., NATO Security through Science Series (2007), 311, doi:10.1007/978-1-4020-5508-9_23.

44. Ibid.

45. Prachi Patel, "Solar-Powered Desalination: Saudi Arabia's Newest Purification Plant Will Use State-of-the-Art Solar Technology," *MIT Technology Review*, April 8, 2010, www.technologyreview.com/news/418369/solar-powered-desalination/.

46. Joe Avancena, "KSA to Go Solar to Raise Water Desalination Plant Output," *Saudi Gazette*, February 11, 2012.

47. C. J. Vörösmarty, P. Green, J. Salisbury, and R. B. Lammers, "Global Water Resources: Vulnerability from Climate Change and Population Growth," *Science* 289, no. 5477 (2000): 284–8.

48. P. A. Davies and C. Paton, "The Seawater Greenhouse: Background Theory and Current Status," *International Journal of Low Carbon Technologies* 1, no. 2 (2006): 183–4, doi:10.1093/ijlct/1.2.184.

49. Ibid.

50. Ibid., 185.

51. Renee Cho, "Seawater Greenhouses Produce Tomatoes in the Desert," State of the Planet blog, The Earth Institute, Columbia University, February 18, 2012, http://blogs.ei.columbia. edu/2011/02/18/seawater-greenhouses-produce-tomatoes- in-the-desert/ (accessed December 5, 2012). See also: "Sundrop Farms Aljazeera English Earthrise Coverage," Earthrise, Aljazeera, April 20, 2012, www.aljazeera. com/programmes/ earthrise/2012/04/ 2012420154516315530.html (accessed December 5, 2012).

52. Sahara Forest Project, "Enabling a Green Future for Jordan," 3, http://sahara forestproject.com/fileadmin/uploads/ SFP_jordan.pdf (accessed December 5, 2012).

53. World Bank, "MENA Regional Water Outlook: Desalination Using Renewable Energy," Part II Final Report (Germany: Fitcher, 2011), 0–2, http://wrri.nmsu. edu/conf/conf11/mna_rdrens.pdf.

54. Ibid., 9–160.

55. Ibid., 5–10.

56. Ibid., 21.

57. California Environmental Protection Agency, "Integrated Regional Water Management Grant Program," State Water Resources Control Board, http:// water.epa.gov/scitech/climatechange/ upload/epa_2012_climate_water_ strategy_sectionIII_final.pdf (last modified August 16, 2011). See also: www. waterboards.ca.gov/water_issues/ programs/grants_loans/irwmgp/index. shtml.

58. G. Wade Miller, "Integrated Concepts in Water Reuse: Managing Global Water Needs," *Desalination* 187, no. 1 (2007): 68.

59. Ibid, 66.

60. B. Durham, A. N. Angelakis, T. Wintgens, C. Thoeye, and L. Sala, "Water Recycling and Reuse: A Water Scarcity Best-Practice Solution" (paper presented at the conference "Coping with Drought and Water Deficiency: From Research to Policy Making," Cyprus, May 12–13, 2005), 4.

61. Philip S. Wenz, "Spigot to Spigot," *American Planning Association* 74 (2008): 9.

62. Jyllian Kemsley, "Treating Sewage for Drinking Water: New California Plant Cleanses Water to Replenish Supply," *Chemical & Engineering News* 86, no. 4 (2008): 71, http://pubs.acs.org/cen/ science/86/8604sci4.html.

63. "About GWRS," Groundwater Replenishment System, www.gwrsystem.com/ about-gwrs.html (accessed December 7, 2012).

64. Wendy Sevenandt, "Old Water Made New: Innovative Project in Southern California Combines Water Purification and Pollution Control," *Pollution Engineering*, January 1, 2006, 10, www.pollutionengineering.com/ articles/85263-old-water-made-new? (accessed July 25, 2012).

65. Groundwater Replenishment System, "The OCWD/OCSD Partnership: How It Began More than Four Decades Ago," www.gwrsystem.com/about-gwrs/ facts-a-figures/the-ocwdocsd-partnership.html (accessed July 12, 2012).

66. Asit K. Biswas and Cecilia Tortajada, eds., *Water Management in 2020 and Beyond*, from Water Resources Development and Management Series (Springer-Verlag: Berlin Heidelberg, 2009), 237.

67. Singapore Public Utilities Board (PUB), "PUB ABC Water," PUB ABC Waters Programme, www.pub.gov.sg/abcwaters/Pages/default.aspx (last updated January 27, 2012).

68. Singapore PUB, "Marina Barrage: 3 in 1 Benefits," www.pub.gov.sg/Marina/Pages/3-in-1-benefits.aspx (accessed January 9, 2013).

69. Singapore PUB, "Overview: Four National Taps Provide Water for All," www.pub.gov.sg/water/Pages/default.aspx (last updated on August 3, 2012).

70. Water Management in 2020 and Beyond," 241.

71. Singapore PUB, "NEWater: History," www.pub.gov.sg/about/historyfuture/Pages/NEWater.aspx (last updated on June 28, 2011).

72. Singapore PUB, "Lowering Energy Consumption of Desalination," www.pub.gov.sg/LongTermWaterPlans/pipeline_LowerEgy.html (accessed January 9, 2013).

73. Noah Garrison, Christopher Kloss, and Robb Lukes, "Capturing Rainwater from Rooftops: An Efficient Water Resource Management Strategy That Increases Supply and Reduces Pollution," Natural Resources Defense Council, November 2011, 15, www.nrdc.org/water/files/rooftoprainwatercapture.pdf (accessed December 4, 2012).

74. Ibid., 12.

75. Ibid., 5–35.

Chapter 8

1. Anastasia Christman and Christine Riordan, "State Infrastructure Banks: Old Idea Yields New Opportunities for Job Creation," *National Employment Law Project* (briefing paper, 2011), 1, www.nelp.org/page/-/Job_Creation/State_Infrastructure_Banks.pdf?nocdn=1.

2. Edward Cohen-Rosenthal, "What Is Eco-Industrial Development?" in *Eco-Industrial Strategies: Unleashing Synergy Between Economic Development and the Environment*, ed. Edward Cowen-Rosenthal and Judy Musnikow (Sheffield, UK: Greenleaf Publishing 2003), 16.

3. The United States Conference of Mayors, "List of Participating Mayors," 2007 Mayors Climate Protection Summit, www.usmayors.org/climateprotection/list.asp (accessed March 25, 2013).

4. Center for Climate and Energy Solutions, "Climate Action Plans," updated November 8, 2012, www.c2es.org/us-states-regions/policy-maps/climate-action-plans (accessed March 27, 2013).

5. At the time of writing, two additional states were considering such arrangements.

6. Elizabeth Daley, "Massachusetts, Eight Other States to Sharply Cut Power Plant Carbon Emissions," *Boston Globe,* Metro section, February 7, 2013.

7. Urban Land Institute and Ernst & Young, *Infrastructure 2012: Spotlight on Leadership* (Washington, DC: Urban Land Institute, 2012), 39.

8. Ibid.

9. Robert Puentes and Jennifer Thompson, "Banking on Infrastructure: Enhancing

State Revolving Funds for Transportation," Project on State and Metropolitan Innovation (Washington, DC: Brookings-Rockefeller, 2012), 7, www.brookings.edu/research/papers/2012/09/12-state-infrastructure-investment-puentes (accessed January 4, 2013).

10. US Department of Transportation and Federal Highway Administration, *State Infrastructure Bank Review* (Washington, DC: 2002), 6.

11. Arizona's Department of Transportation has an SIB, and its Highway Expansion and Extension Loan Program is subject to open meeting laws. See: "Priority Planning Advisory Committee," Arizona Department of Transportation, www.azdot.gov/about/boards-and-committees/PriorityPlanningAdvisory Committee.

12. Rachel MacCleery, "Lessons from California for a New National Bank for Infrastructure," *Urban Land*, November 11, 2010, http://urbanland.uli.org/Articles/2010/Nov/MacCleeryLessons.

13. Ibid.

14. California Infrastructure and Economic Development Bank (I-Bank), "Low-Cost Infrastructure Financing," www.ibank.ca.gov/res/docs/pdfs/IBANK_ISRF_Brochure_for_web_9_10_04.pdf (accessed February 5, 2013).

15. Stanton C. Hazelroth, "California Infrastructure and Economic Development Bank" (prepared remarks before the House Ways and Means Committee Subcommittee on Select Revenue Measures, from public hearing on Infrastructure Banks, May 3, 2010), 3.

16. Office of the Mayor, City of Chicago, "City Council Passes Chicago Infrastructure Trust: Innovative Funding Mechanism Will Allow Transformative Infrastructure Projects" (press release, April 24, 2012).

17. John Schwartz, "$7 Billion Public-Private Plan in Chicago Aims to Fix Transit, Schools, and Parks," *New York Times*, March 29, 2012.

18. Patrick Svtek, "Rahm Emanuel's Chicago Plan for Infrastructure Wins Thumbs Up from Mayors," *Huffington Post*, July 23, 2012, www.huffingtonpost.com/2012/07/23/rahm-emanuel-chicago-plan-infrastructure_n_1696457.html.

19. Deloitte Research, "Closing the Infrastructure Gap: The Role of Public-Private Partnerships," Deloitte Touche Tohmatsu Limited, 2006, 6, www.deloitte.com/assets/Dcom-UnitedStates/Local%20Assets/Documents/us_ps_ClosingInfrastructureGap2006(1).pdf (accessed January 4, 2013).

20. Ibid., 22.

21. Ibid., 11.

22. Kathleen Brown, "Are Public–Private Transactions the Future of Infrastructure Finance?" *Public Works Management & Policy* 12, no. 1 (2007): 324.

23. Ibid.

24. Chu-Wei Chen and Djordje Soric, "Pension Fund Direct Investments in Infrastructure," *Global Infrastructure* 2 (Winter 2012): 107.

25. Clancy Yeates, "US Pension Funds Circle Australian Infrastructure," *Sydney Morning Herald*, December 10, 2012, www.smh.com.au/business/us-pension-funds-circle-australian-infrastructure-20121209-2b3ih.html.

26. Ibid.

27. Clinton Global Initiative, "NYC Teacher Pension Fund Pledges $1 Billion to Investments in Post-Sandy Reconstruction and Other Critical Infrastructure" (press release, December 13, 2012), http://press.clintonglobalinitiative.org/press_releases/nyc-teacher-pension-fund-pledges-1-billion-to-investments-in-post-sandy-reconstruction-and-other-critical-infrastructure/.

28. Emilia Istrate and Robert Puentes, "Moving Forward on Public-Private Partnerships: U.S. and International Experience with PPP Units," Brookings-Rockefeller Project on State and Metropolitan Innovation, December 2011, www.brookings.edu/~/media/research/files/papers/2011/12/08%20transportation%20istrate%20puentes/1208_transportation_istrate_puentes.pdf.

29. Ibid., 10.

30. For California Criteria, see: www.ibank.ca.gov/res/docs/pdfs/01-29-08_BoardApprovedCriteria.pdf; for Chicago Principles, see: www.shapechicago.org/about/operational-principles/.

31. EcoDistricts, www.ecodistricts.org (accessed March 1, 2013).

32. Living City Block, "What We Do," www.livingcityblock.org/what-we-do/ (accessed March 1, 2013).

33. Ken Berlin, Reed Hundt, Mark Muro, and Devashree Saha, "State Clean Energy Finance Banks: New Investment Facilities for Clean Energy Deployment" (Washington, DC: Brookings-Rockefeller, 2012), 1, www.brookings.edu/research/papers/2012/09/12-state-energy-investment-muro.

34. "DSIRE Database of State Incentives for Renewables & Efficiency," www.dsireusa.org (accessed February 5, 2013).

35. John P. Banks et al., "Assessing the Role of Distributed Power Systems in the U.S. Power Sector" (Washington, DC: Brookings-Hoover, October 2011), 47, www.brookings.edu/~/media/research/files/papers/2011/10/distributed%20power%20systems/10_distributed_power_systems.pdf.

36. Peter Rothberg, "The Path to Progress: Ending Fossil Fuel Subsidies," Nation, May 18, 2012.

37. Ken Silverstein, "California's Carbon Caps Are Contentious but Coming," Forbes, July 31, 2012.

38. Bloomberg New Energy Finance, "Crossing the Valley of Death—Solutions to the Next-Generation Clean Energy Project Financing G," Clean Energy Group, June 21, 2010, 8.

39. Ibid., 13.

40. "Connecticut House Bill No. 7432—An Act Concerning Electricity and Energy Efficiency: Sec. 21(1)," January 2007.

41. Ohio has the Northeast Ohio Public Energy Council, a 118-city program. Other examples of CCAs include one in Massachusetts servicing 21 towns and also a consortium of 36 cities forming the Rhode Island League of Cities and Towns. See: Local Government Commission, Sacramento, CA, "Community Choice Aggregation," 3, 2013, www.lgc.org/cca/docs/cca_energy_factsheet.pdf (accessed February 5).

42. Clean Energy Finance and Investment Authority, "Clean Energy Financial Inno-

vation Program," www.ctcleanenergy.com/YourHome/CleanEnergyFinancialInnovationProgram/tabid/624/Default.aspx.

43. Berlin et al., "State Clean Energy Finance Banks."

44. District Energy St. Paul, "History," www.districtenergy.com/inside-district-energy/history/. See also: Maui Smart Grid Project, www.mauismartgrid.com; and Austin Energy Smart Grid Program, www.austinenergy.com/about%20us/company%20profile/smartGrid/.

45. Valerie I. Nelson, "A Soft-Path Water Paradigm Shift: Federal Policies to Advance Decentralized and Integrated Water Resources Infrastructure," Coalition for Alternative Wastewater Treatment of Gloucester, Massachusetts, 2007.

46. National League of Cities, "Water Infrastructure Financing: Overview of Water Infrastructure Needs," www.nlc.org/influence-federal-policy/advocacy/legislative-advocacy/water-infrastructure-financing.

47. US Government Accountability Office, *Water Infrastructure: Approaches and Issues for Financing Drinking Water and Wastewater Infrastructure*, GAO-13-451T (testimony before the Subcommittee on Interior, Environment, and Related Agencies, Committee on Appropriations, House of Representatives, Washington, DC, July 2001), www.gao.gov/assets/660/652976.pdf.

48. Nelson, "A Soft-Path Water Paradigm Shift," 62.

49. Ibid., 57.

50. US Environmental Protection Agency, "The Clean Water State Revolving Fund: Decentralized Systems—Developing Partnerships to Broaden Opportunities," EPA-832-F-12-028, June 2012, http://water.epa.gov/grants_funding/cwsrf/upload/CWSRF-GPR-Fact-Sheet-Decentralized-Systems.pdf.

51. Association of California Water Agencies, "Bill in Congress Seeks Alternative Financing for Regional Water Projects," February 19, 2013, www.acwa.com/news/water-news/bill-congress-seeks-alternative-financing-regional-water-projects.

52. Nelson, "A Soft-Path Water Paradigm Shift," 60.

53. A US EPA program advancing technology transfer of various decentralized wastewater treatment options.

54. Trevor Clements, "Sustainable Water Resources Management: Case Studies on New Water Paradigm," vol. 3 (final report, Electric Power Research Institute, 2010), 6.

55. P. Lynn Scarlett and James Boyd, "Ecosystem Services: Quantification, Policy Applications, and Current Federal Capabilities" (discussion paper, Resources for the Future, 2011).

56. National Association of Clean Water Agencies, Water Environment Research Foundation, Water Environment Federation, "The Water Resources Utility of the Future: A Blueprint for Action," 2013, 1, www.nacwa.org/images/stories/public/2013-01-31waterresourcesutilityofthefuture-final.pdf (accessed July 24, 2013).

57. Roger E. Kasperson, Dominic Golding, and Seth Tuler, "Social Distrust as a Factor in Siting Hazardous Facilities and

Communicating Risks," *Journal of Social Issues* 48, no. 4 (1992): 161–87.

58. Richard G. Kuhn and Kevin R. Ballard, "Canadian Innovations in Siting Hazardous Waste Management Facilities," *Environmental Management* 22, no. 4 (1998): 536.

59. Chris Zeiss and James Atwater, "Waste Facilities in Residential Communities: Impacts and Acceptance," *Journal of Urban Planning and Development* 113, no. 1 (1987): 28.

60. Patricia E. Salkin and Amy Lavine. "Understanding Community Benefits Agreements: Equitable Development, Social Justice, and Other Considerations for Developers, Municipalities, and Community Organizations," *Journal of Environmental Law* 26 (2008): 324.

61. Mark Gerencser, Reginald Van Lee, Fernando Napolitano, and Christopher Kelly, *Megacommunities: How Leaders of Government, Business, and Non-Profits Can Tackle Today's Global Challenges Together* (New York: Palgrave/Macmillan, 2008).

62. US Green Building Council's LEED for Neighborhood Development; ICLEI's Community Star Program.

63. Richard G. Little, "Holistic Strategy for Urban Security," *Journal of Infrastructure Systems* 10, no. 2 (2004): 52–59.

64. Joel B. Smith, Jason M. Vogel, Terri L. Cruce, Stephen Seidel, and Heather A. Holsinger, "Adapting to Climate Change: A Call for Federal Leadership," Pew Center on Global Climate Change (2010), 24.

65. CSA Group, "CSA Group to Develop Four New Standards Addressing Climate Change Impact in Canada's Far North on Behalf of Standards Council of Canada," November 14, 2012, www.csa.ca/cm/ca/en/news/article/csa-to-develop-four-new-standards-addressing-climate-change-impact-in-canadas-far-north. See also: Ian Burton, "Moving Forward on Adaptation," in *From Impacts to Adaptation: Canada in a Changing Climate*, ed. D. S. Lemmen, F. J. Warren, J. Lacroix, and E. Bush (Ottawa, ON: Government of Canada, 2008), 431.

66. Maria Galluchi, "6 of the World's Most Extensive Climate Adaptation Plans," *InsideClimate News*, June 20, 2103, www.insideclimatenews.org/news/20130620/6-worlds-most-extensive-climate-adaptation-plans (accessed June 24, 2013).

67. Barry Bergdoll, "Rising Currents: Looking Back and Next Steps," Museum of Modern Art, blog posting, November 1, 2010, www.moma.org/explore/inside_out/2010/11/01/rising-currents-looking-back-and-next-steps (accessed June 1, 2013).

Index